IMAGIN

THE REDEMPTIVE POWER IN MAN

NEVILLE

The Most Complete Summary
of Neville Goddard's
Core Teaching
in
One Volume

Compiled and Edited
By
David Allen

Published by Shanon Allen

Printed in the United States of America

First Paperback Printing, April 2016

ISBN: 978-0-9972801-4-2

I give you water by telling you how the law operates. Now you must turn it into wine by application.

Neville Goddard

INTRODUCTION

For those who are familiar with Neville Goddard this book needs very little introduction. It is simply a book devoted to his core teaching, Imagination. I have compiled over 640 quotes from Neville's works into one volume on what imagination is and how to use it. If there is one secret above all other secrets on how to achieve anything we desire in life, it lies in one word . . Imagination. Within these pages I believe that you will find what you have been searching for.

David Allen

1. You do not will something to be so, but imagine it and become inwardly convinced that it is so. And if, through your persistence, the world responds, you have found the Lord as your own wonderful human imagination.

2. Tell everyone you meet how the world works. You do not have to have a proper educational or social background to apply this principle; and you cannot fail, for an assumption, though false, if persisted in will harden into fact. Imagining creates reality.

3. Don't hold onto anything on the outside; hold on only in your imagination. If something is taken from you, it is because at one time you assumed its loss and . . for a moment . . wondered what you would do if it were. You forgot the thought, but its message had already been released to fulfill itself. If you want to keep your possessions, you must hold onto them in your imagination and not build barns to house them.

4. The ancients discovered that if they would ever discover really the ultimate reality, it could never be by any instrument made by man. In order to discover the ultimate reality, they would have to set Mind to observe itself, and then to accurately record those observations. For they concluded that no description of Mind made by any science known to man could be an adequate description of the Mind which made that science. So when today we are speaking of taking the imagination to look into the deep, it is looking at itself. You set imagination to observe self and then to accurately record those observations. And you must come to the conclusion, imagination is the central figure 0f the Gospel.

5. If it takes five hundred different beings, male and female, to respond to your imaginal act, they will come and seem to you to be the influence through which your desire is made visible.

6. Prayers are not successfully made unless there is a rapport between the conscious and subconscious mind of the operator. This is done through imagination and faith. By the power of imagination all men, certainly imaginative men, are forever casting forth enchantments, and all men, especially unimaginative men, are continually passing under their power.

7. The statement: You must be born from above or you cannot enter the Kingdom of Heaven is an example. It is literally true, but it is told in metaphor. The rich young man said: How is it possible to again enter my mothers womb and be born a second time? But the womb is below and not above. It is speaking of the birth of the second man, the spiritual man. From Genesis right to the end of the Book, it says that God created all things and that he said: It is good. Seven times he repeats: It is good . . the perfect number. One day you will see the whole vast world, and you will say: It is good! And you will animate it. I know everything depends on the activity taking place in MAN . . and spell it with large letters, for the garments are male-female. You are MAN, this generic man that is God. The whole vast world is man pushed out. Not a man, but MAN. All that you behold though it seems to be without, it is within, in your own wonderful Imagination of which this vegetative world is but a shadow. It is hard at this stage to think that your world is a shadow, and it is cast by you and you are activating it.

8. If tonight you believe your imagination is Christ and you desire to be elsewhere, sleep there in your imagination just as though it were true. Forget the fact that you can't afford it or do not have the time. "I AM" infinity, and all thine are mine and mine are thine. If you really believe in Christ as your own wonderful human imagination, then sleep as the person you want to be. Don't ask me how it is going to come about, for my ways and means are past finding out! A man called me three weeks ago, saying: "Many years ago in New York City you told me that if I wanted to go to

California all I had to do was assume I was there. Well, my wife and I are here now, but I want you to know that I'm not sold on what you teach. I did what you said, but the reason I came here is because the company I worked for opened a factory and transferred me here." He didn't find himself flying through space, but was transferred by his company, so he doesn't believe that feeling is the secret! Well, you take your pearls and throw them before the swine of the world and they pick your wisdom up and drop it down, but you throw it just the same. I know you are warned not to do it, but I have never been able to discriminate as to who will take it and who will not, so I tell it to all who will listen.

9. "All that you behold, though it appears without it is within, of which this world of mortality is but a shadow." If you will but enter a state in your imagination, and assume its truth, the outer world will respond to your assumption, for it is your shadow, forever bearing witness to your inner imaginal activity.

10. You have the capacity to believe. You may believe in something stupid, but you believe and your belief will make it work. The one I speak of as God is your mightier self, yet your slave, for purposes of his own. He waits on you as indifferently and as swiftly when your will is evil as when it is good. He does it by conjuring images of good and evil just as though they were real. Allowing you to imagine whatever you desire, he projects it upon this screen of space in order for you to experience it. You can move into it so naturally and so easily you can forget the thoughtless moment when the seed was planted, and therefore do not recognize your own harvest.

11. If you think in terms of one little being called Jesus Christ, you miss the truth completely; for Jesus Christ is your own wonderful human imagination who is God himself. When you imagine a state, God has imagined it; and just as a sound brings a

response, your world will respond by playing the part it must play to bring about fulfillment.

12. Learn how to pray. Master it and make your world conform to the ideal you want to experience. Stop thinking of, and start thinking from. To think from the wish fulfilled is to realize that which you will never experience while you are thinking of it. When you put yourself into the state of the wish fulfilled and think from it, you are praying, and in a way your reasoning mind does not know, your wish will become a fact in your world. You can be the man or woman you want to be, when you know how to pray. All things are possible to him who believes, therefore learn the art of believing and persuade yourself it is true. Then one day, occupying space and time in your imagination, you will be seen by another, who will call or send you a letter verifying your visit. This I know from experience.

13. Blake saw all possible human situations as "already-made" states, he saw every aspect, every plot and drama as already worked out as "mere possibilities" as long as we are not in them, but as overpowering realities when we are in them.

14. Now, if you test God and prove to yourself that imagination does create reality, tell others. If they try it and it works for them, does it really matter what the world thinks? If they think the idea is insane, it won't be the first time. They thought Einstein was insane. There are those who think I am. That's perfectly all right, for the day will come when God will reveal himself in each individual, and then that one will move from the state of Saul to Paul. There is no other God, for God became Man by assuming all of his human weaknesses and limitations. God is not pretending he is you. When he became your breath, he had to take your unique qualities upon himself. That was his crucifixion. No man was nailed upon a cross bar; your body is the cross Christ wears. He is buried in you and will rise in you. His tomb is the human skull where he lays dreaming. So

awake, you sleeper, who forgot eternity in the pursuit of the moment. Although this moment seems so real, you are its reality and the central being of scripture.

15. By exercising the divine art of imagination, you can prove to yourself that you can go beyond what your eyes, reason, and senses dictate. Exercise this art by daring to assume you are what your reason and senses deny you. Persist, and to the degree you are self-persuaded of its truth, the outer world will change, for it is forever conforming to the belief housed within you.

16. From beginning to end, the Bible speaks only of the creative power of God. You can take that same creative power and use it here in the world of Caesar, for it is your own wonderful human imagination. If you will conjure a scene which would imply the fulfillment of your dream and remain faithful to that vision as Paul was to the heavenly vision, your desire will come to pass. Paul did not expect the vision. It came upon him suddenly, like some great catastrophic earthquake. You cannot conjure the vision, it simply happens. But you can conjure a scene which would imply the fulfillment of your desire, remain faithful to it and it will project itself upon the screen of space. I've done it unnumbered times. Take a simple scene. Would someone congratulate you if they heard of your good fortune? Then allow them to do so. Accept their congratulations, just as you would if they came to you in the flesh. Now remain faithful to that vision. If you need a more complex scene, like two people discussing your success, eavesdrop on them. Listen to their words of praise or envy, then do not forget that vision. Conjured in your imagination, carry it with you, knowing that what it implies will come to pass, for its potency is not in the scene itself, but what the scene implies.

17. Now, not only will this art of revision accomplish my every objective, but as I begin to revise the day it fulfills its great purpose

and its great purpose is to awaken in me the being that men call Christ Jesus, that I call my wonderful human imagination, and when it awakens it is the eye of God and it turns inward into the world of thought and there I see that what formerly I believed to exist on the outside really exists within myself.

18. Now, the words "God" and "Lord" mean I AM! Awareness is the foundation of all life, while the words God and Lord cover it up, like a mask. Rather than calling upon the Lord's name, call with his name. To do that you must say I AM! And because all things are possible to God, anything can be called forth with his name. The minute consciousness is connected to desire, you have called it forth with God's name. If your desire is for wealth, fame, or health, call it forth by claiming: I AM famous, I AM wealthy, or I AM healthy. Do that and you are calling with God's name. We are told to not take God's name in vain; for if we do, he will not hold us guiltless. The minute you say: I am a nobody, I am unwanted, or I am no good, you have taken God's name and conjured exactly what He has assumed . . be it good, bad, or indifferent. Any assumption is yours! Now that you know God's name, put your trust in the true God who is your own wonderful imagination!

19. If man accepts as final the facts that evidence bears witness to, he will never exercise this God-given means of redemption, which is his imagination.

20. "Whatever you ask in prayer, believe that you have received it, and you will." Read it in the 11th chapter of the Book of Mark. "Whatever you ask, believe that you have received it, and you will." "If we know that He hears us in whatever we ask, we know we have obtained the request made of Him." Read that in the First Epistle of John, the 5th chapter, 15th verse. These are statements made by the Awakened Man. Therefore, if the prayer is not answered, you are praying to a wrong god. But if you know that the God to Whom you

pray is your own wonderful human imagination, then instead of begging, you appropriate. You appropriate the state; so I call it the subjective appropriation of the objective hope. What is my objective hope? Well, I appropriate it subjectively. I "go within" and I simply appropriate it. I simply assume the feeling of my wish fulfilled. I appropriate it; and if my wish fulfilled were true, how would I see the world in which I live? and then do everything to make me see it as I would see it if it were: see the people in my world as I would have to see them, and let them see me as they would be compelled to see me if what I am doing is an actual external fact. If they know me and I know them, and something happens in my life that becomes public knowledge, . . well, then, they would know it. Then let them see me as they would have to see me if it were true. So, the subjective appropriation of the objective hope is prayer. You don't beg any one. Don't ask anyone. You simply appropriate it. For, if He is in me, where would I go to ask Him?

21. I'm going to tell you when you begin to awake, you assert the supremacy of imagination and you put all things in subjection to it. You never again bow before the dictates of facts and accept life on the basis of the world without. To you Truth is not confined by facts but by the intensity of your imagination.

22. Knowing what you want, gear yourself towards it, for the act was committed in the wanting. Faith must now be added, for without faith it is impossible to please God. Can you imagine a state and feel that your imaginal act is now a fact? It costs you nothing to imagine; in fact you are imagining every moment in time, but not consciously. But, may I tell you: if you use your creative power by imagining a desire is already fulfilled, when you get it, the circumstances will seem so natural that it will be easy to deny your imagination had anything to do with it, and you could easily believe that it would have happened anyway. But if you do, you will have returned to sleep once again.

23. When I say everything is at your disposal, I mean everything is in your imagination, and you are its creative power. Living in this fabulous world, you can travel unknown seas by gondola and know fruit, trees, birds, and beasts unknown here on earth; and in that world you are in complete control. While walking the earth, man is totally unaware of the food he is mentally eating. Thoughts of horror and anger, jealousy and hate, feed invisible monsters which produce heartaches and pain. There are those who want the spoiled fruit which is part of this age; but when you enter that age, you are in complete control of your power. You realize that everything is a thought and under your control. We are told: "Eye has not seen, ear has not heard and it has not entered into the heart of man the things already prepared by God for those who love him." When you are one with your Father, you will awaken to find yourself in that age which has already been prepared for you. So set your heart fully upon that world which you will enter at the unveiling of Christ from within. As you awaken, one after the other, no two will have a duplicate experience. The symbolism will be there however, as well as the time element. It is always five months between the vision of the birth and the revelation of God's son.

24. Paul tells you that God is found by seeing the phenomena. "All of the invisible things of him are clearly seen from the beginning of time." How? By the things that are made. Did God not say: "I kill, I make alive, I wound, I heal. I do all things and none can deliver out of my hands?" This is not a being on the outside speaking, but the imagination who is the Lord and there is no other God. Don't you say: "I AM?" That's He. So now that you have found God, honor him as God. When what you have imagined happens, honor your imagination as God. At the present time you may think of God as someone up in the sky, but not in your imagination. You know you are capable of unlovely acts, but cannot believe God could do such a thing; yet I say God . . your imagination . . is capable of killing, making alive, wounding, and healing.

25. If someone wants to wallow in self pity, let him. You are not asked to test the man but to test yourself. You are not asked to prove it to another, just yourself. See the world as nothing more than yourself pushed out and everything in it as aiding the birth of your imagination, for the behavior of the world relative to you determined by the concept you hold of yourself! It doesn't really matter what your individual personal life is, the whole vast world is yourself pushed out and everyone in it is there to aid the birth of all of your imaginal acts. Regardless of whether it takes one or one hundred thousand, everyone will play his part, and you don't have to ask his permission for your world is animated by your own wonderful human imagination.

26. As I started this lecture, almost everything in this world is so completely unlike what it appears to be. And I am telling you from my own experience; I am not speculating. I am not theorizing. The power of which I speak is a power within you. That power is not something on the outside; it's your own wonderful human imagination, and you will learn to control it. Your imagination animates the world in which you live. You change your imagination, and you change the world. To attempt to change circumstances before I change my own imaginal activity is to struggle against the very nature of my own being, for my own imaginal activity is animating my world. If I believe that I am injured or that others are against me, I have conjured them in my world, and they have to be against me. If I fully believe that all are working towards the fulfillment of my good, they have to work towards the fulfillment of my good. I don't ask them. I don't compel them. I simply do it only within myself, and the whole vast world exists within me. Therefore, it is myself "pushed out." It's objectified. I don't have to change affairs; I only change it within myself; and then everyone, though I know him or not by name, -- it doesn't really matter, -- it's myself "pushed out."

27. I urge you to use your imagination lovingly on behalf of everyone, and believe in the reality of your imaginal acts. If you have a friend who would like to be gainfully employed, listen carefully until you hear his voice tell you of his new position. Feel his hand clasp yours. See the smile on his lips. Use every sense you can possibly bring to bear into the imaginal scene. Persist until you feel the thrill of reality, then drop it and let that scene fulfill itself on the outside. We are told that the kingdom of heaven is like a mustard seed. Your imaginal act created for your friend in the kingdom of heaven is that seed. Don't pick it up to see if it is growing; just leave it alone, and it will grow and bloom as a solid fact in your world. Then you will have found this hidden cause within you called Christ. Christ, the power and wisdom of God, is in you as your own wonderful eternal being. He will never leave you or forsake you as told us in the 13th chapter of Hebrews. If, perchance, one day you are swept into an unlovely state and go through hell, remember: there is that in you who will not leave you or forsake you; and if you know this principle you can detach yourself from the state and it will vanish, as you move into a more desirable one.

28. So here I share with you what I have discovered. I have discovered that your own wonderful human imagination is the Spirit of God, and that you can enter any state in this world, and on entrance, it ceases to be a flat surface, depicting reality. It is reality. Why? Because you are the reality who dwells in it. Wherever you are, things are real. If you are not in it, then they are not real. They go to their flat surfaces. And all things exist in the human imagination. We are called upon to select that state in which we will dwell . . the state that we will enter and make real in our world. And I do it by simply feeling. What would the feeling be like, were it true? How would I feel, were it true? And how would I see the world, were it true? Then I feel myself into that state, and try to give it all the tones of reality, all the sensory vividness that I can. If I can give it sensory vividness and the tones of reality, even though I do

not see it, it will work; but sometimes it becomes so vivid and so intense, you do see it. The whole thing opens. Your eye opens, and the whole thing is real; and then you are in an entirely different world . . the world of your dreams, for because you entered it, it is real.

29. President Hoover, a man who began his life here on earth in the state of poverty, yet rose to the highest office in our land made this statement at a convention in San Francisco: "Human history, with its forms of governments, its revolutions, its wars, and in fact the rise and fall of nations, could be written in terms of the rise and fall of ideas implanted in the mind of men." We are told in the 8th chapter of Nehemiah that Ezra read from the Book, from the law of God with interpretation, so that the people understood the reading. It is my hope that I can interpret the words of President Hoover and the meaning behind the words from the Epistle of John so that you may understand their meaning. The words are these: "I AM from above; you are from below. You are of this world; I am not of this world. Now I say to you, unless you believe that I AM He you will die in your sins." To sin means to miss the mark, so what he is saying is that unless you believe you already are what you want to be, you will never be it. Would you like to be secure? Then say to yourself and yourself alone: "Unless I believe I AM secure I will die in my sins. I will continue to believe I am insecure; thereby missing my goal in life." Unless you can believe "I AM secure," even though there is not one thing to support it, you will die in your sin and never feel secure, for the name of God is I AM and besides I AM there is no other. Imagination (I AM) is from above. Imagination is not of this world and nothing is impossible to imagine! That is the story of scripture.

30. When you know what you want, assume you have it. Believe your assumption is true. Look at your world mentally and see your fulfilled desire. Do this and you are calling forth a response to your

thoughts, and in the not distant future you will find yourself physically occupying the state imagined.

31. There is only one cause for the phenomena of life. That cause is God. Housed in you, God is a person in the most literal sense of the word. Believe me, for I know this from experience. God, the only creator, is pure imagination working in the depth of your soul. God began a good work in you and He will bring it to completion on the day God's creative power is unveiled in you! God's creative power and wisdom is defined in scripture as Christ. When Christ unveils himself in you, you will know you are God's power and God's wisdom. God, your own wonderful human imagination, underlies all of your faculties, including perception, and streams into your surface mind least disguised in the form of creative, productive fantasy. When you ask yourself what you can do to transcend your present limitation of life, you are dwelling upon the means. God does not ask you to consider the means, but to define the end. Speaking to you through the medium of desire, God asks the question: "What wantest thou of me?" Then he tells you not to be concerned with the ways and means, for his ways are unsearchable. They are inscrutable and past finding out. This statement you will find in the 11th chapter of the Book of Romans. So don't be concerned as to how God will fulfill the end, only know that He will. Can you believe your desire is fulfilled? Can you believe it is true? If you can, it is yours for the taking, for nothing is impossible to one who believes.

32. If you have a genuine desire, voice it then move mentally. You can move on the outside many times and not change. You must move within and view the world from already being the person you want to be. If you do, you have moved from where you were to your desire's fulfillment. The motion is mental, all in your imagination. Now, if the desire is genuine, regardless of what the world will do, remain in that state and you will bring it into visibility. It is

impossible, however, without motion, to bring anything from an invisible state into an outer, visible one. Everyone can do it because everyone has an imagination which is God, and without him not a thing is created, and whatever is created is done by God whether it be good, indifferent, or evil. Take me at my word. I have introduced you to the creator of your life. Now that you know him don't be like the Romans Paul spoke of, who knew God yet did not honor him as God, but exchanged the immortal God for an image resembling Him, and the true knowledge of God for a lie therein, serving the creature rather than the creator, who is the imagination.

33. There are infinite number of states. The state of health, the state of sickness, the state of wealth, the state of poverty, the state of being known, the state of being unknown . . all are only states and everyone is always in a state. We all have one state in which we are very comfortable, so we return to it moment after moment. That state constitutes our dwelling place. If it is not a pleasant state, we can always get out of it. How this is done is the secret I will now share with you. All states are mental. You cannot remove yourself from your present state by pulling strings on the outside. You must mentally adjust your thoughts to proceed from the desired state, all within yourself. You fell into your present state either deliberately or unwittingly; and because you are its life, the state became alive and grew like a tree, bearing its fruit which you do not like. Its fruit may be that of poverty, or distress, heartache, or pain.

There are all kinds of unlovely fruit. But you can detach yourself from your unlovely harvest by making an adjustment in your human imagination. Ask yourself what you would like to harvest. When you know what it is, ask yourself how you would feel if your desire was ready to harvest right now. When you know the feeling, try to catch it. In my own case I find it easier to catch the feeling by imagining I am with people I know well and they are seeing me as they would if my desire were now a fact. And when the feeling of reality possesses me, I fall asleep in that assumption. At that moment I have entered a state. Now, I must make that state as natural as I have made my present state. I must consciously return to my new state constantly. I must feel its naturalness, like my own bed at night. At first the new state seems unnatural, like wearing a new suit or hat. Although no one knows your suit is new, you are so conscious of it you think everyone is looking at you. You are aware of its fit and its feeling until it becomes comfortable. So it is with your new state. At first you are conscious of its strangeness; but with regular wearing, the new state becomes comfortable, and its naturalness causes you to constantly return to it, thereby making it real.

Now most of us, knowing what we want, construct it in our minds eye, but never occupy it. We never move into the state and remain there. I call this perpetual construction, deferred occupancy. I could dream of owning a lovely home and hope to go there one day; but if I do not occupy it now, in my imagination, I postpone it to another day. I may wish my friend had a better job. I may have imagined him having it; but if I don't occupy that state by believing he is already there, I have merely constructed the state for him but not occupied it. All day long I can wish he or she were different; but if I don't go into the state and view him from it, I don't occupy the state, so he remains in the unlovely state relative to me. This is the world in which we live.

You can't conceive of a thing that is not part of a state, but the life of any state is in the individual who occupies it. Life cannot be given to a state from without, because God's name is "I AM." It is not "You are" or "They are." God's eternal name is I AM! That is the life of the world. If you would make a state alive, you must be in it. If you are in a lovely, gentle, kind state, you are seeing another as lovely, living graciously, and enjoying life to the utmost.

Now, to make that state natural, you must see everyone in your world as lovely, kind, and gentle. Others may not see them in that light, but it doesn't really matter what they think. I am quite sure if I took a survey of what people think of me, no two would agree. Some would say I am a deceiver, while others I am the nearest thing to God. I would find a range stretching from the devil to God, all based upon the state in which the person is in when called upon to define me.

You can be what you want to be if you know and apply this principle, but you are the operant power. It does not operate itself. You may know the law from A to Z, but knowing is not enough. Knowledge must be acted upon. "I AM" is the operant power in you. Put your awareness in the center of your desire. Persist, and your desire will be objectified. Learn to use the law, because there is a long interval between the law and the promise.

34. With knowledge of the law of reversibility, the disciplined man transforms his world by imagining and feeling only what is lovely and of good report. The beautiful idea he awakens within himself shall not fail to arouse its affinity in others.

35. When you dream tonight of numberless people and awaken in the morning to find them gone, where did they go? Are they not all in you, created by and acted by you? Then are you not protean? You, all Imagination, are God the dreamer, imagining the many parts you are playing. This very moment is a part of your dream, and those around you are there, playing their parts because you are imagining them. You are playing the part of your husband, your wife, your children, your friends, and your enemies. They are all you, for there is nothing but God (Imagination).

36. To say: "I AM going to be rich," will not make it happen; you must believe riches in by claiming within yourself: "I AM rich."

You must believe in the present tense, because the active, creative power that you are, is God. He is your awareness, and God alone acts and is. His name forever and ever is "I AM" therefore, he can't say: "I will be rich" or "I was rich" but "I AM rich!" Claim what you want to be aware of here and now, and . . although your reasonable mind denies it and your senses deny it . . if you will assume it, with feeling, your inward activity, established and perpetuated, will objectify itself in the outside world . . which is nothing more than your imaginal activity, objectified. To attempt to change the circumstances of your life before you change its imaginal activity, is to labor in vain.

37. Start now to use your talent, which is your imagination. Use it consciously every day, for any time you use your imagination you are pleasing God; and when you do not use it God is displeased. You don't have to sit down and burst a blood vessel pounding out the details of your desire. You can imagine as you walk down the street. A simple assumption is easy and can be lots of fun. A friend called today to thank me for aiding her in the selling of her home. It was an enormous house in Highland Park, which had been empty for some time. She had hired a lady to go to the house and do some cleaning there, when a man came to the door and asked to buy it. Two weeks later the house was sold. What did I do? I imagined hearing her tell me the house was sold. That's all I did. There was nothing else I needed to do; for all things are possible to God, and he so loves me he abides by any request I make of him.

38. Mark tells the parable of the fig tree, which . . having been cursed . . was found withered to its roots. Calling attention to this fact, awakened imagination said: "Have faith in God. Truly I say to you, whoever says to this mountain, 'Be taken up and cast into the sea,' and does not doubt in his heart that what he has said will come to pass, it will be done for him. Therefore I tell you, whatever you desire, when you pray believe you have received it and you will."

Mark 11. Here is an imaginary act which has no support in fact. The tree was not withered at the time it was cursed, but when they returned the next day the imaginal act had been executed. So you see: this law is not limited to being constructive only. It can be used for good, bad, or indifferent purposes; for there are no limitations placed on the possibilities of prayer. Now when you pray you must immerse yourself in the feeling of the wish fulfilled, for the word "pray" means, "Motion towards; accession to; at or in the vicinity of." Point yourself towards the wish fulfilled and accept that invisible state as reality. Then go your way knowing the desire is now yours. You did it and you will not be surprised when it comes to pass. When you first practice this technique you will be surprised when it happens; but when you learn how to completely accept the state assumed, you will know you do not have to do a thing to make it come to pass, as the assumption contains its own plan of fulfillment. You will know that this world is imaginal and that an assumption . . with no external object to support its truth . . will harden into fact when its truth is persisted in. If an imaginal act produces an external fact to support it, then is not this world essentially imagined? If you dare to assume what your reason and senses deny and walk faithful to your assumption, believing in its reality . . and its corresponding effect is produced, can this seemingly solid, real world be anything other than imaginal? Everything is imagined, for you are God . . all imagination! God exists in you and you in Him. The world is all that you have imagined it to be, even though you cannot remember when or how you brought it into being.

39. My experience revealed to me that I am supreme within the circle of my own state of consciousness and that it is the state with which I am identified that determines what I experience. Therefore it should be shared with all, that imagining creates reality, for to know this is to become free from the world's greatest tyranny, the belief in a second cause. Blessed are they whose imagination has been so

purged of the beliefs in second causes they know that imagination is all, and all is imagination. We, by a series of mental transformations, become aware of increasing portions of that which already is, and by matching our own mental activity to that portion of creation which we desire to experience, we activate it, resurrect it, and give it life.

40. I encourage you to control your human imagination; for if you would steer a true course toward a certain goal in life, you must ever be aware of the end that you are shaping by your imaginal activity, and not allow doubt to enter for one moment. When you know what you want, you must think from your belief in its possession, morning, noon, and night. If you do, no power can stop its appearance, because you are the dreamer of your dream, pushing yourself out, shaping your world by your imaginal activities.

41. Men that you and I admire, if they were honest, would admit to implanting in our mind that which would belittle us and ennoble them. Many know what they are doing but they don't know Christ. If they did, they would know they do not have to belittle us to ennoble themselves. If you want to rise, you don't have to put another down in order to feel you have risen. Your reality is I AM. Raise your consciousness and you raise yourself, but you haven't risen when you feel the need to push another down by claiming "I AM better than." Tonight take this law and apply it. I promise you it will not fail. When you go to bed dwell in your own wonderful human imagination and say: "Thank you, Father" as though you were addressing another. You know you are thanking your human imagination, but while assuming you have what you want, thank your Father. You came out from the Father and came into the world. Now you are leaving the world and going to the Father. Eventually you will reach him, and when you do he is yourself. There is no other Father. There is no other God!

42. Tonight when you go to bed just say: "I AM." Add any condition you want to that I AM and believe it. Speak to your imagination as though you are speaking to the God who created the universe and sustains it, for you are. When you imagine something ask yourself who is imagining it, and you will say: "I AM." That's God's name forever and ever. Imagine and fall asleep imagining. Believe that all things are possible to your own wonderful human I AMness. Test yourself! You don't need to get down on your knees and pray to anyone on the outside. There is no need to cross yourself before any icon, for the Lord is your human imagination, your consciousness, your own wonderful I AMness. Nothing can ever cease to be, for God . . he who is in you as your consciousness . . created it in love.

43. "I AM the beginning and the end. There is nothing to come that has not been and is." So look upon creation as finished . . and you and I are only selectors of that which is. By selectors I mean that you and I have the privilege (we may not exercise it) but it is our privilege to select that aspect of reality to which we will respond, and in responding to it, we bring it into existence for ourselves. Not knowing that we are so privileged, we simply go through the world reflecting the circumstances of life, not realizing we have the power to create or to out picture the circumstance of life.

44. When someone comes into your world, don't discard him by turning your back because he is ill, financially troubled, or not successful in his own eyes. Rather, see his desire as clay in your imaginal hands. Take that same vessel (person) and rework him into another state as it seems good to you to do. If he is unemployed, rework him into a man who is gainfully employed and happier than he has ever been in his life. That's all you do. What means will be applied toward his employment is not your concern. Your only desire is to be the perfect potter. The individual came into your

world as a spoiled vessel, not to be discarded, but to be reworked into another vessel as it seems good to you . . the potter . . to do.

45. If you know who you are and how imagination operates, you will learn to control your imaginal activities. If you do not, they will be controlled for you by another, and you will become their victim. Any time you exercise your imagination lovingly on behalf of another you have done the right thing. But if it is not done in love there is a question mark, for God is love. This knowledge is not the result of some philosophic reasoning, but of self-revelation. God unveiled himself within me and now I know that God is Infinite love. Yes, he is Infinite Power and Wisdom as well, but power without love can raise horror. I say to everyone, believe me. The Jesus of scripture and the Jehovah of scripture are your own wonderful human imagination. There is no other God, and God is love. One day you will know this truth.

46. So, the characters of scripture are not historical. To see anyone . . including Jesus Christ . . as a person who walked this earth, is to see truth tempered to the weakness of your soul, and unable to bear the strong light of revelation. Jesus Christ is the perfect state into which you are all moving. And in that state, scripture unfolds to reveal you as God. And who is he? He is your own wonderful human imagination! If all things are possible to your imagination, then all things are possible to imagine! How would you act if God imagined you as you want to be? How would you feel? What would you do? Then do it. Feeling its reality, have faith in your imaginal act. Desire is your hope. Your imaginal act is your subjective appropriation of the hope you want to objectify. Now, faith is the link between God's power and your desire. He doesn't question your desire. He who is all creative power and know-how, simply gives it to you. That is Christ, he who is defined as the power of God and the wisdom of God.

47. Now, all the invisible things of him from the creation of the world are clearly seen by the things that are made, so when they come into your world you can recognize your own harvest. You will bring it in anyway, but . . unaware of what you have been doing you have exchanged the truth about God for a lie. How? By exchanging the immortal God who is your own wonderful human imagination, for an image of a mortal man. Because a man was instrumental in aiding you to bring your desire to pass, you think he is the one who caused it, when that is a lie. If tonight you inherit a fortune don't think that the one from whom it seemed to come was the cause. No. Preceding that event you assumed wealth. He was only the instrument, the actor playing his part in giving you the money. It could have come from a total stranger. You don't need a wealthy uncle, aunt, or grandfather.

48. There is no limit placed upon your human imagination save that which you place upon yourself. Your financial, social and intellectual pictures are as limited as you make them. All within you, you and you alone have the ability to enlarge your concept of causality, plant and reap your every desire. Desires are the sheep of your pasture and the shepherd is your own wonderful human imagination. If your desires have gone astray bring them back into the fold where they really belong. When you go home tonight read the 14th chapter of the Gospel of John. It's such a glorious chapter. The whole Bible is, really. Just to read every verse so thrills me it becomes alive to me. In this chapter, when they asked him to show them the Father, he said: "I have been with you all these years and yet you do not know the Father? When you see me you have seen the Father, how then can you say, 'Show me the Father?'" Then he tells us: "I dwell in you and you dwell in me, we are one and I AM the Father." Man can't quite see it and you can't blame him for that. So I still say: the greatest need is for a new thinking of the human imagination. If man sees his own imagination as Christ, then all the so-called problems of the world will dissolve, leaving only harmony.

There will be no barriers when one sees his own imagination as Christ.

49. God, the Father of all life is in you! Being all imagination, your true name is I AM, and besides you there is no other God. So I tell you: unless you believe “I AM He,” you will die in your sins in the sense that you will continue missing the mark. You must assume that you are now the man (the woman) you want to be and persist in that assumption, for there is no other way for you to be it, as there is only God (imagination) in this world.

50. Test my words, for I know the human imagination is God. Call forth your desire by calling it forth with God's name. Decide what you want and ask yourself what it would be like and how you would feel if it were true. Then dare to assume you have it. Let the people who know you now see you after your assumption. Don't make them see you; let them see the change! Think of the world as a sounding box, echoing and reflecting what you have assumed. Listen to your friends comment on your change. See their faces expressing their pleasure on your good fortune. Wear that feeling as you now wear your present body of belief. Continue to wear that new state and in no time at all your desire will objectify itself and become a fact in your world. Then you will know who the cause of the phenomena of life really is. There is only one source. The world calls it God. That is a lovely name, but don't forget that God is your awareness! No one can see I AM!

51. Victor (Neville's brother) doesn’t smoke and he doesn’t drink; but he sits alone, and in his room he too is carrying on his little inner conversations premises of desires fulfilled. And he can completely control that imagination of his. He can completely control the inner conversation and the things work just as he has determined them. He never goes to church. He’s a religious man in the true sense of the word. He gives generously to charity and to all

people you would never know how many people he helps in the Island because he doesn't publicize it. That works for him because he has found out that inner conversations will do it.

52. Paul tells us: "He loved you and gave himself for you." Loving you, Imagination gave himself to you by becoming you that you may become Imagination, who is Christ. There never was another Christ and never will be another. Put your imagination to the test and see if it is Christ. If it is, do you need anyone to support you? Do you need any anti-poverty campaign? If those on relief could only believe in Christ, what a change they could make in their life! Instead, they go to church and give it a portion of what is given to them through relief. They support emotionalism because they do not know that source of the phenomena of life. Those on relief think their income is coming from Uncle Sam, not knowing he does not exist. No government has any money! The money it has is first taken from you before it can be given to another. In this world the money we earn is taken from us to give to the Mr. Seeons of the world, and if it is stopped, the so-called government will be criticized for stopping the gift. The churches haven't failed, except in not telling the true story of Christ. Rather than giving to the poor, they should tell the poor who Christ really is! If I tell you who Christ is and testing, you find him as your human imagination, does it matter what the world thinks? If there is evidence for a thing, does it matter what anyone thinks? If this can be proved in performance, what does it matter what the world thinks? You do not need to ask any minister, rabbi, or priest what he thinks, if you can test your imagination and prove its creative power!

53. If you would like to live in a lovely home, claim you do. You may think you can't afford the one you want, but that thought is an imaginal act. I would suggest, instead of thinking you can't afford it, to simply sleep in that home tonight mentally, accepting the fact that you have all the funds necessary to pay for it.

54. Remember: God in you creates and sustains your world by the use (or misuse) of your human imagination. There never was another God and there never will be, for Imagination is the only God.

55. Persistent imagination, centered in the feeling of the wish fulfilled, is the secret of all successful operations. This alone is the means of fulfilling the intention. Every stage of man's progress is made by the conscious, voluntary exercise of the imagination. Then you will understand why all poets have stressed the importance of controlled, vivid imagination.

Listen to this one by the great William Blake:

"In your own bosom you bear your heaven and earth,
And all you behold, though it appears without,
It is within, in your imagination,
Of which this world of mortality is but a shadow."

Try it, and you too will prove that your Imagination is the Creator.

56. Now this is how we do it. At the end of my day, I review the day; I don't judge it, I simply review it. I look over the entire day, all the episodes, all the events, all the conversations, all the meetings, and then as I see it clearly in my mind's eye, I rewrite it. I rewrite it and make it conform to the ideal day I wish I had experienced. I take scene after scene and rewrite it, revise it, and having revised my day, then in my imagination I relive that day, the revised day, and I do it over and over in my imagination until this seeming imagined state begins to take on to me the tones of reality. It seems that it's real, that I actually did experience it and I have found from experience that these revised days, if really lived, will change my tomorrows.

57. I will not hear or accept as true anything other than that which contributes to the concept I will hold of myself. For I will see that I AM secure, and maybe a headline would startle the world but I will not accept it, for if I don't admit to it, it can't proceed out of me. For all things when they are admitted are made manifest, not unless they are admitted.

58. When you imagine something it is as though you struck a chord, and everything in sympathy with that chord responds to bear witness to the activity in you. If the world is the responding chord to what you are imagining, and David is a man after your own heart who will do all your will . . is David not the outer world? This is not "will" as the world uses the word. You do not will something to be so, but imagine it and become inwardly convinced that it is so. And if, through your persistence, the world responds, you have not only found David, you have found the Lord as your own wonderful human imagination.

59. An imaginal act is a creative act, for the moment it is felt, the seed (or state) is fertilized. It will take a certain length of time to be born, so start today by assuming you are the man (or woman) you would like to be and let the people in your mind's eye reflect the truth of your assumption. Be faithful to your assumption. Persist in this thought, for persistence is the way to bring your desire to pass. You don't persist through effort or fear, rather knowing that your imaginal act is now a fact; wait for its birth, for it will come.

60. Do not think for one moment, even though you are innocent of what you are saying, that it is an idle word. Because why? You are God, and God's words cannot return unto him empty. They must accomplish that which he purposed and "prosper in the thing for which he sent it." So, even though you are ignorant of the Law, you are the operant power, operating that Law of which you may be

totally unaware, but there is no excuse. You will still reap the results.

61. The late Robert Frost said: "Our founding fathers did not believe in the future, they believed the future in." The most creative power in you is your power to believe a thing in. Our founding fathers did not believe that the passage of time would produce this country as they desired it. They wanted democracy, not a monarchy, and knew that sitting down and hoping it would come to pass wouldn't do it . . they had to appropriate it, so they simply believed it in. How? By faith. They subjectively appropriated their desire.

62. One day I was fired from J. C. Penney Co. Working for a year and a half, running their elevator and being their errand boy, making $22. a week and paying $5. room rent, I could not understand it when they let me go. But my dreams, my desires, transcended my position there, so they had to do what they did in order for my desires to be realized. Believe me, you are the cause of the phenomena of your life . . be it good, bad or indifferent. If, to you the news is distasteful, you are the dreamer of that distasteful storm. But the day will come when you will awake to discover that the storm is over. That there is only one cause, and that is awareness! I know it is easier to give advice and show the other person where he is wrong, than it is to acknowledge that he is only reflecting the wrong in you. It is difficult to accept the concept that the world is bearing witness to your thoughts, but it is true. If you do not like something or someone, do not look at it or them; look within to the one who is causing the image.

63. If you believe you have it you will. Many men can and will come to aid you, even without knowing they are doing it, if you believe. You do not have to persuade others to help you; all you need do is believe you are what you want to be and then let the world (which is nothing more than yourself pushed out) go to work

to make your assumption possible. I promise you: your desire will be fulfilled, for all things are possible to him who believes.

64. We are told in the 14th chapter of John: "Let not your heart be troubled, you believe in God, believe also in me. In my Father's house are many mansions; if it were not so would I have told you that I go to prepare a place for you? When I go and prepare a place for you, I will come again and receive you to myself that where I AM there you may be also." You may think some man is speaking to a group of men as I am here; but these words were spoken by the human Imagination, who . . having come out from the Father, came into the world. Now leaving the world, human imagination is going to the Father's house. He is returning to discover the source, the cause, of the phenomena of life. Jesus Christ, your own wonderful human imagination, is the way to everything in the world . . but specifically to the Father. Tonight we will take this thought on a practical level so that everyone will know how to bring into this world everything he wants, no matter what it is. Today billions of dollars are being spent on anti-poverty programs; yet the one consuming thing we need (which will not cost one nickel) is a new Christology, a new way of thinking of Christ as the human imagination! Christ is the cause of everything, but as long as the churches mislead the world . . by teaching he is on the outside as one who lived and died 2000 years ago to whom you should turn and pray . . you will never find him. Poverty can never be overcome on the outside, no matter how much money is given to the poor. Only when the poor man is told that he is the source of all life and taught how to turn and pray to himself, will he overcome poverty. So the outstanding need is to teach this new Christology, to tell everyone you meet that Christ is the human imagination, for without this knowledge . . I don't care what you do . . you will never bring your desires into fulfillment.

65. When I speak of imagination I am referring to God in you, of which there are two sides: imagining and contacting. Contacts are what imagining is all about. When you imagine, you contact a feeling, and the feeling you imagine, you create. You are the same God who created the world and all within it, but while you are clothed in a garment of flesh and blood your power is keyed low. I do hope you understand the rules to the game of life; and . . because there is a positive as well as a negative rule . . I urge you not to curse anyone. Ecclesiastes used the words "king" and "rich" because they are the ones most often envied. A person need not be a millionaire, however, to be envied. He could simply be a little bit better off than another. Someone could live in a better neighborhood, pay more rent, maybe even go to a better restaurant, or buy better clothes, to be envied. So we are warned not to curse the king or the rich in our thoughts, for they cannot be concealed, as all thoughts are completely one; and by a law divine they mingle in one another's being. Awareness seems to be scattered, as everyone on the outside is aware. But no one needs ask another to aid in the change of his world if he changes it on the inside. If another is necessary to bring about the change, he will . . with or without his consent. You do not have to single out the individual to play the part in bringing about the change you have imagined. He will play his part if necessary because we all intermingle. All you have to do is stand at the end, from within.

66. The world belongs to you and it is always expressing your inner thoughts, your imagination.

67. Jesus, your own wonderful human imagination, is your hope of glory, and there is no other Christ. Defined as God's power and wisdom, Imagination is in travail until Christ is formed in you. On that day your history will be changed from BC to AD, and every year thereafter will be the year of the Lord. Having been formed in you, Christ is born, and the words of Isaiah become yours: "For to

you a child is born and a son is given. The government shall then be upon your shoulders, and you will be the Wonderful Counselor, Mighty God, Everlasting Father, Prince of Peace. And of your reign there shall be no end." Start now to look upon the great mystery of creation as the subjective appropriation of your objective hope. Dwell upon my words. Put them into practice, and you will experience their fulfillment, for all things exist within you!

68. You are told that everything proceeds out of your own consciousness, but what you and you alone accept as true, that will externalize itself and mold itself in your environment. All the conditions that you will encounter will simply bear witness of the state you have accepted.

69. All things are possible to you, because you are all imagination and imagination creates reality. Knowing what you want, imagine you have it. Knowing what you want to be, imagine you are it. Subjectively appropriate your objective hope and you have assumed a virtue you did not have. Ask no one to help.

70. You can always tell the truth of any concept by the feeling of certainty which it inspires. When you imagine seeing the world as you desire it to be and are inspired as to its truth, it doesn't matter what anyone else thinks. I don't care what it is; when you know what you want, you can make your desire so real, so natural that you will reach a feeling of certainty which no power in the world can stop. When that feeling is yours, drop it. Don't ask anyone if what you did was right or wrong; you did it and that's all that is necessary.

71. "Fear not, you meant evil against me, but God meant it for good." So everything works for good when there is time to reflect upon the act. I could go back to my own small family. There came a moment in our life when it seemed as though the world had come to

its end. My father's partners, desiring to take control of the little equity he had in the business, succeeded and our world collapsed. We had nothing and even our friends made themselves scarce. But what appeared to be an evil thing turned out to be a blessing, for by detaching ourselves from this partnership . . which was small in the sense that they couldn't think big . . my father started on his own with sons who could imagine. The family has now turned our business into a large enterprise of many kinds of businesses with no outside partnerships, dwarfing anything we thought possible forty years ago when it happened. It has taken time and reflection, but now we can see that . . although my father's partners intended evil against him . . God meant it for good.

72. Imagination is the redeeming power in man. This is the power spoken of in the Bible as the Second Man. "the Lord from Heaven". This is the same power personified for us as a man called Christ Jesus.

73. When you tell me what you want, do not try to tell me the means necessary to get it, because neither you nor I know them. Just tell me what you want that I may hear you tell me that you have it. If you try to tell me how your desire is going to be fulfilled, I must first rub that thought out before I can replace it with what you want to be. Man insists on talking about his problems. He seems to enjoy recounting them and cannot believe that all he needs to do is state his desire clearly. If you believe that imagination creates reality, you will never allow yourself to dwell on your problems, for you will realize that as you do you perpetuate them all the more.

74. Every dream contains within itself the capacity for symbolic significance. A fish is the symbol of the power of the human imagination. Imagine yourself depressed, and imagination will throw you into the pit of depression. Imagine yourself free, and your imaginative power will bring you out, for your imagination is the

savior of your world. When you become lost in the reasoning world, your imagination is not fed with your desire, for reason negates its flow. Christ, being your human imagination, is not limited by the reasoning world and all things are possible to him. If you would ignore the facts and walk in your imaginal acts as though your wish were already fulfilled you are feeding Christ, and he becomes alive within you once more.

75. Everything is geared towards the awakening of the imagination.

76. I tell you that imagination creates reality and I ask you to imagine a state, any state, which would imply the fulfillment of your desire. It doesn't really matter what anyone else thinks; it's what you think that matters to you! If you create a scene which implies the fulfillment of your desire and dwell in it until you have an inner conviction that it is real, what does it matter what another thinks?

77. The Bible is not just beautiful poetry; it is the inspired word of God. Written by poets, they have given enlarged meaning to normal words. When you put your body on the bed and assume you are elsewhere, are you not all imagination? In the act of imagining, you depart the dark caverns of this body and appear where you imagine yourself to be, because you are God . . all imagination . . and cannot die.

You cannot go to eternal death in that which cannot die, and your immortal being is imagination! You are the central being of scripture . . the one called Jesus Christ, who is the Lord God Jehovah . . who descended here for a purpose. While here, you must pay the price of living in the world of Caesar. You may criticize our politicians and protest any raise in taxes, but you will continue to be taxed. All you have to do is learn the art of prayer and make more money. I am reminded of a story told of the late President Kennedy.

It seems his father . . who had, in one generation, made something like four-hundred million dollars . . complained that his children were spending too much money. At a banquet, President Kennedy said: "The only solution to this problem is for father to make more money." One day a friend told me that when she was a child, her father would say: "If you have but a dollar and it was necessary for you to spend it, do so as if it were a dry leaf, and you the owner of a boundless forest." If one really knows how to pray, he could spend his dollar and then reproduce it again. You see, this world is brought into being by man's imagination, so it is very important to learn the secret of prayer. If you are still desiring, stop it right now! Ask yourself what it would be like, were your desire a reality. How would you feel if you were already the one you would like to be? The moment you catch that mood, you are thinking from it. And the great secret of prayer is thinking from, rather than thinking of. Anchored here, you know where you live, your bank balance, job, creditors, friends, and loved ones . . as you are thinking from this state.

But you can move to another state and give it the same sense of reality, when you find and practice the great secret of prayer. Take my message to heart and live by it. Practice the art of prayer daily, and then one day you will find the most effective prayer is: "Thank you Father." You will feel this being within you as your very self. You can speak of it as "thou" yet know it is "I." You will then have a thou/I relationship, and say to yourself: "Thank you, Father". If I want something, I know the desire comes from the Father, because all thought springs from Him. Having given me the urge, I thank Him for fulfilling it. Then I walk by faith, in confidence that he who gave it to me through the medium of desire will clothe it in bodily form for me to encounter in the flesh. Don't get in the habit of judging and criticizing, seeing only unlovely things.

You have a life . . live it nobly. It is so much easier to be noble, generous, loving, and kind, than to be judgmental. If others want to do so, let them. They are an aspect of yourself that you haven't overcome yet, but don't fall into that habit. Simply thank your heavenly Father over and over and over again, because in the end, when the curtain comes down on this wonderful drama, the supreme actor will rise from it all and you will know that you are He.

78. If I gave a Stradivarius to one who had mastered the violin he could lift me to the nth degree of joy, but if I put the same violin in the hands of one who could not play it, he would shortly drive me insane. It's the same violin, yet one brings harmony while the other brings discord. You kill and make alive out of the same instrument, which is your own wonderful human imagination. You may make many discords until you 1earn how to play. We are here in this world of educated darkness learning to play the instrument which is God. You may not know anyone who would give you $10,000 right now, but if you believe a11 things are possible to God and you know that God is your human imagination, you can imagine you have the money, persist in your belief and you will have it. How, I do not know; I only know that according to your belief will it be done unto you.

79. The day I realized this great truth . . that everything in my world is a manifestation of the mental activity which goes on within me, and that the conditions and circumstances of my life only reflect the state of consciousness with which I am fused . . is the most momentous in my life.

80. Do you believe that all things are possible to God? And do you believe that he is your own wonderful human imagination? Knowing that God is all love, and you are capable of imagining unlovely things, you may not believe your imagination is God, but if that is true then God is not all-powerful. If you can imagine

something that God cannot, then you transcend him. If God strikes only harmonious notes and you can strike chords that produce discord as well as harmony, then you are greater than he because you can do something he can't. But I tell you: your own wonderful human imagination kills and makes alive, it wounds and heals, for all things come out of the human imagination. While learning to use and believe in your human imagination you may make alive that which you do not want. You may wound yourself in the process, but what you create in your imagination you can uncreate.

81. Believe me, imagining does create reality. Take me seriously. You will never know Jesus until you know the secret of imagining, for your imagination is He. If you really believe in God, believe in your own imagination, for it is the power of God and the wisdom of God. I tell you, there is only one power in the universe. We call it by the name of God or Jesus. But if you think of Jesus as someone on the outside, who lived 2,000 years ago, you will never know him. Nor will you ever know God, if you think of him as some impersonal force. God is a person because you are a person. He became you, as he became us all, that we may become as He is. Take my message to heart and apply it from now on. You can be the man you would like to be. Don't start dreaming about it. Awake and think from it. Do not concern yourself about trying to meet the so-called "right" people. They are simply reflections of the activity you have placed within you. Change your thoughts and you will change the behavior of those who surround you for they are nothing more than yourself made visible.

82. An imaginal act is an immediate objective fact. Functioning on low intensities as we are, an imaginal act is realized in a time process. And so every vision as it stands there I assume that I AM; but at the moment reason denies and my senses deny, but I assume that I AM. And if I assume it and it seems to me real and natural, when I break the spell I know I have planted it, and then it has its

own appointed hour. Every vision has its own period of gestation, as we are told by the prophet: "It has its own appointed hour, it ripens, it will flower, if it seems slow then wait, it is sure, it will not be late." If you see it clearly in your mind's eye, if you were really in the image, it will become just as objective as this room is now . . and again I am speaking from experience. Sitting in my chair at home or reclining on a couch or in my bed, suddenly . . without my eyes being physically open . . I see a world that I would not see if I know where I am physically, and I can't deny it. It's just as real as you are. It's objective, it is seemingly solidly real, and consciousness follows vision and I step into the world that I am observing. And stepping into my image it closes around me, and this world which is seemingly the only world I should know is shut out, and I am part of the world I contemplated, I am in it. I explore that world and it is just as solidly real as this world.

83. Test yourself, and you will discover that your imaginal act was the cause of the response of the world relative to you.

84. Everything in your world that you behold, though it appears without, it is within, in your imagination. And this wonderful imagination of yours is Christ Jesus. Imagination is the actual habitation of every created thing. No matter what you see in the world, it springs from your imagination.

85. But I do know that God's law reflects all the way down to this world of Caesar. I do not know how long it takes for each egg to hatch in a nest, but I do know each one will hatch in its own time. And so it is with an assumption. If I desire to be wealthy, I may not know how long it will take me to reach the conviction that I possess great wealth, but when I feel wealth is mine I have conceived. Conception is my end. The length of time between my desire and its conception depends entirely upon my inner conviction that it is done. A horse takes twelve months, a cow nine months, a chicken

twenty-one days, so there are intervals of time; but it comes down to the simple fact that the truth concerning every concept is known by the feeling of its certainty. When you know it, not a thing can disturb your knowingness!

86. What is an idea to sleeping man, the unawakened imagination, is a fact to the awakened imagination, an objective fact, not an idea.

87. If you will construct mentally a drama which implies that you have realized your objective, then close your eyes and drop your thoughts inward, centering your imagination all the while in the predetermined action and partake in that action, you will become a self-determined being.

88. It is the highest wisdom to know that in the living universe there is no destiny other than that created out of imagination of man. There is no influence outside of the mind of man. Man creates himself out of his own imagination.

89. If it is difficult to control the direction of your attention while in this state akin to sleep, you may find gazing fixedly into an object very helpful. Do not look at its surface, but rather into and beyond any plain object such as a wall, a carpet or any object which possesses depth. Arrange it to return as little reflection as possible. Imagine, then, that in this depth you are seeing and hearing what you want to see and hear until your attention is exclusively occupied by the imagined state. At the end of your meditation, when you awake from your controlled waking dream you feel as though you had returned from a great distance. The visible world which you had shut out returns to consciousness and, by its very presence, informs you that you have been self-deceived into believing that the object of your contemplation was real; but if you remain faithful to your vision this sustained mental attitude will give reality to your visions

and they will become visible concrete facts in your world. Define your highest ideal and concentrate your attention upon this ideal until you identify yourself with it. Assume the feeling of being it . . the feeling that would be yours were you now embodying it in your world. This assumption, though now denied by your senses, "if persisted in" . . will become a fact in your world. You will know when you have succeeded in fixing the desired state in consciousness simply by looking mentally at the people you know. This is a wonderful check on yourself as your mental conversations are more revealing than your physical conversations are. If, in your mental conversations with others, you talk with them as you formerly did, then you have not changed your concept of self, for all changes of concepts of self result in a changed relationship to the world. Remember what was said earlier, "What you see when you look at something depends not so much on what is there as on the assumption you make when you look." Therefore, the assumption of the wish fulfilled should make you see the world mentally as you would physically were your assumption a physical fact. The spiritual man speaks to the natural man through the language of desire. The key to progress in life and to the fulfillment of dreams lies in the ready obedience to the voice. Unhesitating obedience to its voice is an immediate assumption of the wish fulfilled. To desire a state is to have it. As Pascal said, "You would not have sought me had you not already found me." Man, by assuming the feeling of the wish fulfilled and then living and acting on this conviction changes his future in harmony with his assumption. To "change his future" is the inalienable right of freedom loving individuals. There would be no progress in the world were it not for the divine discontent in man which urges him on to higher and higher levels of consciousness.

90. Satan is the doubter. It is he who doubts the reality of your imaginal acts. If you can't believe in the reality of your unseen imaginal act, you may turn to another and believe in him; but you are always imagining, for imagination is God, and imagination . .

imagining . . is the power of the world. In the beginning you heard, but as your eyes see the result of your inner hearing you believe, and in the end everything taken from you will return one hundred-fold.

91. May I tell you: before you entered this world of tribulation and death you were God the Father, but you did not know it. You had to come into this experience in order to know that the world is yours and all within it. And, since it is all the Father's, the only way you can know it is all yours is to become the Father. You could own the earth, but if you did not know everything in it was yours for the taking, you could die of starvation, not knowing how to appropriate it.

92. When you imagined you were the person you wanted to be and heard your friends rejoice at your good fortune, you entered that state and prepared a place in which to dwell; for at that moment Christ in you was speaking to the outer, rational you. As your own wonderful human imagination Christ is telling you that he knows you are afraid, that you have obligations in life which must be met, but to not be afraid for "I will go and prepare a place for you." Knowing this, close your physical eyes upon the world round about you and let not your heart be troubled, neither let it be afraid, for all things are possible to Christ (imagination) in you! Let him prepare the state, for he is the way to its fulfillment.

93. Blake identified the human imagination with the divine body of the Lord Jesus Christ, saying: "Babel mocks saying there is no God or son of God, but thou, O human imagination, O divine body art all a delusion, but I know thee, O Lord." Knowing exactly what he had experienced and how he traveled across the bridge of incident which led him back into this mundane state called the waking world, he knew . . when he opened his weary eyes . . that he had returned. But in that realm, whatever he imagined happened; and he knew the power of the creator. He knew that all things were

made by imagination, and without imagination was not anything made that was made. If you awake in a dream and know exactly who is imagining it, you can control your dream. The same thing is true in this world. Become aware that it, too, is a dream. Awake! Remember who is imagining it, and control your day. Then one day you will completely awake to find yourself in that body which is the Lord Jesus Christ, to know that everything is your imagination pushed out. The restriction you imposed upon yourself when you came here was for the purpose of expansion, for you could not expand until you first reached the limit of contraction and opacity called man.

94. Nothing has ever happened to you that you did not set in motion in your imagination. I tell you: you can be anything you want to be, but when you voice your request, your desire must be genuine. You must so want it that you are willing to remain faithful to your change in position. You cannot assume you have your desire for one little moment and then return to your former state, for if you do you are a double-minded man and will not receive anything from the (Imagining) Lord (as told us in the Book of James). If you want to be successful in business, you can. I don't care how many creditors you owe, or what the bank says you have; if you assume success and persist in that assumption you cannot fail. This is the law by which everyone lives.

95. Remember the story of the prodigal son? The first son did not leave his Father, but the second . . asking to be given what was his . . went into the world and wasted all. When the second one, having experienced the world of death, remembered his Father, he turned around and the Father gave him the robe, the ring and prepared a fatted calf for a merry reception in honor of his son who had returned. When the first son complained, the Father said: "Son, you are always with me. You never detached yourself, but have always remained here and all that is mine is yours." Because of this

the first son knew nothing of the power of imagination. Everything was his, but he didn't know how to appropriate it. Tonight you could have a billion dollars in the bank and die of starvation if you didn't know it was there. All that the Father has is yours, but you will never know it until you use your imagination to appropriate it! You and I have departed from the Father. It was his will to subject us to this world of futility. He did it in the hope that we would be set free from this world of decay where everything dies, and obtain the glorious liberty of the sons of God . . those who exercise their power of imagination lovingly.

96. Take me seriously! Know what you want and then claim you have it. Tell a friend about it and feel his excitement for you. Persuade yourself that what you are imagining is true. Believe in its reality and it will come to pass as an objective fact on this level, I promise you. Then when the image is perfect, you will return to your ancestral self, and time will no longer be necessary between the imaginal act and the fact.

97. A friend of mine, maybe, is unwell; or maybe he's unemployed, or maybe he is not earning enough to meet the obligations of life. All right, he is in me. As I think of him, he's in me. He need not be physically present for me to think of him; he's in me. I think of him; I conjure him. Well, can I change his entire picture in me? I assume that he is talking to me, and he's telling me that he has never had more, he has never felt better; and as I believe in what I am seeing in my own mind's eye, . . I believe in him. That is Christ in me, and all things are possible to Christ. Well then, test it and see if it works. See if you do not see him in the not too distance future earning more, looking better; and everything in the world that you have done within you, he responds to. He need not praise you or thank you. You don't need his praise; you don't need his thanks. You don't need confirmation from him, other than he does conform to what you have done in yourself concerning him. You ask no one

to thank you. Thank nothing. You are simply exercising the power of God within you. "And the power of God and the wisdom of God is Jesus Christ". And there is nothing in the world but God. It is all God in you "pushed out," and God is your own wonderful human imagination. He can't be closer. God is never so far off as even to be near, for nearness implies separation. He's not separated. God actually, literally became as I AM, that I may be as He is. He is not something on the outside. No matter how near He is, He can't even touch me. He actually became me, with all of my weaknesses, all of my limitations; and now I am trying to struggle within myself to find out who I AM, -- and that's His name. My name is in Him. What's your name? "Go and say I AM has sent you." "Is that your name?" "Yes, forever and forever it is my name." "What name? Jehovah?" "No." "The Lord?" "No, I AM." That's His name. That is His name forever and forever.

98. If the Lord (your imagination) claimed that David (the world) always does his will, and you, by a simple imaginal act, command the outer world to respond . . are you not the Lord?

99. Persist in your imaginal acts and the world will respond. The world does not cause, it only responds to your imaginal acts, for only God acts and God is in you as your own wonderful human imagination. Now, before you judge it, try it. If you do, you cannot fail, and when you prove imagination in the testing, share the good news with your brothers. Tell everyone you meet how the world works. You do not have to have a proper educational or social background to apply this principle; and you cannot fail, for an assumption, though false, if persisted in will harden into fact.

100. Imagination, which is Christ in man, is not subject to the necessity to produce only that which is perfect and good, it exercises its absolute freedom from necessity by endowing the outer physical self with free will to choose to follow good or evil, order or disorder.

101. See a situation as something on the outside, and you become entangled in its shadows . . for everyone who responds to your imaginal act is a shadow. How can a shadow be causative in your world? The moment you give another the power of causation, you have transferred to him the power that rightfully belongs to you. Others are only shadows, bearing witness to the activities taking place in you. The world is a mirror, forever reflecting what you are doing within yourself. If you know this, you are set free and a series of events will unfold within you to reveal the story of salvation.

102. Let us set ourselves, here and now, a daily exercise of controlling and disciplining our imagination. What finer beginning than to imagine better than the best we know for a friend. There is no coal of character so dead that it will not glow and flame if but slightly turned. Don't blame; only resolve. Life, like music, can by a new setting turn all its discords into harmonies. Represent your friend to yourself as already expressing that which he desires to be. Let us know that with whatever attitude we approach another, a similar attitude approaches us. How can we do this? Do what my friend did. To establish rapport, call your friend mentally. Focus your attention on him and mentally call his name just as you would to attract his attention were you to see him on the street. Imagine that he has answered, mentally hear his voice . . imagine that he is telling you of the great good you have desired for him. You, in turn, tell him of your joy in witnessing his good fortune. Having mentally heard that which you wanted to hear, having thrilled to the news heard, go about your daily task.

Your imagined conversation must awaken what it affirmed; the acceptance of the end wills the means. And the wisest reflection could not devise more effective means than those which are willed by the acceptance of the end. However, your conversation with your friend must be in a manner which does not express the slightest doubt as to the truth of what you imagine that you hear and say. If you do not control your imagination, you will find that you are hearing and saying all that you formerly heard and said. We are creatures of habit; and habit, though not law, acts like the most compelling law in the world.

With this knowledge of the power of imagination, be as the disciplined man and transform your world by imagining and feeling only what is lovely and of good report. The beautiful idea you awaken in yourself shall not fail to arouse its affinity in others. Do not wait four months for the harvest. Today is the day to practice the control and discipline of your imagination. Man is only limited by weakness of attention and poverty of imagination. The great secret is a controlled imagination and a well sustained attention, firmly and repeatedly focused on the object to be accomplished.

103. Knowing that every desire is ripe grain to him who knows how to think *from* the end, he is indifferent to mere reasonable probability and confident that through continuous imagination his assumptions will harden into fact.

104. Men believe in the reality of the external world because they do not know how to focus and condense their powers to penetrate its thin crust. Strangely enough, it is not difficult to penetrate this view of the senses. To remove the veil of the senses, we do not employ great effort; the objective world vanishes as we turn our attention from it. We have only to concentrate on the state desired to mentally see it; but to give reality to it so that it will become an objective fact, we must focus our attention upon the desired state until it has all the sensory vividness and feeling of reality. When, through concentrated attention, our desire appears to possess the distinctness and feeling of reality; when the form of thought is as vivid as the form of nature, we have given it the right to become a visible fact in our lives. Each man must find the means best suited to his nature to control his attention and concentrate it on

the desired state. I find for myself the best state to be one of meditation, a relaxed state akin to sleep, but a state in which I am still consciously in control of my imagination and capable of fixing my attention on a mental object.

105. The imaginative image is the only thing to seek.

106. Let nothing come between you and that foundation of which Paul speaks and defines as the creative power of God and the wisdom of God, no matter what it may appear to be. Allow no one to come between you and God, for God is your own wonderful human imagination, and who can lead you there? Every moment of the day you are thinking. Be careful what you think, for your thoughts will be tested by fire, and if they survive you will receive a reward. Your thought (your imagination) is fireproof. But if you believe fulfillment is conditioned on a chain letter, another person, or going to church and praying to an unknown God, then something has come between you and the one foundation. Nothing must come between you and your imagination (thought), who is the Lord Jesus Christ.

107. It may startle you to identify the central figure of the Gospels as human imagination, but I am quite sure you will be convinced that this what the ancients intended that we should know, but man has misread the Gospels as history and biography and cosmology, and so completely has gone asleep as to the power within himself.

108. Assume your wish through the sense of feeling. That assumption, subjectively appropriated and believed to be true, is faith. Can you believe in its reality? Knowing all things are possible to him who believes, can you persuade yourself that, although your reason and senses deny it, your assumption will make it so? Blake, in his wonderful "Marriage of Heaven and Hell," said: "I dined with

Isaiah and Ezekiel and asked: Does a strong persuasion that a thing is so, make it so? and Isaiah replied: All prophets believe it does, and in ages of imagination a firm persuasion moved mountains, but many today are not capable of a firm persuasion of anything." Everything here was once only a desire, believed. This building, the clothes you wear or the car you drive were first a desire, then believed into being.

109. The man of imagination knows that the world is a manifestation of the mental activity which goes on within himself, so he strives to determine and control the ends *from* which he thinks.

110. Forgiveness is, in fact, experiencing in imagination the revised version of the day, experiencing in imagination what you wish you had experienced in the flesh.

111. In the world you must go on the outside to light your way. You may light a candle, a lamp, or use electricity; but one day you will turn within to discover that you are the light of the world. Then you will know you are God, the light of infinite love, infinite power, and infinite wisdom. You will expand into these states as you break the barriers of reason and senses. I challenge you to examine yourself. Are you holding to the state you desire to experience? Test yourself, and as you do you are testing Christ (imagination), for he is God's power and wisdom. It doesn't cost anything to test him, so try it.

112. You can test your creative power based upon your desires. You may desire something you think you cannot afford, or you don't have the time or the know-how to enjoy it. You can think of a thousand reasons why its possession is impossible; but . . hearing that imagination creates reality . . you can imagine you have it. But to imagine is not enough; you must have faith enough in your imaginal act to believe in its reality. When you imagine you are the

person you want to be, you must firmly believe you already are it; then wait in faith for your assumption to appear in your world, for that imaginal act has its own appointed hour. It will ripen and flower. If it seems long to you . . wait, for it is sure and will not be late.

113. The mystic calls a change of consciousness "death", by death he means, not the destruction of imagination and the state with which it was fused, but the dissolution of their union.

114. So, you either believe in your own wonderful human imagination or you do not, for that is Christ. An event took place 2,000 years ago, but it didn't take place once, never to take place again. His birth is taking place in the lives of everyone who hears and believes. So what must you do? Believe in him whom he has sent. I did not come into the world to make you think I am a holy man, but to tell you that I have awakened from the dream of life. I have finished the race. I have fought the good fight, and I have kept the faith. It doesn't really matter when I drop this garment, for this world is over for me. I will tell you of my experiences while I am here, in the hope that you will believe . . not in Neville, but in your own wonderful human imagination whom you sent! Your true name is I AM, and your creative power is called Jesus Christ. Because all things are made by your imagination, test yourself and see. Put your powerful imagination to the test.

115. You will find tonight to be a very practical and yet a very spiritual hour, for I am going to speak to you of the Creator. In Paul's letter to the Romans he said: "All the invisible things of God are clearly seen, being understood by the things that are made." Man is called upon to look at the made, in order to discover the invisible God. How? By questioning himself. Look around you and try to remember when there was nothing to support your belief in the present, but you had a thought and dreamed a dream that one day

you would have what is now yours. If you can remember, you have found the Creator to be your own wonderful human imagination. Could that be God? Now, in the very next verse Paul claims: "Although they knew God they did not honor him as God." Having found the relationship between the things seen and the imaginal act, do you honor your imagination as God? Or do you turn to images resembling mortal man, birds, animals, or reptiles and believe that they are the cause because they seemed to aid in bringing your unseen act into being? If you turn and think something on the outside is the cause of your good fortune (or your misfortune) you are giving up the truth about God for a lie, and worshiping the thing created instead of the Creator. Rather, you should relate your outer world to an imaginal activity within. If you do not accept the fact that God is the cause of everything in your outer world, then you do not honor your imagination as God.

116. So when man "dies," he cannot die; only the garment that he "wears" can die. But that Being that he really is, is all imagination. And as He enters, wherever He enters, it takes on cubic reality. That I have proven. The Immortal You cannot die. It did not begin. So when you leave this world, because you are all imagination, . . the very moment that you depart, you are in some state; but, you being there, you give it cubic reality. That world is just as real as this world. It's terrestrial, just as this world is; and no one in this world can "die." Everything dwells in your own wonderful human imagination. The purpose, now, is to awaken that Being in you, so He is fully conscious at all times. That is the purpose of life. He who came down and took upon Himself the weaknesses and the limitations of this garment and confined Himself to it, is destined to awaken while He walks this earth. And by "this earth," I mean this earth to the senses; but it does not end where my senses cease to register it. It doesn't terminate at the point called "death," because the Being in it goes on, and He is still in the world.

But His entrance into that state gives it a cubic reality just like this room now because we are in it.

117. The being you really are is the God in scripture who is your own wonderful human imagination. There is no god besides your own wonderful human imagination.

118. I tell you it is possible to be anything you want to be, for the believer and the God of the universe are one. Don't divorce yourself from God, for he is your I AMness. Believe in your I AMness, for if you do not you will never fulfill your desire. Only by assuming you already are the one you would like to be will you achieve it. It's just as simple as that.

119. I couldn't tell you the atoms of my body, but it is my body. I couldn't tell you if you took the hand off that it's my hand I am looking at, any more than I could tell you your name or anything about you; yet, you are myself "pushed out," as this body is the body I wear. And so, as the body obeys my mind, you -- my "pushed-out" body -- will obey my mind too. All I have to do is to concern myself with what I want in this world, and try to keep it within the frame of the Golden Rule; doing unto others only that which I would want done unto me, -- nothing more than that; hurting no one, doing not a thing to anyone other than that which I would want done unto me. If you want all the lovely things done, -- do only the lovely, and do it all in your own wonderful human imagination. Then you will realize this tremendous secret of imaging. It is the greatest of all secrets, to the solution of which everyone in the world should aspire, because Christ is the answer.

120. A friend recently shared a vision with me, in which I appeared and said: "The story of Jesus is persistent assumption." If this is true, and we are told to imitate him as a dear child, I must dare to assume I am the being I want to be. I must continue in that

assumption until that which I have assumed is objectively realized. And if I am one with everyone, how can anyone be greater than I? Do not believe that someone is greater than you because of some influx of spirit or validity. Your imagination is the only God, and there is no other being greater than He! Claim you are what you want to be. Persist in that assumption. Continue to assume that role until that which you have assumed is reflected in your world.

121. Believe in the reality of your own imaginal acts, for faith is loyalty to unseen reality. Have faith in your imaginal act. Although unseen by the outer world as an external fact, your loyalty to its unseen reality will cause the unseen to become seen by the world.

122. Everything I am telling you is from the Bible. "I kill and I make alive. I wound and I heal and there is none that can deliver out of my hand. I, even I AM He and there is no God besides me. I AM the Lord your God, the holy one of Israel, your Savior and besides me there is no savior." These are the words of God, revealed through his prophets of old. Their prophecy is fulfilled in the New Testament as: "Whatsoever you desire, believe you have received it and you will." That's how easily you apply it, for an assumption, though false and denied by your senses, if persisted in will harden into fact.

123. Your I AMness is He. Say: "I AM secure, I AM wealthy, I AM free." This may not be true based upon your senses, but I am simply asking you to say the words, for the moment you do you are subjectively appropriating security, wealth, and freedom. Reason will try to take these from you, so I ask you to play a little game with me. Go through the door and walk as though you are secure, wealthy, and free. Sleep this night as though it were true. If you do, you will not fall asleep seeing the world as you did last night, you will see it differently. If this morning someone gave you a check for $20,000 and you deposited it to your account, you would be $20,000 richer, therefore you could not sleep tonight as you did before. Now,

without waiting for someone to physically give you the money, go to bed as though it were true. Put Christ to the extreme test. If all things are possible to God and if all things are possible to the believer, can you believe? I am not saying you will succeed the first night, or even the second. Having been trained to accept only what your reason and senses dictate, you may find it difficult, almost impossible, to believe what you could believe . . but you can!

124. Everything must first be imagined before it can become a fact, and that capacity to imagine is God.

125. Everything can be resolved, even though while learning, horrible mistakes are made. Don't condemn yourself for anything you have ever done, are doing, or may do, as you learn to play the instrument who is God himself and your own wonderful human imagination, for there is no other creative power.

126. You can be the man (or woman) you want to be, but not by simply wishing. You must make the effort to look at the world mentally and see it reflect your fulfilled desire. And when it does you must remain in that state until you reach the inner conviction that what you are seeing, touching, tasting, smelling, and hearing is true, clothe yourself in the feeling of its reality . . and explode! Do that and you are pregnant. And what do you do after pregnancy? Nothing! You simply wait for its birth to appear in its own appointed hour. And it will! When you least expect it your desire will objectify itself in the world for you to enjoy, whether it be health, wealth, or fame. That's how God's law works.

127. When someone born into poverty persists in dreaming he possesses great wealth and his dream comes true, his wealth seems perfectly natural to those who do not know his dream. You are dreaming. If you try to make your dream come true while doubting its possibility, you are heading toward a nervous breakdown. But if

you go all out in your wonderful claim, you will fulfill it, for all things are possible to the God you are, for you are the God of whom the Bible speaks.

128. There is only one reality, and that is Christ . . Human Imagination, the inheritance and final achievement of the whole of Humanity.

129. If you would say: "I remember when I couldn't afford to spend $400 a month for rent," you are implying you can well afford it now. The words: "I remember when it was a struggle to live on my monthly income," implies you have transcended that limitation. You can put yourself into any state by remembering when. You can remember when your friend expressed her desire to be married. By remembering when she was single, you are persuading yourself that your friend is no longer in that state, as you have moved her from one state into another.

130. In his infancy, man thinks everything outside of himself is the cause of the phenomena of life. Many believe in astrology. I must confess at one time I did also. Years ago I taught astrology to a dear friend who was a retired school teacher. Desiring to augment her retirement income, she became an astrologer. One day I found her in tears. It seemed that she was sitting next to an open window when a breeze blew the papers, causing her to draw the chart of a man who was born ten years later than her customer. Not realizing this, she convinced herself . . and the man . . that his business venture would be a success. The customer promised to wire her $100 if this were true. Norma saw in the chart what the man wanted to hear, and she believed her little hieroglyphics. That is all that mattered. She was self-persuaded, so the whole thing was done. This is based upon the foundation: "Whatever you desire, believe you have received it and you will." By this time I had outgrown my belief in monkey bones, astrology, teacup leaves, numerology, or

anything outside of my own wonderful human imagination; for having tested myself, I knew that all things were possible to the imagination. Although I told Norma this, I could not console her. But that evening I was there when a Western Union messenger brought her a check for $100 from the man who had promised it. Even though Norma understood the truth of the one foundation, astrology brought her a small income, so she remained a professional astrologer until her death. Norma is not alone. Many a minister, priest, or teacher, knows that what he teaches is not true; but he is not willing to stand on his own feet and believe in the one foundation, human imagination.

131. When man has the sense of Christ as his imagination, he sees why Christ must die and rise again from the dead to save man . . why he must detach his imagination from his present state and match it to a higher concept of himself if he would rise above his present limitations and thereby save himself.

132. Now I ask you to continue to test your creative power . . imagination . . by practicing revision. If you hear something that is unlovely, don't accept it, but instantly revise it. Hear the words that ought to have been spoken and persuade yourself, to the best of your ability, that it is so.

133. It's time for man to stop believing in something on the outside and start believing in his human imagination. It's time to stop all the outside icons. "You shall make no graven image unto me, or have no other gods besides me, your own wonderful human imagination." You may have no education, no money or social background, and find it difficult to believe in yourself; but because all things are possible to him who believes, and with God all things are possible, you can go outside of your senses and believe anything into being. Test your imagination, and if it proves itself in performance, what does it matter what the world thinks?

134. If you want something don't ask yourself if you are qualified, but is your request genuine. Do not concern yourself as to how and when it will happen, simply assume that you are there already and in a way that no one knows it will take place. Your business will grow, your family will grow, everything will be as you have imagined. You can stand perfectly still and so move that you can be seen at the point in space where you have imagined you are. I have done it. Wanting my sister in Barbados to see me although I was physically 2,000 miles away, I moved in my imagination, and when she entered the room of her son she saw me lying on the bed. She wrote me that very day and told me of her experience, so I know that all things are possible, for you and God are one. Take me at my word. It is impossible without motion to bring anything into being, and the motion is within you. Knowing exactly what you want, view the world from the premise that you have it. If the world remains the same you haven't moved. Only when it can be seen after the change, can you know you have moved. Now, continue thinking from the new state, for motion can be detected only by a change of position relative to another object. A friend is a good frame of reference. Looking at his face, let him see you as he would if your desire were fulfilled. He would see you differently, would he not? If he is one who would congratulate you, accept his congratulations. Extend your hand mentally and feel the reality of his hand. Listen and hear the reality of his words of congratulations. Then have faith in your unseen reality, for if you do, no power can stop it from coming into your world.

135. Recognizing the power of feeling, let us pay strict attention to our moods and attitudes. Every stage of man's progress is made through the exercise of his imagination and feeling. By creating an "ideal" within our mental sphere we can feel ourselves into this "ideal image" till we become one and the same with it, absorbing its qualities into the very core of our being. The solitary or captive can, by the intensity of his imagination and feeling, effect myriads so that

he can act through many men and speak through many voices. Extend your feelers, trust your touch, participate in all flights of your imaginations and be not afraid of your own sensitivities. The best way to feel another's good is to be more intensely aware of it. Be like my friend and have "more of a feeling" for the health, the wealth, the happiness you desire. Ideas do not bless unless they descend from Heaven and take flesh. Make results or accomplishments the crucial test of true imagination. As you observe these results, you will determine to fill your images with love and to walk in a high and noble mood.

136. There are those who try to rush everything into being. They try to force birth from conception, but it cannot be done. There are many experiences not recorded in scripture, and I am not here to stand in judgment of anyone as to whether they have experienced scripture or not. But I do know from experience that on this level, if you dare to assume you are what you want to be, your inner conviction, your feeling of certainty will bring it to pass. When you embrace the desired state, you have assumed its impregnation, and its fulfillment has its own appointed hour. It will ripen and flower. If the state is slow in objectifying itself wait, for it is sure and will not be late.

137. As the Word, you sent yourself into the world to fulfill all that you said you would. In the beginning you were the Word which was with God and was God. You are the Word which went forth from God's mouth and will not return void, but must accomplish that which you purposed and prosper in the thing for which you were sent. Coming out from the knowledge of being the Father, you brought with you the pattern of salvation. This you will fulfill, as it is this pattern that takes you back to the knowledge of being the Father you have been seeking. You came out from yourself and entered the world of men by falling asleep to your true awareness. You will return to that awareness when you learn to trust the one

and only God, who is your own wonderful human imagination. Forget all the little isms; there is only God! When you say I AM, you are speaking as God. Add any word and you have placed a limit on an infinite being. That which is unlimited, abides by his own law and becomes that which he believes himself to be . . whether it be unwanted, sick, helpless, or poor. Believe in a world of your own creation, and . . because all things are possible to imagine . . the moment you become aware of anything, you have given it the power to project itself on your screen of space.

138. As you represent another to yourself as you would like to see him, you are lifting his burden and fulfilling God's law. And when your time is fulfilled you will enter the temple and find the sign of the birth of your creative power as a child wrapped in swaddling clothes. Then the arm of God, who creates everything, is unveiled in you and from that day on whatever you imagine will come to pass . . I don't care what it is. I ask you to dwell upon this thought and follow the pattern of Simon. Lift the burden of someone today, and maybe tomorrow you will be able to do it to two. Don't let another remain carrying his burden, because there is no other. Lift his burden from yourself and follow Jesus Christ, your own wonderful human imagination.

139. Prayer is the elevation of the mind to that which we seek. The very first word of correction is always "arise." Always lift the mind to that which we seek. This is easily done by assuming the feeling of the wish fulfilled. How would you feel if your prayer were answered? Well, assume that feeling until you experience in imagination what you would experience in reality if your prayer were answered. Prayer means getting into action mentally. It means holding the attention upon the idea of the wish fulfilled until it fills the mind and crowds all other ideas out of the consciousness. This statement that prayer means getting into action mentally and holding the attention upon the idea of the wish fulfilled until it fills the mind

and crowds all other ideas out of the consciousness, does not mean that prayer is a mental effort . . an act of will. On the contrary, prayer is to be contrasted with an act of will. Prayer is a surrender. It means abandoning oneself to the feeling of the wish fulfilled. If prayer brings no response . . there is something wrong with the prayer and the fault lies generally in too much effort. Serious confusion arises insofar as men identify the state of prayer with an act of will, instead of contrasting it with an act of will. The sovereign rule is to make no effort, and if this is observed, you will intuitively fall into the right attitude.

140. Leave the state containing poverty and move into the state containing wealth, and wealth will take on reality. This room has reality and substance because you are thinking from it. Think of a room, however, and it is but a shadow. Think of a state and it seems a mere possibility. But enter it by thinking from the state, and it is the only reality. Blake said: "If the spectator could only enter into the image in his Imagination; if he could make a friend and companion of his image, he would rise from the grave and meet the Lord in the heavens." Now, buried in a state, you are a spectator of other states. But if you will rise from your present state and bury yourself in another, you will express it. If you can be what you want to be, why not become it? Why sit in a state you dislike and argue, when you can move into another state in your imagination? But once you have moved into the state of your fulfilled desire, don't be like Lot's wife. Don't look back at your former state and preserve it, for salt is a preservative.

141. Everything is within you and can be brought into being by this simple technique. Desiring to visit my family in Barbados, I slept in New York City as though I were in Barbados and thought of New York City as 2,000 miles to the north. Then I received a letter from my brother justifying the trip and enclosing a draft to cover my personal expenses. I had not written my brother to ask him for this

money, but while I was physically sleeping in New York City and imagining myself in Barbados, my brother had the impulse to write and give me reasons why I should come home. I hadn't been there in twelve years and the family needed me to complete the link. He justified his letter; justified the draft and justified the expenses he would incur, while I . . without a nickel . . simply imagined I was already in Barbados. I knew exactly what I had done, and I believe that all things are made by God . . Imagination . . and without him is not a thing made that is made; so I have found God to be my human imagination. Now, am I going to fall into the trap and not honor him (Imagination) as God but turn to an image resembling a human being and say he was the cause of my trip? Am I going to give credit to my brother who sent me the draft and notified the steamship company to issue me a ticket? Or am I going to remember the God . . Imagination . . that I discovered? This is what Paul is asking everyone who reads his letter. Having found God, are you going to honor him as God? Or are you going to exchange the truth about God for a lie?

142. The Bible begins on this note: "In the beginning God created the heavens and the earth." Here we see that God created the within, (for we are told that heaven is within and God is in his heaven) and he created the earth, which is without. How did God bring the earth into existence if it is on the outside and He is in heaven on the inside? By the act of movement: "The spirit of God moved upon the face of the waters." Here we find that motion is the cause, that without motion it is impossible to bring forth anything. And how does God move? Through the act of imagining. Now, motion can only be detected by a change relative to a fixed frame of reference. What would you do to move from where you are now and what you are now, to where you want to be? Would your friends see a change in you? Would your outside world look different? Take time to sort out your desire, and when it is clearly defined move in

your imagination. How do you know you have moved? By mentally looking at your world and seeing its change.

143. In the Book of Psalms, you are told to; "Commune with your own self." Sit quietly. Be at peace with yourself and suddenly thoughts will begin to flow within you, from God. In the beginning you were God! And in the end, you and I and the whole vast world of billions will be regathered into the one God. One imagination fell into this fragmented world of seeming others, yet the whole is within each one of us. A man's enemies are those of his own household, for they are all within him. Not knowing this, man fights within himself until he realizes there is no other, just himself. Then he tells others in the hope he can convince himself. And as he rises from within, he is called back into the one being he was before that the world was. The fall into division was deliberate for God's expansion into unity.

144. Start now to put your imagination to the test. Jesus Christ is in you and you will not fail if you call your desire forth with God's name. Sleep in the assumption that you already are the person you desire to be, and firmly expect the evidence to appear in your world. The last bold statement in the Book of John is: "I AM the true vine." If God's name is I AM and it is synonymous with God Himself, then I . . the vine . . will grow and produce the fruit I AM aware of. If you dare to remain conscious of any state, it must appear! Claim for yourself that which you would like to experience. Then put your hope fully upon the grace that is coming to you at the unveiling of Christ within you. When the first act takes place, count the days, and you will discover the last act will appear exactly 1,260 days later. After that, you will linger to tell your story to those who will listen. Not everyone will, for they are interested only in things of this world. Show them how to get their things until they hunger for the promise. Then Christ will unveil himself in them and they will

discover they are God the Father. Yes, I AM the way, the truth, the life, and the vine. But when I come to the end, I AM the Father.

145. I tell you, if you want someone to change, you must change your imaginal activity, for it is the one and only cause of your life. And you can believe anything in if you will not accept the facts your senses dictate; for nothing is impossible to imagine, and imagining . . persisted in and believed . . will create its own reality.

146. I say to everyone: the whole vast world is now in your human imagination, and you can bring any desire out of it by believing it into being. First, you must know what you want, then create an image that fulfills it. Would your friends know and talk about it? Imagine they are with you now, discussing your fulfilled desire. You could be at a cocktail or dinner party that is being given in your honor. Or maybe it's a little get-together over tea. Create a scene in your mind's eye and believe its reality in! That invisible state will produce the objective state you desire, for all objective reality is solely produced by imagination.

147. Your life is nothing more than the out picturing of your imaginal activity, for your imagination fulfills itself in what your life becomes.

148. Always remember that the Bible is addressed to the man of imagination and not to any mortal man.

149. Continue to revise and not to be afraid of the responsibility of this tremendous power to imagine; for life itself is nothing more than an activity of imagination. When I speak of Christ being your life, I am saying he is your imagination, for life is an activity of imagination. Ask yourself what you are imagining right now and you will discover what Christ has created. For by imagination all

things are created, and without imagination is not a thing created that is created.

150. I had discovered that my imagination was the only God who ever existed, yet in spite of this discovery I had not fed it. Rather I continued to use the rational approach to life by planning my life on a reasonable basis. Knowing of a power that did not need reason was not enough; I had to exercise this power within me. And then I was determined to exercise my imagination on behalf of myself and others. You must exercise your powerful imagination morning, noon, and night and never neglect it. It must be exercised daily and then one day you will discover the Christ within you, who is God the Father.

151. The story of Jesus is a wonderful mystery that cannot be solved until you discover, from experience, that he is your own wonderful human imagination.

152. That which you experience in imagination is an actual creative act. It is a fact in the fourth dimension of space and will make its appearance in this three-dimensional world just as surely as planting a seed will result in the growth of a particular plant. Once you have planted this seed in your imagination, do not uproot it by being anxious about how it will be accomplished. Each seed has its own appointed time. Some seeds take a few days; others a little longer. Feel confident that what you have planted will appear in your world. Your imagination will draw all that it needs to make your dream an actual reality.

153. Prayer is nothing more than the subjective appropriation of an objective hope. Imagine by giving objective reality to your hope. Bring your hope so close that you can feel what it would be like if it were objective to you. Clothe yourself in that feeling . . and you have clothed yourself in its reality. The world will not immediately

reflect your feeling, but you have set your desire in motion and cannot take it back. You have given a subjective state your blessing by giving it objective reality. Now it must fulfill its destiny so that you will be blessed in all that you are doing. If you don't give your subjective hope objective reality, you can't be blessed in its fulfillment. You must clothe yourself in the feeling that your wish is fulfilled. Your desire is waiting to be clothed in the feeling of external reality. Catch the feeling, and you have clothed your desire with the external reality. Now deceive yourself into believing that your desire is externally real, and give it your blessing by subjectively appropriating your objective hope. You cannot see what you are asking for in your outer world. It's a hope and you are blind to it. But when you clothe yourself in the feeling of its fulfillment, you are eating the feeling of satisfaction. Feast upon this feeling morning, noon, and night, and in a way you do not know your desire will become an objective reality in your world.

154. Tonight take a mere wish and see it in your mind's eye as fulfilled. Contemplate it. Merge and lose yourself completely in it. Allow your wish to take on objectivity, all the various tones of reality, so that it seems now to be the only reality. Then break it and return once more to merge in this section of your dream, and reflect upon that which was so real only a moment before. Do that and no power on earth or in the universe can stop that which you have imagined from objectification. Simply rest in confidence that it will be objectified, and keep the Sabbath. The Sabbath is simply that moment when you do not make any effort to make it so, because you know it is already so! Do not labor to add to it or take from it. It is going to happen just as you judged it as good and very good. You try it. If all things were made by God, and without Him was not anything made that was made, and you imagined and it came to pass . . then you must come to the conclusion that what is done grows from what is finished. In the beginning it was only a wish, but in the end it became a fact. So what is done grows from what is finished.

The creative power of the universe stems from imagination . . the real man . . for man is all imagination, and God is man and exists in us and we in Him. The eternal body of man is the imagination, and that is God Himself. Imagination is not a God afar off, but a brother and a friend.

155. I invite you now to go all out and imagine you really are the man or woman you want to be. But do not doubt, for the minute doubt steps in, a mental division descends, as doubt is the devil. If you will believe that regardless of what the world tells you, you are the man you want to be, you won't go mad. Instead, you will become that man. Your dream world will rearrange itself to fit your new image into it without any difficulty or help on your part.

156. Man expresses himself through his human imagination, just as God expresses himself through his Divine Imagination. There is no clear-cut separation between God and Imagination, or man and his imagination. I tell you, Imagination is God Himself. He is the divine body Jesus, of which we are his members. Identifying Divine Imagination with Jesus, Blake claims Imagination became Man, that Man may become God's power and wisdom, called Christ. Any Christ other than he who is crucified, buried, and rises in an individual is false, for there is no Christ other than man's own wonderful human imagination.

157. The dictionaries define meditation as fixing one's attention upon; as planning in the mind; as devising and looking forward; engaging in continuous and contemplative thought. A lot of nonsense has been written about meditation. Most books on the subject get the reader nowhere, for they do not explain the process of meditation. All that meditation amounts to is a controlled imagination and a well sustained attention. Simply hold the attention on a certain idea until it fills the mind and crowds all other ideas out of consciousness. The power of attention shows itself the sure

guarantee of an inner force. We must concentrate on the idea to be realized, without permitting any distraction. This is the great secret of action. Should the attention wander, bring it back to the idea you wish to realize and do so again and again, until the attention becomes immobilized and undergoes an effortless fixation upon the idea presented to it. The idea must hold the attention . . must fascinate it . . so to speak. All meditation ends at last with the thinker, and he finds he is what he, himself, has conceived. The undisciplined man's attention is the servant of his vision rather than its master. It is captured by the pressing rather than the important.

158. Inner talking mirrors our imagination, and our imagination mirrors the state with which it is fused.

159. There is no fiction. What is fiction today will be a fact tomorrow. A book written as a fictional story today comes out of the imagination of the one who wrote it, and will become a fact in the tomorrows. If you have a good memory or a good research system, you could find today's facts. Not every fact is recorded, because not every thought is written; yet every person imagines.

160. My friend saw tiny, magnetic seeds swirling around his feet, causing the outer world to appear so large. These seeds of contemplative thought are so tiny they are often ignored and even scraped off; but awareness causes them to reform themselves instantly to magnify their new formation in the outer world. If imagination's seeds did not reform themselves, the outer world would vanish and leave not a trace behind; but they do, for the seeds are contained in man. You have the power to rearrange your thought-seeds to produce a different pattern in your outer world. This is done by a change of attitude. Think of the world as different, and as you do, you have scraped off the little magnetic seeds, thereby causing their rearrangement. This is the world in which we live. Now, when imagination lifts us up from the pit and places our

feet upon the Rock, we stand on our own feet. No longer will we stand upon the foot of another, giving the other either our praise or blame. We can, however, be gracious and kind and thank another for the role he played in our drama. But when we stand on our own feet, we realized that everything that happens . . be it good, bad or indifferent . . is because of our attitude towards life.

161. When imagination matches your inner speech to fulfilled desire, there will then be a straight path in yourself from within out, and the without will instantly reflect the within for you, and you will know reality is only actualized inner talking.

162. Tonight I ask you to take the most fantastic thing in this world and find an inner conviction within yourself that it is yours, for the truth of any concept is known by the feeling of certainty which that conviction inspires. Once you have that inner feeling of certainty, don't ask me to confirm it. What would it matter what I think? Do not be disillusioned if your experience has not been mine. Believe in yourself and trust your inner feeling. Test yourself and if it works on this level it will work in the depths of your being.

163. Do you know what you want? I will tell you a simple way to get it. Simply catch the feeling that you have it and sustain that feeling. Persist in acknowledging the joy of fulfillment. In your imagination tell your friends your good news. Hear their congratulations, then allow him who heard your friends and felt your joy of fulfillment, bring it into your world, for he who can do all these things is within you as your own wonderful I AMness, your Imagination, your consciousness. That is God. Test God, for he will not fail you. Then, when he proves himself in performance, tell a friend, and continue telling others as you exercise this law. And walk knowing all the other I AM statements are yours. Prove this in the world of shadows and you will prove the other in the world of reality. Your I AMness is the true eternal reality. Living in a world

of shadows, as you declare your I AMness you are declaring eternal truth. When you say, "I AM the resurrection," that is eternal truth. "I AM the life" is eternal truth, as well as "I AM the way." All of these bold certainties preceded with the "I AM" are eternal truths. So, do not listen to anyone who screams at you from their tower of Babel and tells you of another way, for there is no other way. You don't have to give up meat or only eat fish on Friday in order to enter the way, for the way to the cause of all life is within you. Believe in your I AMness for there is no other God.

164. When I say all things exist in the human imagination, I mean infinite states; for everything possible for you to experience now, exists in you as a state of which you are its operant power. Only you can make a state become alive. You must enter a state and animate it in order for it to out picture itself in your world. You may then go back to sleep and think the objective fact is more real than its subjective state into which you have entered; but may I tell you: all states exist in the imagination. When a state is entered subjectively, it becomes objective in your vegetative world, where it will wax and wane and disappear; but its eternal form will remain forever and can be reanimated and brought back into being through the seed of contemplative thought.

165. You may not be aware of who you are, where you are, or what you are; but you do know that you are. Aware of what your senses and reason dictate, you may believe that you are limited, unwanted, ignored, and mistreated; and your world confirms your belief in your imaginal activity. And if you do not know that your awareness is causing this mistreatment, you will blame everyone but yourself; yet I tell you the only cause of the phenomena of life is an imaginal activity. There is no other cause.

166. Every person, place, or thing, is animated and rearranged from within; for as He is, so are we. A good Christian would call

that statement blasphemy; yet I am quoting the first epistle, the fourth chapter of the Book of John: "As he is, so are we in this world." This thought follows on the heels of the definition of God as love. And because God is love, He will not change your imaginal act, but will allow it to be externalized. If God changed the act, there would be two of you: one who imagines, and one who changes the imaginal act. But, being all love, God instantly plays the parts designated in your imaginal acts and suffers with you because He is dreaming. But one day Love will awaken within your skull. He will resurrect and you will begin the real drama, which is to discover your true identity. Coming out of your immortal skull, all of the imagery of scripture will surround you. The child and the witnesses will be there; but they will not see you, for you will be spirit. While witnessing your spiritual birth, they will speak of you and identify the child as yours, but you will be invisible to their mortal eye. As the great drama unfolds, it appears to take place externally; yet it is within, for you contain eternity within yourself.

167. When man discovers that his world is his own mental activity made visible, that no man can come unto him except he draws him, and that there is no one to change but himself, his own imaginative self, his first impulse is to reshape the world in the image of his ideal.

168. Why is the Bible more Entertaining and Instructive than any other book? Is it not because it is addressed to the Imagination, which is Spiritual Sensation, and only immediately to the Understanding or Reason." Tonight I will use scripture, but my premise will not be along any orthodox concept of Christ, for scripture is a mystery. It is God's secret, which cannot be read with complete understanding, but must be experienced. When you read in the Book of Revelation, "Jesus Christ, the faithful witness, the first born from the dead," you may think . . as the world does . . of a unique being who came into the world two thousand years ago. But

the word "Christ" means "the Lord's anointed." This is not one man called 'the Lord" and another man called "the anointed," but one who knows himself to be the Lord's anointed. Who is the anointed? Your own wonderful human imagination! That's the only Jesus and the only God. When a friend asked Blake what he thought of Jesus, Blake replied: "He is the Only God, but so am I and so are you." This statement is true, but man will not accept the fact that his human imagination is God. He cannot grasp the idea that the God who created and sustains the universe is one with his human imagination, but Blake meant his statement to be taken literally. Your own wonderful human imagination is Jesus, the Only God . . and so am I.

169. Act as God, and simply let it be so. God said: "Let there be light, Let the sun appear. Let the moon appear." After his imaginal act, God let everything appear, sustaining it by faith, knowing that without faith it is impossible to bring it to pass. "Faith is the assurance of things hoped for, the evidence of things not yet seen." If you have faith in the reality of your imaginal act, it must objectify itself in your world.

170. It is impossible for man to see other than the contents of his own consciousness, for nothing has existence for us save through the consciousness we have of it. The ideal man is always seeking a new incarnation but unless we, ourselves, offer him human parentage, he is incapable of birth. We are the means whereby the redemption of nature from the law of cruelty is to be effected. The great purpose of consciousness is to effect this redemption. If we decline the burden and point to natural law as giving us conclusive proof that redemption of the world by imaginative love is something that can never come about, we simply nullify the purpose of our lives through want of faith. We reject the means, the only means, whereby this process of redemption must be effected. The only test of religion worth making is whether it is trueborn . . whether it

springs from the deepest conviction of the individual, whether it is the fruit of inner experience.

No religion is worthy of a man unless it gives him a deep and abiding sense that all is well, quite irrespective of what happens to him personally. The methods of mental and of spiritual knowledge are entirely different, for we know a thing mentally by looking at it from the outside, by comparing it with other things by analyzing and defining it. Whitehead has defined religion as that which a man does with his solitude. I should like to add, I believe it is what a man is in his solitude. In our solitude we are driven to subjective experience. It is, then, that we should imagine ourselves to be the ideal man we desire to see embodied in the world. If, in our solitude, we experience in our imagination what we would experience in reality had we achieved our goal, we will in time, become transformed into the image of our ideal. "Be renewed in the spirit of your mind . . put on the new man . . speak every man truth with his neighbor."

The process of making a "Fact of being a fact of consciousness" is by the "renewing of our mind." We are told to change our thinking. But we can't change our thought unless we change our ideas. Our thoughts are the natural outpouring of our ideas, and our innermost ideas are the man himself. The end of longing is always to be . . not to do. Be still and know "I am that which I desire." Strive always after being. External reforms are useless if your heart is not reformed. Heaven is entered not by curbing our passions; but rather, by cultivating our virtues. An old idea is not fickly forgotten, it is crowded out by new ideas. It disappears when a wholly new and absorbing idea occupies our attention. Old habits of thinking and feeling . . like dead oak leaves . . hang on till they are pushed off by new ones.

Creativeness is basically a deeper receptiveness, a keener susceptibility. The future dream must become a present fact in the mind of anyone who would alter his life. Every great out-picturing is preceded by a period of profound absorption. When that absorption is filled with our highest ideal, . . when we become that ideal . . then we see it manifest in our world and we realize that the present does not recede into the past, but advances into the future. This is essentially how we change our future. A "now" which is "elsewhere" has for us no absolute meaning. We only recognize "now" when it is at the same time "here." When we feel ourselves into the desired state "here" and "now" we have truly changed our future.

171. First of all, most of us do not even realize our own harvest when it confronts us. And if we do remember that we once imagined it, reason will tell us it would have happened anyway. Reason will remind you that you met a man (seemingly by accident) at a cocktail party who was interested in making money. When he heard your idea, he sent you to see his friend, and look what happened . . so really, it would have happened anyway. Then, of course, it is easy to ignore the law, but "Blessed is the man who delights in the law of the Lord. In all that he does he prospers."

172. The man of imagination puts his whole trust in the feeling of the wish fulfilled and lives by committing himself to that state, for the art of fortune is to tempt him so to do.

173. The sixth disciple is called Bartholomew. This quality is the imaginative faculty, which quality of the mind when once awake distinguishes one from the masses. An awakened imagination places the one so awakened head and shoulders above the average man, giving him the appearance of a beacon light in a world of darkness. No quality so separates man from man as does the disciplined imagination. This is the separation of the wheat from the chaff. Those who have given most to Society are our artists, scientists, inventors and others with vivid imaginations.

174. Life is a controllable thing to the man of imagination.

175. Who is this being who bears our sins, our infirmities, and our diseases? Christ! Our wonderful human imagination! When you are in pain, or experiencing deep sorrow, your imagination is doing the suffering. If a friend tells you he is not feeling well, or is in great pain, and you tell him that his imagination . . called Christ . . is doing the suffering, your friend would not believe you, because he conceives Christ to be someone other than himself. But Christ is the human imagination, and until man discovers this for himself the Bible will make no sense to him whatsoever.

176. On this level you can start from here, right now, and fulfill any dream. May I tell you: you are going to live the life that you are imagining, so imagine well! Imagine the most glorious thing in the world and . . no matter how wonderful it is . . may I tell you it is nothing compared to the being that you really are. Nothing in this world can come close to the being you really are. This world of Caesar is only a tiny section of your infinite being, but while you are here, dream nobly. Dream lovely dreams, for you can realize everything if you are willing to imagine that you have them now. Begin now to imagine you are the man (the woman) you would like to be, and regardless of what happens tomorrow, next week, or next month, if you persist in the assumption that you already are that which you want to be, you will become it in this world of flesh and blood. Everything here will vanish, yes . . but why not test your creative power? Then you will begin to taste the power latent within you, and you will discover that you can conjure out of your own depth things that are seemingly impossible, conjured by the mere act of assumption. If you dare to act and persist in acting as though it were true and it becomes a fact, then you will know the truth of your creative power.

177. Remember: everything you see, although it appears on the outside it is within you. You do not have to be concerned about influencing individuals if you make goals. If you want a great deal of money, see the money within you. Then claim it is yours!

178. Now tonight you believe it, though everything in the world denies it. Reason denies it, your friends will deny it, and you dare to assume you are the man . . already the man, already the woman . . you would like to be, and that things are already what you would like them to be. And as you dare to assume that you are, and you walk in that assumption just as though it were true, in a way that no one knows you will be led across a series of events toward the fulfillment of that assumption, and no power in the world can stop it if you are persistent in that assumption. Believe that imagining creates reality. "Therefore I tell you, whatever you ask in prayer, believe that you receive it, and you will." Just as simple as that . . but how to believe that I receive it? If at this very moment I believe that I have received what today I deny, I would look at the world differently. I wouldn't see it prior to that fulfillment. I would now mentally look at the world, and I should see it as I would see it, were it true that I have become the man I want to be. I would commune with my wife, my daughter, my friends, from that assumption, and though no physical thing in the world could force me, I still should persist in the belief it is done, and carry on that assumption, and sleep in the belief that it has taken place just as though it were true. And if I do, may I tell you: I know from experience it will come true on this level. It is already true the very moment I believe it; at that moment is the creative act. But man's memory is very short and he doesn't remember the act, so when he reaps the harvest he denies that it is his. He didn't plant it, and yet we have a law established in the very beginning called the law of "identical harvest." "While the earth remains, seedtime and harvest, cold and heat, summer and winter, day and night, shall not cease." Everything will bear according to its nature; it cannot bring forth other than its nature.

179. Now I urge you to put his teaching into practice. He taught you to simply appropriate a subjective state which is your objective hope, and know it must externalize itself in your world. Do that and it will. Ask in faith, without a doubt, for those who doubt are like the wave of the sea that is driven and tossed by the wind. They are double-minded, for they know what they are while desiring to be something else. You must be single-minded by dropping what you believe you are and assuming that you are already what you desire to be, for you cannot desire something you already possess. Look into the wonderful law of liberty which sets you free, and you will see your freedom in the faces of your friends. Persist in your assumption and it must come to pass.

180. The link between your imaginal act and its fulfillment is your faith, which is nothing more than your subjective appropriation of your objective hope. Hoping your desire . . subjectively appropriated . . is true, faith is your link to its objectivity.

181. The only Christ who ever existed is within you as your own wonderful human imagination.

182. The law is simple: "As you sow, so shall you reap." It is the law of like begets like. As you imagine, so shall your life become. Knowing what you want, assume the feeling that would be yours if you had it. Persist in that feeling, and in a way you do not know and could not devise, your desire will become a fact.

183. To believe your desire into being is to exercise the wonderful creative power that you are. We are told in the very first Psalm: "Blessed is the man who delights in the law of the Lord. In all that he does, he prospers." This law, as explained in the Sermon on the Mount, is psychological. "You have heard it said of old, thou shalt not commit adultery, but I say unto you, anyone who lusts after a woman has already committed the act of adultery with her in his

heart." Here we discover that it is not enough to restrain the impulse on the outside. Adultery is committed the moment the desire is thought!

184. People think that Man is not God, but I tell you that Man is all Imagination and Imagination is God.

185. An imaginal act is a creative act, for the moment it is felt, the seed (or state) is fertilized. It will take a certain length of time to be born, so start today by assuming you are the man (or woman) you would like to be and let the people in your mind's eye reflect the truth of your assumption. Be faithful to your assumption. Persist in this thought, for persistence is the way to bring your desire to pass. You don't persist through effort or fear, rather knowing that your imaginal act is now a fact; wait for its birth, for it will come.

186. So, in the Father's house are many states of consciousness. Pick a state, enter and occupy it. Your Father is the good shepherd and your desires are his sheep. When the good shepherd comes, he gathers all of your desires for yourself and others together and brings them into the field. How is this done? In your imagination! A friend's desire may not be your desire for him, but if it is not in conflict with your ethical code and you are a good shepherd, you will represent your friend to yourself as telling you that he (or she) has it. That way your sheep, having heard your voice, will follow you into the fold. In the 10th chapter of John we are told that the good shepherd goes first and his sheep follow. Signs follow, they do not precede. Take your desire into the fold by putting yourself into the desired state. Remain there until you feel its reality. Knowing that imagining creates reality, thank your Father and drop it. Now, do nothing on the outside to make it so, only know your desire is yours the moment you do it! Do not expect immediate birth! There are always intervals of time between pregnancy and its fulfillment. One seed may take 21 days, another five months, nine months, a

year, or even more. Do not be concerned with the interval of time between the fertilization of the seed and its hatching; only know the seed of desire has been planted in the mind. And if at times you find your sheep have gone astray, bring them back into your fold when you know who the good shepherd is. But if you don't, you will find many shepherds who will fleece you!

187. Man's inner talking mirrors his imagination, and his imagination is a government in which the opposition never comes into power.

188. Inner talking reveals the activities of imagination, activities which are the causes of the circumstances of life.

189. "The wise men of old, the prophets and the kings would have given anything to have heard the things that you have heard and to see the things you have seen, and they did not." And so in our State Department . . or the Foreign Office of England, or in the foreign office of any power in the world . . they are not hearing what you are hearing. This doesn't make sense to them; they must be rational beings and play the game as they played it for unnumbered centuries, with all the mistakes and replaying all the silly things all over again. I tell you: don't forget it, because God doesn't forget it, and we create by our imaginal acts. What are you tonight imagining? I don't care what it is; one day you are going to be shocked beyond your wildest dreams when you see the other side. Like the story of "Lazarus laughs." He returns from the dead and all the values were changed, and the rich were poor, and the poor were not poor. All the values on this side were completely reversed on that side and everything was changed when Lazarus returned, and he laughed at some things we are doing here. So I tell you: don't forget God's law, for "Blessed is the man who delights in the law of the Lord, for in all that he does he prospers."

190. Jesus Christ is your own wonderful human imagination and his story is all about you. Told in the third person, it is written as though another is doing all the suffering for you; yet you know you are the one who is suffering. I tell you, that unless you believe your awareness of being is God you will continue to miss your mark, thereby remaining in sin.

191. You don't have to broadcast what you want; you simply assume that you have it, for . . although your reasonable mind and outer senses deny it . . if you persist in your assumption your desire will become your reality. There is no limit to your power of belief, and all things are possible to him who believes. Just imagine what an enormous power that is. You don't have to be nice, good, or wise, for anything is possible to you when you believe that what you are imagining is true. That is the way to success.

192. Imagine, and then watch the mystery of creation unfold in terms of faith, by remaining loyal to the unseen reality of that which already exists.

193. In the Book of Luke, the story is told of a man who came to a house at the midnight hour, and said: "A friend has arrived who is hungry. Would you let me have three loaves of bread?" The man upstairs replied: "It is midnight. My children are in bed asleep and I cannot come down and give you what you want." Then this statement is made: "But because of the man's importunity, he was given all that he desired." The word “importunity” means "brazen impudence." Having a desire, the man would not take no for an answer! When you know what you want, you don't ask God as though he were another; you ask your individual self to bring about your desire, for you are he! And God . . your own wonderful human imagination . . will respond when you will not take no for an answer, as your denial is spoken from within and there is no other. It is within your own being that you persist in assuming you have

received what you want. The story is, even though it was midnight and the family was asleep, the father came down and gave what was needed. The God of a Blake, a Shakespeare, or an Einstein, does not differ from the God housed in you, as there is only one human imagination. There cannot be two. He is not a dual God. You and your imagination are not less than anyone, but you must learn to be persistent.

194. If Christ is your own wonderful human imagination and all things. . be they good, bad, or indifferent . . are made by him, you can imagine unlovely things and perpetuate their image. To say that Christ makes only the good and a devil makes the evil is false. When you doubt the power of Christ in you . . that's the devil. Unless you actually believe that "I AM" is the being you are seeking and pray only to him by exercising your human imagination, you will never reach your desire, for awareness is the only power that can give it to you. imagination.

195. I tell you, you are all imagination and not a prisoner of anything or anyone, rather you have imprisoned yourself. You have brought all of your experiences into being and you can change them now that you know who you are. When you hear the word Lord, don't think of another. The word is Yod Hey Vav Hey and means I AM, as do the words Father and potter. Your awareness of being is your I AM, your potter who molds your world. To him and him alone lies all of the responsibilities for what is done in your world. Your own wonderful human imagination is the cause of the restrictions on the freedom that you enjoy today. There is no other cause but the Lord, who is the Father, who is the potter, and if he is your own wonderful human imagination, to whom can you turn to praise or blame for the circumstances of your life? The blind leaders of the blind blame society or the government for the causes of the phenomena of their life. But I tell you, there is no other cause; for there is no one outside of self. Society, the government, your family,

or friends, are all within you. Although they appear to be pushed out, there is not a thing that does not now exist in you; as Divine Imagination (the Lord God Almighty) has reproduced Himself in you . . the human imagination; and Divine Imagination contains all things within Himself.

196. Whatever you are beholding in your mind's eye, you will produce in your outer world. It is just as simple as that. I hope you are beholding your fulfilled desire in your mind's eye; for scripture tells you that: "Whatever you desire, believe you have received it and you will." This is telling you that, to the degree you are self-persuaded, you will become what you have assumed you are.

197. You can put God to the test, and if He proves himself in the testing then you will know God is your own wonderful human imagination. If you want the joy of marriage, a love affair, or a romance, you can test God by assuming the one you desire is with you now. And to the degree you persist in that assumption, it will be yours to experience. Do not be concerned as to how or when it will happen; simply persist in the assumption that it has happened, and when it does you will know who God is.

198. If to you a storm is raging remember, it is only raging because you are not aware of your imaginal activity. By disciplining your thoughts, you rise from the sleep of unawareness, and become aware of what you want to imagine. Then the world will change to conform to the change in you. The storm will subside and there will be a perfect calm. Do not look for God outside of the temple, for you are God's temple, and the spirit of God dwells in you. Ask the average person where he thinks God's temple is, and he will point to a synagogue, cathedral, or church; but God does not dwell in houses made with hands. God is spirit and dwells in his living temple! Imagine . . and God is acting. Believe in the reality of what you are now imagining! Rearrange those little clusters around the foot, and

when they are fixed with feeling, relax in the knowledge that your outer world will conform to the new fixation. Although the world appears external, its reality is within, as you are its creative power, dreaming the world into being; for you are an immortal being, wearing a garment of mortality. One day you will awaken from this fantastic dream, to find yourself enhanced by having experienced the mystery of death.

199. You need not be concerned about how this will be accomplished. Your imagination will use whatever natural means are necessary to bring it about. "I AM the beginning and the end." "My ways are past finding out." What you do in imagination is an instantaneous creative act. However, in this three-dimensional world, events appear in a time sequence. Make your inner conversations conform to your imaginal act. You have planted a seed and you will soon see the harvest of that which you have sowed.

200. It is possible to resolve every situation by the proper use of imagination.

201. I firmly believe, from my own experiences, that this God of whom the Bible speaks is our own wonderful human imagination; that God and the human imagination are one; that all natural effects in the world, though they are created by the Spirit of God, are caused by Spirit. So, "every natural effect has a spiritual cause, and not a natural. A natural cause only seems; it is a delusion of our" . . fading, I would say, "memory." (Blake, from "Milton") For here in this world I can't quite remember when I imagined that which is now taking place in my world. I do not recall it. I can't quite remember when I set it in notion. But if this is Law, . . and a Law that no man can break, . . at some time, somewhere, I imagined what I am now encountering; that my present moment is not really receding into the past; it is advancing into the future to confront me,

but I forgot it. And I now think it has a natural or physical cause, and it does not have a natural cause. "Every natural effect has a spiritual cause," or the Bible is completely wrong. For we are told: "By Him all things were made," . . without exception; "and without Him was not anything made that was made." And: "He is Spirit," and "the Spirit of God dwells in me." Well, if He dwells in me, I have identified Him with my imagination. Only on this level, I do not remember having imagined it; but along the way, I must have if this is Principle.

202. I AM is the key to scripture. Called Jesus Christ in the New Testament, God the Father's name is revealed in the Old Testament as I AM. Having come into the world to fulfill the word, you cannot return empty but must accomplish that which you purposed and prosper in the thing for which you sent yourself. After inspiring the prophets to tell your story, you came not only to fulfill their prophecy, but to share your experiences to encourage others.

203. I remember a man in New York City during the Second World War, who claimed he despised Roosevelt. Every morning when the man shaved, he would talk to himself in the mirror, imagining he was telling Roosevelt everything he disliked about him. The gentleman attended my meetings, and when I confronted him with his imaginal acts, he said: "I pay $10 to see a Broadway show which does not give me the joy I receive during that ten minutes in the morning." Well, this man created his own storm, for the venom that he spewed out every morning returned to him. He lost his New York City home, then went to Florida, where he lost everything there. I tried to tell him to awake, that he was sleeping and only dreaming that Roosevelt was the cause of his world. But he could not believe me. He came from a Germanic background and could not get over the fact that we were at war with Germany. He blamed Roosevelt, even though he knew Germany had declared war on us. He could not see the war as a bad dream, and he was

confusing it, making the storm rage by the pleasure he received telling Roosevelt off as he shaved. It's entirely up to you what you think. If you want to hate someone, you can augment it through intensity and persistence. The same thing is true if you want to love someone; for your human imagination is the only God you will ever know, and he is in his temple . . that temple you are!

204. All that has been built up by natural religion is cast into the flames of mental fire., yet, what better way is there to understand Christ Jesus than to identify the central character of the Gospels with human imagination . . knowing that, every time you exercise your imagination lovingly on behalf of another, you are literally mediating God to man and thereby feeding and clothing Christ Jesus and that, whenever you imagine evil against another, you are literally beating and crucifying Christ Jesus?

205. Here is a story of a man who learned to turn to no one on the outside for help, for all help came from within him. As a very young boy he was one of a very poor family of five who lived in Russia. At the age of eight he was running errands to earn money to help feed the family. Having never had a square meal, a new shirt, slacks, or shoes, he knew the horror associated with a minority group, as his family were Jews. This lad had a job taking large amounts of money to a bank to be exchanged into small denominations. One day he noticed that the teller's copper coins resembled the silver ones, and as he returned the money to his employer he began to play a little game with himself. Assuming the teller had given him silver instead of copper, he dreamed of the wealth that would be his, had the mistake been made. The very next day the teller made the mistake. Giving him silver instead of copper, the young lad pocketed the money, went to another bank and changed it into the right denomination then, returning to work he gave his employers the money they expected. Having been taught what was right and wrong, the boy wrestled all through the night

with his conscience, but in the morning he took the money, bought a new pair of shoes, a new shirt and pants. Then he went to a restaurant and ate to his heart's content. No, he never returned the money, but he learned a great lesson from this experience. The world, upon hearing this story, would say he was wrong; but when we came out from the Father we ate of the tree of good and evil, and there isn't one person in this world who has not violated that code. He may not have the courage to violate the moral code openly, but the drama of life is psychological. The child was hungry. Having entered the world of experience, he learned how to use the creative power of his own wonderful human imagination. In the interval he has given back to society ten thousand times more than the small amount taken, not to compensate, but because of the lesson learned. After the First World War Russia collapsed and, penniless, he came to Paris to work as a street cleaner. Then he remembered what he had done so many years ago, and from that point on he rose and today is a multi-millionaire in a legitimate business, applying this simple principle that an assumption, though false, if persistent in will harden into fact.

206. I remember visiting my family in Barbados, when I was told I could not leave the island for seven months; but I wanted to leave on the next boat out. To me, being on that boat was my end; so . . while sitting on a chair in my parent's home . . I entered the boat in my imagination and viewed the island as I was departing. I did not know how I would get on it, but a week later when the boat left the island I was there. This I know from experience. In your desire to go anywhere you must first go there in your imagination, and even those who may deny your request will aid you when the time is right. I got out of the army that way. Knowing I wanted to be honorably discharged and in my apartment in New York City, I slept as though it had already happened and I was already there. Then my captain . . who had previously disallowed my discharge . . had a change of heart and aided in my release. Anyone can do it. This

game is easy to play and can be lots of fun in the doing. Think of an object you would like to hold. Think of a place you would desire to be. Then find an object in that room and feel it until it takes on sensory vividness. Don't make it a lamp, but that lamp; not a table, but that table. Sit in that chair until you feel the chair around you. View the room from that chair and you are there, for you are all imagination and must be wherever you are in your imagination. Now, cast your bread upon the water by feeling the relief of being there, and let your genie . . who is your slave . . build a bridge of incident over which you will cross to sit in that chair, hold that lamp, and touch that table.

207. Tonight learn to fine-tune your imagination. Knowing the voice of your friend, tune him in. Determine the words you want him to say and listen carefully. Tune him in until his words are fine and clear, then believe you heard him. Think it really happened. If you will, it will come to pass. When, I cannot say, for every imaginal act is like an egg and no two eggs (unless they are of the same species) have the same interval of time for hatching. The little bird comes out in three weeks, a sheep in five months, a horse in twelve months, and a human in nine months. Your imaginal act has its own appointed hour to ripen and flower. If it seems long, wait . . for it is sure and will not be late for itself.

208. But until individual man believes in his own wonderful human imagination, God remains imprisoned within him. If you do not harvest God's promise it is only because you do not believe!

209. It may take a thousand times to persuade yourself that things are as you desire them to be, and not as they appear to be. But, to the degree that you are self-persuaded that you have done it in your imagination, will the outer world reflect its harmony. William James, a professor of psychology at Harvard, is one of our great educators. He said: "The greatest revelation in my generation

is the discovery that human beings, by a change of inner attitude can produce outer changes in harmony with their inner convictions."

210. Your own wonderful human imagination is the actual creative power of God within you. It is your savior. If you were thirsty, water would be your savior. If you needed a job, employment would be your savior. Your imagination is the power to save you from whatever circumstances you now find yourself. You can experience your heart's desire through the use of your imagination. Nothing is impossible to your imagination. Your imagination is unlimited in what it can accomplish. If you can imagine something, you can achieve it.

211. Faith in any power other than He (imagination) who is within you is false, and anyone who teaches a power on the outside is a false teacher. Christ (imagination) in you is your hope of glory, and there is no other power.

212. Continue to imagine what you want until you have actually obtained it. You do nothing else to obtain your desire. If it is necessary to take some action, you will be led to do so in a normal, natural manner. You do not have to do anything to "help" bring it about. Remember that it is God, Himself, who is doing the work and He knows exactly how to accomplish it. If you think of your desire during the day, give thanks that it is already an accomplished fact . . because it is!

213. There is no limit to your creative power. The most horrible problem will be resolved if you will but conceive a solution in your mind's eye. Anyone can do it. It doesn't take an Einstein to imagine a problem is resolved. Do not limit your creative power by determining the ways and means for it to come about, for imagination has at its disposal ways that are past finding out. Do not be concerned as to how, when, or where . . only the end. If you are

in debt, what is the solution? That you win the lottery or an uncle dies and leaves you his fortune? No! The end is that you are debt-free. How would you feel if all of your bills were paid? Assume that feeling and let imagination harden that feeling into a fact!

214. Every problem has a solution. Imagine the solution and assume it is true. What would you see and do were it true? How would you feel? Persist in that feeling and in a way no one knows the solution will come to pass. There is nothing impossible to God, and God is crucified on you as your own wonderful human imagination! There never was another and there never will be another God, and all things are possible to him. If you can imagine the end, knowing all things are possible to imagination and remain faithful to that assumption as though it were true, imagination will harden into fact. Remember, creative power will not operate itself. Knowing what to do is not enough. You, imagination's operant power, must be willing to assume that things are as you desire them to be before they can ever come to pass. How long will it take for a state to become objective? As long as it takes the nature of that seed to hatch. All you are called upon to do is to go into the state and remain there psychologically. Although you will continue to physically walk the earth as one person, as you think from your desired psychological state, it takes on physical tones and becomes a fact in your world.

215. Now I know I AM the center of creative power. The day will come when you, too will awaken and exercise your creative power, knowingly. That is our destiny, for we all will awaken as God and use this power to create in the true sense of the word. Try to remember that there is no limit to God's creative power, or your power of belief. Persuade yourself that things are as you desire them to be. Fall asleep in that assumption, as that is your act of faith. Tomorrow the world will begin to change, to make room for the garment of your assumption. If it takes one person or ten thousand to

aid the birth of your assumption, they will come. You will not need their consent or permission, because the world is dead and what would be the purpose in asking dead people to help you? Simply know what you want, animate the scene and those playing their parts will begin to move towards the fulfillment of your desire. Try it before you pass judgment upon it. I know it doesn't make sense, but it will prove itself in performance and then it will not matter what the world thinks. If there is evidence for a thing, does it really matter what someone else thinks about it? I encourage you to try it, for if you do you will not fail.

216. Begin now to believe in your true Being who is God, and whatever you imagine to be so, firmly believe it is so, and it will be so.

217. Knowing what you want, close your eyes and enter its fulfillment, knowing that God (consciousness) is seeing what you are seeing. That He is hearing what you are saying; and what God (consciousness) sees and hears and remains loyal to, He externalizes.

218. Now here is the story. He said, "Except you be born again, you cannot enter the kingdom of heaven." The wise man said, "How is it possible a man my age may once again enter my mother's womb and be born again?" He said, "You, a master of Israel and you do not know? Except you be born of water and the spirit, ye can in no wise enter the kingdom of heaven." Then he gives this clue, "As Moses lifted up the serpent in the wilderness, even so must the son of man be lifted up." …As Moses lifted up the serpent… do you think a man lifted up a brazen serpent as told in the story and that everyone who looked on it was instantly healed and those who would not look were not cured? It's not any serpent. A serpent is a symbol of the power of endless self-reproduction. For the serpent sheds its skin, and yet does not die. Man must be like the serpent,

who grows and outgrows. So I must now learn the art of dying that I may live, rather than, I would say killing that I may survive. I die, by laying down all that I now believe, and I lift myself up to the belief that I am what I want to be. That's how I do it.

219. I ask you to test your creative power every moment of time. Live with absolute faith in Jesus Christ (your Own Wonderful Human Imagination). He is a person because you are a person. As you imagine a state, the creative power of the world will bring it into reality. Claim a glorious future for yourself by making the future the present. Have your friends congratulate you on your good fortune now, and have faith in Jesus Christ, knowing he is your Own Wonderful Human Imagination!

220. I say: you are God, the only actor in this world. No matter what you imagine, God is acting. He is the only actor, acting by imagining. You can imagine anything, cover the act with faith by believing in its reality, and it will come to pass.

221. If you want to test God, you may. Your immortal eyes and ears need not be open to test your creative power. Simply assume you are the one you want to be. Remain faithful to your assumption and, although everything denies it, you will become it. It does not matter who you are or what the world thinks of you; anything is possible to the "I" of imagination.

222. If you test your creative power on this level, the statement: "Whatsoever you desire, believe you have received it and you will," will no longer be a great theory given lip service, but will be known from experience. Believe you are the man (or woman) you want to be. Catch the feeling that you have already arrived. Look at your world from that assumption, knowing its truth. Now, believe your assumption has its own appointed hour to flower. Persist in your

belief and no power on earth can stop it from hardening into fact. This is Christianity!

223. When I first stumbled upon this principle, I thought it was stupid. The idea that imagining creates reality was nonsense. How could anyone believe a thing into being without any external evidence to support it? How could any imaginal act be the causative fact, which fuses and projects itself? Although I did not believe it could, I imagined, and got that which I did not want! So I acquaint you now with what I know about this principle of imagining and lead you to your choice and its risk. There is always a risk, for you may not want what you have imagined after you get it, so I warn you to select wisely.

224. Look at your world mentally. Your present level of objective fact may be the same as it was before, but in your imagination hear your friends congratulate you on your good fortune. Then believe in the reality of this unseen experience. Like Paul, look not to things seen, but to things unseen; for the things seen are temporal, while the things unseen are eternal.

225. The dream of life unfolds on this level, as well as on a higher one. On this level we see things happen and are given reasons for wars and revolutions, as well as the geological causes for the convulsions of nature. But we do not know and cannot perceive their hidden cause, for it lies in the imagination of man. All things spring, not from the ostensible causes to which they are attributed, but from that which is hidden . . man's own wonderful human imagination! In the April issue of the Atlantic Monthly, there is an article by General David M. Shoop, retired commandant of the Marine Corps. In this article, he claims that there is an ambitious elite of high-ranking officers who are turning this country into a militaristic and aggressive nation. They are promoting war in the belief that through it they will receive the promotions and glory they desire and cannot

achieve while serving in a peacetime army. They dream of a war they can command in glory. Where? In their own wonderful human imagination, the hidden cause of all life! Imagination can be used infernally . . as these men are doing . . or towards the kingdom of heaven. This is done by thinking of a friend and hearing him tell you his good news. You can watch his facial expression change as he speaks to you. You can see him stand erect, wearing clothes he is proud of, as you feel the thrill of his change. And if you will believe that what you are now seeing is real, you can relax in the knowledge that one day your friend will conform to what have you done in your imagination!

226. All things exist in the human imagination, and all phenomena are solely produced by imagining. Where there is no imagining, everything vanishes. If lack is now in your world, and you cease to be aware of it by imagining plenty, lack disappears; therefore, any modification in your body of belief will cause a change in your life.

227. Do you know what you want from life? You can be anything you want to be if you know who you are. Start from the premise, "I AM all imagination and pass through states," for eternity (all things) exist now! Having experienced a state and moved into another one you may think the former state has ceased to be, but all states are eternal, they remain forever. Like the mental traveler that you are, you pass through states either wittingly or unwittingly, but your individual identity is forever. Whether you are rich or poor, you retain the same individual identity when you move from one state into another. If you are not on guard, you can be persuaded by the press, television, or radio, to change your concept of self and unwittingly move into an undesirable state. You can move into many states and play many parts, but as the actor, you do not change your identity. When you are rich, you are the same actor as when you are poor. These are only different parts you are playing.

228. The clue to purposive living is to center your imagination in the action and feeling of fulfilled desire with such awareness, such sensitiveness, that you initiate and experience movement upon the inner world.

229. To realize your desire, an action must start in your imagination, apart from the evidence of the senses, involving movement of self and implying fulfillment of your desire.

230. The world was constructed in the mind's eye, out of things unseen by the mortal eye, and made alive by faith. Eternity exists and all things in eternity, independent of the creative act, which is the assumption of unseen reality and loyalty to its assemblage. In spite of denial by your senses and reason, if you will be faithful to your unseen assumption, it will externalize itself. That is how all worlds come into being, but men do not understand this. Structuring their world based upon the evidence of their senses, they continue to perpetuate that which they do not desire.

231. On this basis, imagining creates reality. That is my premise. And don't think for one moment you can imagine idly because the record is there. And so, as a man plants, so he's going to reap. There isn't a thing in this world that comes into your world that comes by accident. But you don't remember the moment in time when you actually did it. And so you can't relate it to the natural effect. But the natural effect always has a spiritual cause and not a natural cause. The natural cause only seems. It is a delusion. So don't let anyone tell you that you can trace it to some physical cause. The physical cause, which is the natural cause, is not a cause. It's only an effect. All causes are spiritual and by spiritual I mean imaginal. For man is all imagination and God is man and exists in us and we in Him. The eternal body of man is the imagination and that is God Himself. And God is the only source. There is no other source. In that 87th Psalm that I quoted tonight, "when this one was born

there," it ends in a very lovely note. "And the singers and the dancers alike said, you are our springs." There is no other spring, no other source, no other cause. Whether you be the dancer or the singer of the world. You are our springs. We have no other source.

232. Man begins to awake to the imaginative life the moment he feels the presence of another being in himself.

233. Construct mentally a drama which implies that your desire is realized and make it one which involves movement of self, immobilize your outer physical self, act precisely as though you were going to take a nap, and start the predetermined action in imagination.

234. Every natural effect has a spiritual cause and not a natural. A natural cause only seems. It is a delusion of the perishing, vegetable memory. We do not remember these moments in time when we imagined certain states. So when that imaginal state takes form so we can see it with the outer eye, we do not recognize our own harvest and deny that we had anything to do with these natural effects that are taking place in our world. Because our memory is faulty, we do not remember.

235. You can't get away from your own imagination. You can't get away from it because that's your own being. That is the reality. But it suffers with you. He is the Lord Jesus Christ within you. Now test Him tonight. Test Him for the good. Do you want a better job when they say they are letting people out? Forget what the papers say. Forget what anything says. "All things are possible to the Lord Jesus Christ." (Matthew 19:26) If you don't have enough money, forget what the paper says, you assume that you have it. "All things are possible to God." He sets no limits whatsoever on the power of believing. Can you believe it? Well try to believe it. Try to believe, first of all, in God. Well God is your own imagination. Well believe

in Him; that whatever you can imagine is possible. Can you imagine that you have now the kind of a job that you want? The income that would come from it? The fun in the doing of the work? Well then walk as though it were true; and to the best of your ability believe that it's true. And that assumption though denied by your senses, -- though the world would say it is false; if you persist in it, it will harden into fact. This is the law of your own wonderful imaging. Believe it, and it will become a reality.

236. The man of imagination dwells in the end, confident that he shall dwell there in the flesh also.

237. The only source of all causation is found in man as man's own wonderful human imagination. So you take it to heart and then you never can pass the buck. You can't blame anyone in this world for anything that happens to you. There isn't one in the world you can turn to and say, "well now, you are the cause of it." Don't let anyone turn to you and say that. If they do, just ignore it. Because they're bringing it into their own world by what they imagine morning, noon, and night. So, one sits down to imagine unlovely things of another, unlovely things of a group, well then they're going to simply produce it. Not in the group, but in themselves.

238. I give you water by telling you how the law operates. Now you must turn it into wine by application. I only ask you not to just continue drinking water. As you're told in the Book of Timothy, "Drink no longer water, but use a little wine for your stomach's sake and your many infirmities." So, it's good to know what to do but we are the operant power. And, therefore, we must do it, not just know what to do but we must do it. So when I do it, I stop drinking the water and I drink wine. Because the minute I begin to apply it, I'm using wine. But if I know what to do but don't do it, well, I have the water but I'm not turning it into wine. So, let everyone here, practice

it and put it into a daily practice. And, may I tell you it cannot fail you. It cannot fail you.

239. The very first creative act recorded in scripture is when the spirit of the Lord moved upon the face of the waters. Here is motion. If you would like to be elsewhere, all you need to do is close your senses to the room you now occupy and sense the room where you would like to be. Open your eyes, and your senses will deny any change, for yours was a psychological motion. By closing your eyes the obvious here vanishes, and through the act of assumption, there becomes here. Seeing the world related to your new position, you breathe reality into the state and, having moved from where you are to where you want to be, you have created it. I know this doesn't make sense, but as Douglas said: "The secret of imagining is the greatest of all problems, to the solution of which every mystic aspires, for supreme power, supreme wisdom, and supreme delight lie in the solution of this far-off mystery." How is this mystery unraveled? By claiming you are all imagination. Then wrapping yourself in space, and mentally seeing your world relative to your assumed position in space. Do that and you have moved.

240. I would like to give you an immense belief in miracles, but a miracle is only the name given by those who have no knowledge of the power and function of imagination to the works of imagination.

241. Test Jesus Christ, God's creative power in you as your Human Imagination! Do you want a better job? More money? Whatever you want claim it just as simply as I did the rose. Put on the feeling of possession and wear it as though it were true right now. If it is a better job you want, where would you sit if you had it? How would your mate see you? Sit behind that special desk and let your wife (or husband) see you there. Live as though it were true

and have faith in Jesus Christ, your own wonderful human imagination, the creative power and wisdom of God.

242. By sleeping in my father's house in my imagination as though I slept there in the flesh, I fused my imagination with that state and was compelled to experience that state in the flesh also.

243. The world was created by the Word of God, who is the Human Imagination!

244. Jesus Christ is he who created the world and all things within it, be they good, bad, or indifferent. And who is He? Your own wonderful Human Imagination! God's creative power . . as pure imagining . . works in the depth of your soul, underlying all of your faculties, including perception. He streams into your surface mind least disguised in the form of creative fancy.

245. Imagining oneself into the feeling of the wish fulfilled is the means by which a new state is entered.

246. What are you imagining right now? Is it something disastrous? Or is it a wonderful thought that has caught fire within you? No matter what your thoughts may be, they will come to pass, for there is nothing in this world but that which was first imagined.

247. By imagination, we are all reaping our destinies, whether they be good, bad, or indifferent. Imagination has full power of objective realization and every stage of man's progress or regression is made by the exercise of imagination. I believe with William Blake, "What seems to be, is, to those to whom it seems to be, and is productive of the most dreadful consequences to those to whom it seems to be, even of torments, despair, and eternal death. By imagination and desire we become what we desire to be. Let us affirm to ourselves that we are what we imagine. If we persist in the

assumption that we are what we wish to be, we will become transformed into that which we have imagined ourselves to be. We were born by a natural miracle of love and for a brief space of time our needs were all another's care. In that simple truth lies the secret of life. Except by love, we cannot truly live at all. Our parents in their separate individualities have no power to transmit life. So, back we come to the basic truth that life is the offspring of love. Therefore, no love, no life. Thus, it is rational to say that, "God is Love."

248. God's creative power is buried in you. Just as a seed buried in the womb of woman must bring forth after its own kind, God's power is brought forth as your spiritual birth. Your imagination is spirit buried in you. God . . being spirit . . has planted his seed, which will erupt one day, and you will experience a spiritual birth.

249. As a physical man called Neville I can do nothing, but I can do anything that I imagine! Imagining a thing and thinking it is done, is saying amen in the belief that, because I imagined it, it must come to pass. How it will happen, I do not know. I only know it will.

250. Turn to the only God, who is your own wonderful Human Imagination! Learn to adore him. All things are possible to God, therefore, all things are possible to imagine! Knowing what you want, ask yourself if you believe that your imaginal acts are committed by God. I tell you, they are!

251. Now I ask you to examine yourself. When confronted with a problem, do you turn to someone on the outside for its solution, or do you believe that all power resides in your human imagination? Do you believe in the hydrogen bomb, meeting the right people, or living on the "right" side of the street? Or do you believe in your own wonderful human imagination? I have found he of whom

Moses and the law wrote, Jesus of Nazareth, to be my human imagination and I turn only to him for the solution of my problems. I do it by asking myself what I would see if my problem dissolved and its solution rose in its place. What would I hear? How would I act? Having discovered Jesus to be my imagination, I act as though the problem was solved, and have found from experience that I have brought things not seen by mortal eye into the world to be seen by all. I have proved it and encourage everyone to try it. Examine yourself to make sure, really sure, that you have completely accepted Jesus Christ as your human imagination, so that when confronted by any challenge you turn to the only Jesus Christ and not to a false one. If you turn to anyone outside of yourself you have turned to a false Jesus Christ and failed the test. Turn only to God and not to anyone or anything on the outside. No one can tell your future, for your future is to fulfill Scripture, and you have no other!

252. To passively surrender to appearances and bow before the evidence of facts is to confess that Christ (Imagination) is not yet born in you.

253. By its nature, reason is restricted to the evidence of the senses; but imagination, having no such limitation, can satisfy our desires.

254. You know, people are totally unaware of this fantastic power of the imagination, but when man begins to discover this power within him, he never plays the part that he formerly played. He doesn't turn back and become just a reflector of life; from here on in he is the affector of life. The secret of it is to center your imagination in the feeling of the wish fulfilled and remain therein. For in our capacity to live IN the feeling of the wish fulfilled lies our capacity to live the more abundant life. Most of us are afraid to imagine ourselves as important and noble individuals secure in our contribution to the world just because, at the very moment that we

start our assumption, reason and our senses deny the truth of our assumption. We seem to be in the grip of an unconscious urge which makes us cling desperately to the world of familiar things and resist all that threatens to tear us away from our familiar and seemingly safe moorings.

255. There is only one creator. It is the Human Imagination who kills and makes things alive, wounds and heals. Whether you use or misuse your creative power, the same being will bring it to pass. So if you desire lovely things, you must imagine lovely thoughts. Your friends are your own lack or limitation made visible. Like Job, pray for your friends and your own fears will be lifted.

256. The one creative power of the universe is buried in humanity. It is the same creative power in all. God allows you to misuse Christ (Imagination), his creative power. But in the end He will awaken and all violence within you will cease to be, for you will discover yourself to be infinite love, infinite wisdom, and infinite power. Then the world will become a shadow, and you will know there is no need to fight shadows.

257. If all things are possible to your imagination, and you are all imagination, you should be able to accomplish anything and fulfill every desire. But first you must be willing to believe you are all imagination! It's entirely up to you. Do you believe you are mortal man . . or all imagination?

258. Here is the "outer man" called Neville who came into the world first. This is the "Esau" of Scripture. And then after that, comes another one, . . my own wonderful human imagination; and that's the "Jacob." This is the "twin" that comes into the world. They aren't two separate little boys. This is the story; this is an adumbration of that which comes later into the New Testament; that the one who could say, "I AM from above and you are from below;

you are of this world; I am not of this world." So the Being that is speaking is your own wonderful human imagination that in Scripture is called "Jesus Christ." And the "thing below" is the body that you are "wearing," and that is "of this world." You see, we are dealing with the most fantastic mystery in the world, the mystery of imagining. That's what Fawcett said: "The secret of imagining is the greatest of all problems, to the solution of which every man should aspire, for supreme power, supreme wisdom, supreme delight lie in the far-off solution of this mystery," . . because you are actually solving the problem of God. If you can solve the problem of imagining, you are solving the problem of God!

259. Man finds it difficult to identify himself with his imagination, but the word "logos" . . translated "Word" means a purpose; a plan; a pattern. The Word which was with God in the beginning is Divine Imagination, through which all things are made. There is not one thing in the world today which was not first imagined. Perhaps you cannot grasp the idea that nature was first imagined, but you cannot deny that man's clothing, home, business, and transportation, were imagined.

260. All happiness depends on the active voluntary use of imagination to construct and inwardly affirm that we are what we want to be.

261. So tonight I ask you to exercise your own wonderful human imagination. Since your friends are only yourself out pictured, put them in a glorious light. Don't justify their actions by saying: "It serves them right", because all things exist in you. There is no one out there, but all in you! So if you fail a thousand times, saying: "How often Lord must I forgive my brother who sinned against me?" the answer will come: "Seventy times seven." May I tell you: you can't say "sin" in any other way than as recorded in the 51st Psalm, the 4th verse: "Against thee, O Lord, thee only have I sinned

and done that which is evil in thy sight; therefore thy justification is in order."

Who is this being in whom I have sinned? His name is I AM! How have I sinned against thee and thee only? By seeing someone in my world that is in need and allowing them to remain there, for I cannot sin against another as I am the one seeing it. So I must change and represent him to myself as someone I desire to see. And I must persist in that belief until he conforms to the image I have created. That is what you are called upon to do, for you were made subject unto vanity and live alone in your world, so if you desire it to change, you alone must change it and live in the state of the desired change.

I know this from experience, because the night that I was lifted up to the state of perfection I came upon this infinite sea of human imperfection, and as I glided by all were made perfect in harmony with that state to which I was lifted. So you must lift yourself to the state you desire your world to reflect, because everything in it is yourself made visible. The whole vast world is projecting God, and God's name is I AM! Believe my visions, for they have never betrayed me. I may betray my vision by not accepting its message, but when I was lifted up I was shown that everyone I encounter is myself. And when I represent that seeming other to myself as I would like him to be, to the degree I persist in that assumption, he conforms to that state.

262. Imagination can not only bring things into being, it can take things away! It can uncreate whatever it creates. In this wonderful world we have created nightmares which we cannot endure forever, so they will have to be uncreated. That is why I urge everyone to live nobly. Sow your mind with ideas worthy of recall, because the day is coming when that which is built on any foundation other than Imagination will be consumed or uncreated. We bring all kinds of

unpleasant things into our world and live with them until we discover we can uncreate them. You have the power to create and uncreate. Having brought something unlovely into your world, you can uncreate it if you are willing to create something in its place, and persist until your desire becomes your reality.

263. Every stage of man's progress is made by the conscious exercise of his imagination matching his inner speech to his fulfilled desire.

264. When I speak of my imagination there appears to be two of us: Neville, and my imagination. I know imagination cannot be seen, yet I also know I cannot separate myself from it. I cannot separate myself from my creative power. I cannot, for my imagination is my very being. I can speak of my imagination, but I cannot separate myself from it any more than God can be separated from Divine Imagination, for through Divine Imagination's creativity God creates and sustains the world. Should God change his imagining the world would cease to exist, because it must be, and is supported by an imaginal act. The same thing is true in your world. It will change only when you cease to continue to dwell in your current imaginal state!

265. No one owes me a living; all I have to do is trust Jesus Christ, trust my human imagination! I have no desire to pile up a lot of money. Why pile up a million shadows? My desire is to tell you who Jesus Christ really is. He is your own wonderful human imagination. There never was another Christ and there never will be another. If you will trust him . . and I use “him” advisedly because God’s creative power and God is a person (and you are that person) . . you will never fail, for he will never fail you! Tonight if you know what you want, just believe that you have it. Sleep as though it were true, and because Christ, your own human imagination, is in

everyone, he will use as many as necessary to aid the birth of your assumption.

266. Living in infinite states, the basic state from which we operate is our body of belief. If you believe you are limited, your thoughts flow from that belief. But if this principle is true, and you place a modification on that body of belief, you should produce a corresponding change, as your outer world is forever reflecting your inner thoughts. You are all Imagination.

267. Through imagination, man escapes from the limitation of the senses and the bondage of reason.

268. Although this world appears so very real, it is a vision. "All that you behold, though it appears without, it is within, in your Imagination of which this world of mortality is but a shadow." If life is in God and God is your imagination, then what the world calls life is only an activity of your imagination. If you stop imagining and arrest that which seems to be animated and independent of your perception, you will prove to yourself that it can be done. Then you will know who Christ is, for you will have discovered that "In him is life and his life is the light of men." God animates Man within himself. Although humanity appears to be independent, with life in themselves, their life is but an activity of imagination, for that is what I AM!

269. In his 14th chapter, John tells you that imagination is his spirit of life, saying: "You believe in God? Believe also in me." Can you believe your imaginal acts will come to pass? That your desire is real, and live as though it were? If you imagine . . and imagining does create reality . . you will see your desire appear in your world. If it does not, then you have proved that the principle is false. I tell you the principle is true . . according to your belief! There is no limit placed on your ability to believe or on what belief can accomplish.

No matter what you desire, when you believe you have received it, you will. Can you believe that the only true God is in you?

270. Well, I appeal to you to try it. If you try it, you will discover this great wisdom of the ancients. For they told it to us in their own strange, wonderful, symbolical form. But unfortunately you and I misinterpreted their stories and took it for history, when they intended it as instruction to simply achieve our every objective. You see, imagination puts us inwardly in touch with the world of states. These states are existent, they are present now, but they are mere possibilities while we think OF them. But they become overpoweringly real when we think FROM them and dwell IN them. You know, there is a wide difference between thinking OF what you want in this world and thinking FROM what you want.

271. Every state is already there as "mere possibility" as long as you think *of* it, but is overpoweringly real when you think *from* it. Thinking from the end is the way of Christ (Imagination).

272. Our imagination connects us with the state desired.

273. You are destined to know the power of stopping and starting time. Possessed by the Spirit, you will be taken into a room. Knowing intuitively who you are and the power you are feeling, you will arrest that activity within you and everything will stand still. As you examine that which was so alive and seemingly independent of your perception only a moment ago, you will discover it is all dead. Then, releasing their activity in your imagination, everything will once more become animated and continue its purpose. If a bird was in flight when you arrested it, it will continue to fly when released. If someone is carrying food to a table when arrested . . although you can keep them in that position for as long as you like . . when you release the power you know yourself to be, they will continue to serve the meal as if nothing had happened. Can you imagine doing

that? I tell you it is true, but as long as you identify yourself with a body of death and believe it is you, you will not realize you are your own hope of glory. The body you care for and keep well is dead, while I . . the awareness who entered it . . AM a living being, who will experience scripture while in this dead body. I came into the world and took upon myself the body of a slave when I was born in the likeness of man. Now, wearing the human form, I AM obedient unto death, even death upon the cross of man. While in this state, I will experience the word I inspired the prophets to write, for I AM the God in you!

274. Dwell upon my words, for you will find them most stimulating and, far from not being practical, they are the most practical words you have ever heard. The Bible is far more exciting than anything you heard or read today, for not a thing said by any person could compare to the words you have heard tonight. All of the plots and plan of men concerning bringing this world to an end are not part of the divine plan. Divine Imagination's plan is to reproduce Himself in the human imagination, for God is only begetting Himself. Divine and human imagination are not two, but one imagination, which differs only in the degree of intensity. The purpose of it all is that you will be able to wish anything into realization. I have come that you may have life and have it more abundantly. No longer will you be a slave to the world or afraid of anything, for you will know that you are one with its creator. In that awareness, you will ask and receive instantaneous return. All this will be yours when the complete revelation of what I have told you this night is fulfilled.

275. I tell you: there is only one cause, and that is the Human Imagination. When you change your body of beliefs, everyone must and will play their part to produce evidence of that change in you. One who was formerly an enemy will play the part of a friend.

Dream nobly! Think of lovely things you want to recall, and you will experience them in your tomorrows.

276. If there is only one cause, then he who quelled the wind and the sea is the one who caused the storm. There cannot be another. If there is confusion in your life, and you resolve it in your imagination, and the world bears witness to what you have done . . you caused the change. And since there is no other cause, then did you not cause the confusion also? There is only one God and Father of us all who is above all, through all, and in all. If He is in every being who says I AM, and there is only one God, no one can accuse another; for God's name is not he is, but I AM. No matter what appears on the outside, I am its cause. Assume full responsibility for the things you observe, and if you do not like what you see, know you have the power to change them. Then exercise that power and you will observe the change you caused. If you are truly willing to assume that responsibility, you are set free.

277. Everyone imagines! Can you believe that Christ, Imagination's power, is in you? If so, then God is in you! And if God is in you, you cannot be lost for then God would be lost. Everyone has to be redeemed. Everyone will be saved because God . . the savior of each individual . . is redeeming himself, bringing the individual awareness in whom He is buried back into the kingdom with him.

278. Tonight I give you a principle: God is the great artist, who . . as your own wonderful human imagination . . is perfecting his work through the ages in the making of his own image in you. Do you have an image? Name it. Now, are you willing to simply assume that you have it, and wait for its objectification? Every image has its own appointed hour to ripen and flower. If it be long, wait, for its appearance is sure and will not be late. Are you willing to wait for the happiness you now seek, or are you going to try to go

on the outside and make it so? If you are willing to apply this principle and let it happen, you will become the successful businessman, doctor, minister, or whatever you desire to be. If you will assume your desire and live there as though it were true, no power on earth can stop it from becoming a fact, because you are God and your only opponent is yourself. There is nothing but God, but man . . not knowing this . . creates opposition and calls it Satan or the devil, both of which are just as nonexistent as St. Christopher. Millions believe in them and give them power they do not possess. But I urge you to believe in nothing but God, who is your own wonderful human Imagination.

279. Imagination is the very gateway of reality.

280. Begin now to practice the art of imagining every day. A concert pianist must constantly practice. for if he does not and he is called upon to give a concert he would not be ready. You must practice the art of imagining day after day so that when you are faced with a problem you will not put it aside, but will do something about it.

281. If you have a desire to supplant what you have now, you must start by assuming it is a dream. And when it objectifies itself and enters the stream of reality, may I tell you: it will still be dream. Imagination is the creative power which can cause that which was not, to be! It can also cause that which is, not to be; therefore, it not only creates, but un-creates. This power is God.

282. Let us return now to the interpretation of scripture. Being all imagination, take any passage and put yourself in the central role, for in the volume of the book it is written of you. Don't think of some man who lived 2,000 years ago. Christ in you is the hope of glory. That is the Christ of whom the scriptures speak. Enter the state of Abraham as you read the story of Abraham and Sarah. Then

become Sarah when she is the center, and Rebecca when she appears, for the Book is written of you! Do this and you will have the key which will unlock the most difficult passages of scripture. Don't give up. Dwell upon each story as though it were happening to you now, and your eyes will open.

283. All things were made through imagining, and without awareness was not anything made that was made.

284. If you want something, it is not going to come into being by saying: "I will have it someday." That is deferring your hope and making your heart sick. But if you believe that imagining creates reality, you will build a stage, paint the scenery, and place lovely images there. Then you will let them interweave so that when you bring that scenery back into your mind, the actors will come alive and say the words you had dictated for them to say.

285. Believing and being are one. The conceiver and his conception are one. Therefore, that which you conceive yourself to be can never be so far off as even to be near, for nearness implies separation. "If thou canst believe, all things are possible to him that believeth." Faith is the substance of things hoped for, the evidence of things not yet seen. If you assume that you are that finer, nobler one you wish to be, you will see others as they are related to your high assumption. All enlightened men wish for the good of others. If it is the good of another you seek, you must use the same controlled contemplation. In meditation, you must represent the other to yourself as already being or having the greatness you desire for him. As for yourself, your desire for another must be an intense one. It is through desire that you rise above your present sphere and the road from longing to fulfillment is shortened as you experience in imagination all that you would experience in the flesh were you or your friend the embodiment of the desire you have for yourself or him. Experience has taught me that this is the perfect way to achieve

my great goals for others as well as for myself. However, my own failures would convict me were I to imply that I have completely mastered the control of my attention. I can, however, with the ancient teacher say: "This one thing I do, forgetting those things which are behind, and reaching forth unto those things which are before . . I press towards the mark for the prize."

286. If any two agree... So, I say to you, I am telling you of a principle . . a Law that cannot fail. You don't have to do anything on the outside, and you don't even need another one. You can say to yourself, and then listen; the two could be within yourself. "State it in a bold, positive mariner what you have," . . which is really what you hope to have. "I hope to have it," . . don't state it as a hope. State it as a fact, because we are living in an imaginal world. This world is one's own imagination "pushed out." The whole vast world is all imagination; that all these so-called objective realities were simply first imagined, and then they become what you and I call "realities." So, "All things are possible to him who believes"; and "With God all things are possible." Therefore, the human imagination is equated with God! God and the human imagination are one.

287. You may not immediately see the effect of what you have done in your imagination; but it must come, because there is no other creator to stop it. All things are made through awareness, and without it is not anything made that is made. It is imagination who claims: "I kill and I make alive, I wound and I heal. I form the light and create darkness. I form the evil and I make the good, the weal and the woe, and there is no other."

288. The world and all of its conflicts appear to show us that Imagination can and does run amok. Imagination is the only foundation. It is the Rock upon which one builds his house. No matter what happens, blame no one, but remain on that Rock; for

Christ (your own wonderful Human Imagination) is He, and the only cause of the phenomena of life. Accept this truth and you will have a firm foundation upon which to build. As you dwell upon this power vested in you, you will discover it will help you far beyond your wildest dreams. You will realize that you do not need the help of anyone. All you need do is assume you have what you want. Then dare to walk in that assumption; and if it takes a thousand people to aid its birth, they will appear and play their parts, not knowing why or what they do. They will do it without their permission or consent, just as I did in my friend's dream.

289. Desire exists to be gratified in the activity of imagination.

290. If you claim you are solely responsible for the phenomena of your life, you will find it much easier to live. But if, at times, life seems too hard to bear, and you find a secondary cause, you have created a devil. Devils and Satans are formed from man's unwillingness to assume the responsibility of his life. To see another other than self, is to build a golden image. Asking a priest for forgiveness. Calling him father in spite of being told to call no man on earth father. Seeing him as an authority, man goes whoring after a man-made false image.

291. Today in the New York Times, Brook Atkinson has this article. He just returned from Leningrad. They were not concerned, when he started through, to examine his baggage concerning liquor or tobacco, which is the item they all look for, for it brings in revenue. They were only concerned about ideas. They said: "Do you have any magazines?" He said "No, none." "Do you have the Bible?" He said, "No." That is the only thing they questioned the second time. "Do you really mean that? Do you have a Bible?" It is the only thing they really wanted to prove beyond doubt he did not bring into Russia. And they could read . . they know the Hebrew tongue, the Greek tongue; they have the different concordances.

They could look back and find the true meaning of God and find it really means "imagination." That is exactly what the word means. The word "potter" in Hebrew means imagination. And who makes anything? If God made me out of the clay, out of the dust, was he not a potter? And I . . the made, and he . . the maker. The maker was the imagination, and then imagination sunk himself in the thing made and then gave me himself.

292. It never failed me if I would give the mood, the imagined mood, sensory vividness. I could tell you unnumbered case histories to show you how it works, but in essence it is simple: You simply know what you want. When you know what you want, you are thinking of it. That is not enough. You must now begin to think FROM it. Well, how could I think from it? I am sitting here, and I desire to be elsewhere. How could I, while sitting here physically, put myself in imagination at a point in space removed from this room and make that real to me?

293. So, "Be still and know that I AM God." As we are told: "Unless you believe that I AM He, you will die in your sins." So, the "I AM" in you is your own wonderful human imagination, and you can put it any place in the world. You need not be anchored to where your senses tell you that you are.

294. As we control our inner talking, matching it to our fulfilled desires, we can lay aside all other processes, then we simply act by clear imagination and intention.

295. If we assemble the right sequence and experience it in imagination until it has the tone of reality, then we consciously create circumstances. This inner procession is the activity of imagination that must be consciously directed. We, by a series of mental transformations, become aware of increasing portions of that which already is, and by matching our own mental activity to that

portion of creation which we desire to experience, we activate it, resurrect it, and give it life.

296. Quite easily. My imagination puts me in touch inwardly with that state. I imagine that I am actually where I desire to be. How can I tell that I am there? There is one way to prove that I am there, for what a man sees when he describes his world is, as he describes it, relative to himself. So what the world looks like depends entirely upon where I stand when I make my observation. So, if as I describe my world it is related to that point in space I imagine that I am occupying, then I must be there. I am not there physically, no, but I AM there in my imagination, and my imagination is my real self! And where I go in imagination and make it real, there I shall go in the flesh, also. When in that state I fall asleep, it is done. I have never seen it fail. So this is the simple technique upon how to use your imagination to realize your every objective.

297. I tell you that Jesus Christ is your own wonderful human imagination, who is the eternal creative power of God. If you do not know that, you do not know Jesus Christ! You may say: "He is a person." Well, you are a person, aren't you? Jesus Christ is God the Father and God the Father is Spirit, And those who worship him do so in Sprit through the art of feeling! I have imagined a state and seen it externalize itself and become a physical fact that I may share with another. This I have done unnumbered times and taught others to do it. So I have found him and know him to be the only creative power of the universe. Everything in your world which is now a fact to be shared with others was once only imagined. And if you know that Jesus Christ is the creative power that brings things into this world, that all things must be first imagined, then you have found him. Having found him, you must learn to trust him and live by this principle. Do this and you will find yourself moving into the stream

of eternal life by fulfilling scripture and knowing that "All power in heaven and earth is given unto me."

298. We are all careless and often think a problem will take care of itself, but it will not. The power to change anything will lie dormant unless we operate it, as Imagination does not operate itself.

299. You must imagine yourself right into the state of your fulfilled desire,

300. In the beginning was the unconditioned awareness of being, and the unconditioned awareness of being became conditioned by imagining itself to be something, and the unconditioned awareness of being became that which it had imagined itself to be; so did creation begin. By this law, first conceiving, then becoming that conceived, all things evolve out of nothing; and without this sequence there is not anything made that is made.

301. In the 12th chapter of the Book of Numbers, we are told: "If there is a prophet among you, I the Lord will make myself known unto him in a vision and I will speak with him in a dream." A scriptural prophet is not one who tells your fortune, but one who hears the Word of God and fulfills it. If you asked me if I were a prophet I would answer in the affirmative. I am not one who prophesies by looking into a crystal ball, teacup leaves, cards, or astrology, but one who has fulfilled scripture. I know I am the central figure of scripture called "the Father." I came into the world to fulfill scripture and share my revelations, my experiences concerning the power to create. In this simple way God revealed his power to create, his power to remember when! Having nothing, you can become aware of being surrounded by wealth, and feeling wealthy you can say: "I remember when I had nothing." Does that statement not imply that the state of poverty no longer exists for

you? I remember when I was unknown. I remember when I couldn't sell a book. I remember when I couldn't sell anything I wrote. I remember when....Now you fill in the events, the desires and the fulfillments. I remember when. Do not those words imply memory? I hope you will put yourself in an I Remember When mood and trust your memory, because memory is your own wonderful human imagination, the one and only creative power of God scripture calls Jesus Christ.

302. Here is a very healthy and productive exercise for the imagination, something that you should do daily: Daily relive the day as you wish you had lived it, revising the scenes to make them conform to your ideals. For instance, suppose today's mail brought disappointing news. Revise the letter. Mentally rewrite it and make it conform to the news you wish you had received. Or, suppose you didn't get the letter you wish you had received. Write yourself the letter and imagine that you received such a letter.

303. When you find the Lord as your own wonderful human imagination, and you want something, simply imagine you have it, and walk in that knowledge. I promise you, when you find the Lord and really trust him, you will know a peace you have never known before. You will never again bow before anything or anyone. Knowing that only your own wonderful human imagination is holy, He will be the only one you will ever serve!

304. Men go to church and pray to a god who does not exist, when the only God makes man alive, for man could not breathe, were God not housed within him. So when you find God, trust him implicitly; but let me warn you: He will not accept your orders! Only as you imagine the wish fulfilled, will He act upon it. Tonight, as you put your head on that pillow, snuggle into the mood of the wish fulfilled in absolute confidence, and trust that God has ways and means your surface mind knows not of. I urge you to believe

me, that you also may say with Paul: "I know whom I have believed." You will not fail, when you find the Lord your God, who is your own wonderful human imagination. You will learn to trust him completely. Knowing there is no need to help God by devising the means to fulfill your desire, you will move under compulsion, when the time for its fulfillment appears.

305. Through imagination, we disarm and transform the violence of the world.

306. I firmly believed that Jesus Christ was my own wonderful human imagination, that he was one with God, and that all things were possible to him. I knew I could not compel God to do anything. That He would act only as I imagined!

307. You must believe in your human imagination and make him the rock upon which you stand. He is the Lord your God, and the only one whom you serve. If you are going to serve another, then you do not know God. If your boss tells you to do what he says and eventually you will get a raise, and your trust is in your boss, then you don't trust the Lord your God. Put your faith in anyone outside of your own wonderful human imagination and you don't trust God, for there is no other creative power!

308. Will you accept the fact that your own wonderful human imagination is He whom the world calls God? Will you accept this idea and allow it to ferment? Acknowledge your true self and live in that belief? Or will you say: “It’s easier to live with my wife (or husband) if I don’t confess it. I tried, but it upsets the household, so we continue to go to the same church and do the same things we have always done in the outer world.” You must be willing to acknowledge me (your own wonderful human imagination) before men, for if you are ashamed of me, the Father who sees only the heart will deny you. But when you make any modification in your

basic belief, it will take precedence over your beliefs of the past. If you say: "I AM rich" and your concept of God remains as before, you are speaking from the surface of your being; but when you change the core and speak from your new concept of God, your world changes. If you believe what I have confessed openly to you, do not be ashamed to acknowledge it openly before men. Although you may not at the present time have the experiences to support your claim, do not be ashamed of the good news that you have heard from me.

309. Do you realize that if you would begin to imagine something entirely different concerning your life instead of accepting that the so-called wise people say it must be, your world would rearrange itself to reflect the change? You, all imagination, are in the world which you made; yet the world does not know that imagination made it.

310. The cause of all of the phenomena of life is the Human Imagination. There is only one source of all creation. "By him all things were made, and without him was not anything made that was made." If anything or anyone comes into your world, remember the cause is your Human Imagination, who is the God of scripture and the dreamer in you.

311. In the meanwhile you can exercise your power on this level if you will accept this challenge. Examine yourselves and make sure you are faithful to your imaginal act! Let no one else examine you, but test yourself! Have you completely accepted the fact that Jesus Christ is in you? If you can answer, "not quite" then you have failed the test. If, like one billion Christians, you believe in some other Jesus Christ, you have a false Christ. And you will never find him by going to church or giving to the poor, for he is not on the outside, but in your own wonderful human imagination! Let no one prophesy for you! The only prophecy you are destined to fulfill is scripture.

When someone tries to tell me what some astrologer or medium said I get so annoyed I want to shout: "Have you ever heard me?" Believe in all that nonsense, and you worship false Christs! If you want to be famous in this world of men, use this principle and you will shine for your little moment, but I ask you: are you in the mainstream of fulfilling scripture? Do you really believe in the only Jesus Christ, who is your human imagination? I say: there never was another Christ and there never will be another Christ.

312. I tell you a mystery: Christ in you is the hope of glory, for God, your human imagination became man that man may become God. This is a mystery that we are called upon to test, for the power that created the world became as you are, that you may know yourself to be all creative power, as He is! I did not receive this knowledge from a man. I did not read it in a book, nor did I ever hear of it from another. It was revealed to me that God, in man, is his own wonderful human imagination!

313. Apply this principle to the little things of life and let no one tell you it is too material; the same ones will ask you for whatever it is when you discard it. You are here in this schoolroom to create out of your imagination and to do it by faith. Imagine and create the noblest concepts for yourself or for others and live in [them], and in a way you do not know, you will influence the lives of everyone in the world, and everyone who will be needed to bring about your dream will be drawn into it and brought to you. Even those who seek to stack the cards against you and think they are doing so very cleverly will find that the very thing they did will instead stack the cards against themselves. You are influencing everyone in this world when you are imagining. Who knows what being now in solitary is not disturbing the whole vast world. He will never be accused, for he is not out. They can find approximate cause, but they cannot blame him for he was in a cell. Yet he could cause a wave of hate out of the depth of his own being. That is why it is so important

to imagine wisely. There is only one being awakening and that is God, and we were put into this schoolroom in love even though many a night, like the children, we cry. Loving fathers here have sent their unwilling children to school; a loving heavenly father sent you here on earth. You apply it and use the greatest talent in the world, which is himself. That is Imagination.

314. If you see a Jesus Christ as other than your own wonderful Human Imagination, you have made a graven image. But when you find the true Christ . . called the Rock . . and start building on it, no rumors or arguments can knock your house down. Build on the sand and your house will slip away, but if you create your world believing in your own wonderful Human Imagination . . called Jesus Christ . . nothing will destroy it. Your Imagination is Christ, dreaming in you and creating your world. Feed him noble thoughts. Become selective and dare to assume something wonderful for yourself.

315. Whatever your desire may be, imagine it is fulfilled, and trust the Lord your God implicitly. If it takes a million people to play the part they must play in order to produce what you have assumed you are, they will do it. This is the world in which we live. Jesus Christ is your own wonderful human imagination! Believe me.

316. Functioning on this level, it takes a little while to persuade ourselves when reason denies it and our senses deny it. Were we functioning on higher levels, everything would be immediately subject to our imaginative power. On this level it takes a little while, and so it takes persistence, it takes patience, it takes diligence. These are the things we pay, the price we pay for the fruits we are seeking to reap in this world. Here we always bear in mind the distinction between states and the occupant of the state. You are an immortal being occupying a state. That state may be poverty, wealth, health, sickness; it may be to be known in this world or to be unknown . .

but they are only states. You are neither known or unknown . . you are immortal; you are neither rich or poor –these do not really define you at all. You can assume that you are, and to the degree that you are persuaded you are, you bear the fruit of that state . . but you are neither rich or poor. You are immortal, destined eventually to inherit the whole vast universe, for it is God's purpose to give you himself as though there were no other in the world, just God and you . . and not even God and you . . just God, and you are he. That is the purpose.

317. Tonight test yourself! I will not test you. I am not here to test anyone. I only urge you to examine yourself to see if you are really keeping the faith, or are you going to call a friend and tell him how horrible things are and appeal to him on the outside? I ask you: are you really keeping the faith? Do you always turn to your imagination and, no matter what happens, do you remain faithful to the state imagined? If you do, you have passed the test. But if every little rumor, doubt, or fear can move you around like a pawn on a chessboard, then you are not keeping the faith! It's entirely up to you. Are you testing yourself or not? Can you say within yourself: "I always turn to my imagination when confronted with a problem and solve it there. Then I remain faithful to that imaginal act." If you can, you have passed the test. It's just as simple as that.

318. Believe me when I tell you that God is love, for I stood in his presence and he embraced me. But do you know that love, divided from imagination, is eternal death? I'll show you why. I have a friend who is unemployed, without funds, and burdened beyond measure. I can't deny I love him, and when I think of him my memory tells me how poor he is, that he is unemployed, without funds and burdened. I will keep him in that state forever, through love, unless I know how to use my imagination. So, no one can ever know imagination who has not tasted the cup of experience. Entering this world we love our mothers, fathers, husbands, wives,

children, and friends, but do not know how to change them from what they are into what they ought to be, unless we drink the cup of experience and practice the great secret of imagining. That is why I say: love divided from imagination is eternal death. Imagination is God's great gift. He is love, yes. He is infinite power and wisdom, but his creative power is imagination. Giving you his creative power, he gives you his Son Christ, defined in the second chapter of Paul's letter to the Corinthians as "The power of God and the wisdom of God." And because of this great gift, when you see one that you love dearly as unemployed, without funds and in great need, embarrassed and unclothed, you can represent him to yourself as gainfully employed, beautifully clothed, happy, and debt-free. Then as you persist in exercising your imagination concerning your friend, the world will remold itself and shape him in the likeness of one who is gainfully employed, debt-free and happy. All this is possible because of God's great gift to you.

319. May I tell you: we remain in this world of death until we enter the mainstream and come to the climax. You can't believe how much this world is really a world of death, whose life is in you as your human imagination. Life itself is an activity of imagining where everything is a symbol. Your closest, dearest friend, your wife, your mother, father, brothers and sisters are all symbols, all dead symbols revealing to you who you really are.

320. You wonder why he called himself the vine? He said, "I AM the vine and ye are the branches. Unless the branch be rooted in the vine, it has no life." Well every man in the world is a branch, rooted in me, the vine, and he ends in me as I am rooted in and end in God. Now that can be said of every man in the world. While you look at me and can hear me, you too can say it. Although I have just made the claim, "you are rooted in me," you can claim that I am rooted in you and I end in you as you are rooted in and end in God. If you know it, then it is your duty to lift up every man in this world.

Not one must be discarded. Everyone must be redeemed and your life is the process by which this redemption is brought to pass. Discard no man. Every man can be changed. And you have the power to change him by taking the man and seeing him as he seemingly is and then asking what he would like to be instead of what he seems to be. When you know what he would like to be, then you imagine that he is that being already. Turn to a loved one and commune with the loved one concerning this man, just as though it were a fact. When you do it, trust it, touch it and believe it, and I will tell you that man will become the embodiment of what you have imagined him to be.

321. Determined imagination, thinking from the end, is the beginning of all miracles.

322. You are the Christ written of in scripture. You are your own hope of glory. Jesus Christ is in you as your human imagination, so why call upon another for help? Why not call upon yourself in whom imagination dwells? I tell you: there never was another Jesus Christ other than he who dwells in you as your human awareness.

323. Now this is how a man is born of water and of the spirit. If I told you now that an assumption, though false, if persisted in, will harden into fact, that is a truth, that is water. But water is not enough. You must catch the spirit of it and apply that truth. Well, if I know that if I assume that I am the man I want to be and persist in that assumption, I would gradually become that. If I have that knowledge, that's marvelous. But not to do it is to try to bring this being to birth by water only. We are told this is the one who came by water and the blood. Not by water only, but by water and the blood. In other words, I have the knowledge, but I cannot bring to birth my ideal by bare knowledge. I must put it into action, I must do it. Then when I do it, I take my savior and I crystallize him by the

doing. This is the story of our wonderful Easter. This is your own wonderful human Imagination.

324. How many people today can pinpoint their success or failure to their imagination? The average man will say: John Brown did it, or the storm, or the president. Only a few will confess that their success or failure was created in their imagination. But I tell you: Christ in you creates your life, for you are all imagination and your imagination can be used for good or for evil. When you think of God as a man of imagination, you are recognizing the power behind the mask God wears. Rather than giving credit to the mask, praise the wearer, who is Christ. It is Christ who erupts from within us. Christ is the one who bears the name I AM, which is what the words Jesus, Joshua, and Jehovah really mean.

325. Although this teaching (that Christ is our imagination) shocked and repelled me at first . . for I was a convinced and earnest Christian, and did not then know that Christianity could not be inherited by the mere accident of birth but must be consciously adopted as a way of life . . it stole later on, through visions, mystical revelations, and practical experiences, into my understanding and found its interpretation in a deeper mood. Not one stone of literal understanding will be left after one drinks the water of psychological meaning.

326. Now, if Christ is the one quoted as radiating from within you, and by him all things are made and without him is not anything made that is made (even the bad), then you must find him. If there is only one maker, is it not He who made your awful day, your awful month, your awful year? If you are brutally honest with yourself, you will admit that what happened was related to your imaginal acts. When you recognize and acknowledge this, you have found him. And because He is a person and you are a person, you know exactly who He is. Now, walk with your head up high, knowing that you

have learned from your mistakes; and from now on try to imagine the best as you perceive the best to be, knowing that these acts must project themselves in this world. Then you will awaken and rejoin the brothers, for "I AM not a God afar off, in me lo we are one, forgiving all evil and seeking no recognition." If we are one, why should I demand recognition? Why not forgive all, for they know not what they do.

327. So, you look into your own mind's eye and know exactly what you want in this world. When you know what you want in place of what you are, then you are seeing your savior, your Jesus. The story is, don't let Him go, but let all else go. Disengage yourself from the whole vast belief that you formerly entertained, and hold on in your imagination to the concept that you ARE the man that you want to be. That will lead you toward Calvary. Calvary means fixing in your own mind's eye that state, and that will lead towards Easter or this wonderful day that we speak of as the Resurrection. For you will resurrect and make alive the state that began only as a concept. If you remain faithful to the concept you will be led right into the fulfillment of that state. It is called, in the Bible, rebirth.

328. In the 13th chapter of 2 Corinthians, Paul invites you to test God, saying: "Come, test yourself. Do you not realize that Jesus Christ is in you?" That's quite a challenge. If Jesus Christ is in you and you know he is your human imagination, which you believe creates reality, you can test him by imagining that you are what . . at the moment . . your reason denies and your senses deny. Now, can you believe in your imagination? Can you awaken your faith in the true God who is your human imagination? Try it. Walk as though you were the person you desire to be. Ask yourself how you would feel if it were true, for feeling creates life. This is brought out in scripture. We are told that Isaac was blind when he said: "Come close, my son, that I may feel you." He could not see what he was assuming, so he sought the feeling. Throughout scripture you find

the blind father calling his son to be felt and touched. When Joseph placed his sons before Jacob (who admitted being blind), he crossed his hands as he blessed the boys, then justified his act. Now I ask you: what would the feeling be like if your desire could be felt? How would you feel now if you were the man you want to be? Catch the feeling and believe in Jesus Christ, knowing he is your imagination. Everything is possible to imagine, but it takes faith to create its reality. Just as I said earlier: first you must hear then acceptance will come through faith.

329. Jesus, your I AM, is the Word that was sent to transform you into himself. He is the creator of it all, for although you seem so limited and unable to create anything here, you can see everything made perfect in your imagination. You can imagine a state, remain faithful to it and it will be made alive for you. Now, if I am made everything and you know you imagined it before it appeared, and it appeared because you imagined it, then you have found Jesus Christ to be your own wonderful human imagination.

330. "He was in the world and the world was made by him and the world knew him not" Do you know that imagination made the entire world? Do you know that a change in imagination will change the entire world? Do you realize that if you would begin to imagine something entirely different concerning your life instead of accepting that the so-called wise people say it must be, your world would rearrange itself to reflect the change? You, all imagination are in the world which you made; yet the world does not know that imagination made it.

331. So I warn you of the law and leave you to your choice…and its risk, because you can use it unwisely. But my hands are now washed of that. I cannot stop it. I can’t be like a mother over you, stating that you should not do this. As you are told in the Book of Deuteronomy: “I place before you this day good and evil, life and

death, blessing and cursing; choose life." He suggests you choose life but he can't take from you the right, having set you free, to choose anything you want; it is all spread before you. If you imagine something unlovely of another, he'll come to that. It will boomerang too, but it will come to pass, for you are entirely free to imagine anything in this world, for imagining creates reality. A man imagined . . if he imagines it and persists in that imaginal act, it will come to pass. And that's the law.

332. For the "Wisdom of this world is foolishness in the eyes of God." Not a thing that man knows here through his efforts will in any way function where he is destined to be. For he is rising into a world that will be completely subject to his imaginative power. Everything in the world will be under his control. Because God, having given himself to man, God being all-wise he'll be all-wise. God being all-powerful, all-loving, he'll be all-powerful, all-loving, for he gives himself to man. And so, you will not be replaced by anyone and all will be equal in the eyes of God, because it is himself. He can't be more than what he gave you. And one will not be greater because you can't get more than what God gave you, for he gave you himself, as though there were no others in the world, just God and you. And finally only you.

333. He is in the world, the world was made by him, yet the world knows him not. Man, walking the streets, is imagining the world around him; yet he is unable to recognize his own harvest.

334. "Born, not of blood or of the will of man, or of the will of the flesh but of God." Here we see an entirely different birth, which will take place in the one who finds Imagination, believes in him, holds onto and trusts him implicitly. To prove that imagination causes change, you must first change your imaginal structure; and when your world out pictures your thoughts, you have found him. Then you will realize the truth of that 14th verse, for you will have

found the one called the Word. Having become flesh, the Word is dwelling in you full of grace and truth. Jesus Christ is not some historical being on the outside. He became flesh and dwells in us.

335. There is not a thing you can imagine but what already is. Eternity exists. When you imagine, you claim that which already exits by identifying yourself with the state you desire to dream into objective reality. Just as the lady slipped into a section of her past and relived it as though it happened for the first time, you can slip into any section of time and live an event you desire to externalize here. We are dreaming the dream of life until we awake. So I say, advisedly: God . . your own wonderful human imagination . . dreams in you.

336. If you would only realize that the depth of your own being (which is your human imagination) is trying to instruct you, trying to persuade you, to get you aroused, as my friend's dream of the other night. Starting from the center God is working towards the surface, so it takes a while for Him to awaken and reach your surface mind. But while he is moving He is influencing your surface mind, and when He arrives you and He are no longer two, but one! You can tell when He is moving toward the surface, for He begins to question the reality of the world in which he lives.

337. So is Christ your imagination? I say Christ is the power and the wisdom of God, and this power and this wisdom creates everything in the world. I can trace to my own being an imaginal act that became fact, then I repeated it and it became fact. If I can repeat it and repeat it, and these imaginal acts externalize themselves in facts, then I have found it. Found that power in myself, for the Bible calls him Christ and personifies it and speaks of [this] presence as a man . . but that man is Jesus. Jesus Christ is simply the resurrected being that is God now, because he has resurrected the power within him, which is Christ. Now he is called "the Lord," and everything

should bow before him when it happens. I say to you: the day will come you will have the experience, and you will be startled. No one will believe you; they aren't going to believe you anymore than they believed the first person to whom it happened. He is the first that rose from the dead, but no one believed him. Up to the very end who would believe the story? They were looking for a different kind of Messiah, a conquering hero who would come just like a man out of some glorious background of warriors, and then conquer the enemy of Israel and lead Israel to some victorious end. They always look for that kind of a Messiah. We have them all over the world today, these false Messiah's who promise the nations they will lead them to some victory, even a little temporary victory. That's not Messiah. Messiah hasn't a thing to do with this world; he is resurrected out of this world. This world is vanishing, wearing out just like a garment. Christ in man is the power and the wisdom; and then, that in man that is man's imagination, becomes a mercy because he exercises it lovingly.

338. Scripture urges you to examine yourself, to test yourself and see if Jesus Christ is now in you. And if all things are made by him and without him is not a thing made that is made, who is he? I'll tell you who he is. He is your own wonderful human imagination. How do I know this to be true? By imagining a state, remaining faithful to it and watching it come to pass in my world. Believing that God makes all things, I made my desired state alive and can now trace its maker back to my imagination.

339. So I tell you: the God that you formerly dreamed in you was your own wonderful human imagination. Put him to the test. Conceive a scene implying the fulfillment of your desire and . . to the best of your ability . . merge with it. If you succeed in moving right into the scene, do you know it will become objective before it is seen in this section of time? It will become as objective as this world. Then when you break the spell, that which was objectively

real only a moment before will be to you as a dream, but you will know it to be. Then wait in confidence that it will happen here, and when it does share it with others, that they may believe or not believe you; but tell them, because we are all one, so in the end you are simply telling yourself. That is the eternal story.

340. Here is a vivid experience of a duplicate dream, and scripture tells us that if the dream repeats itself the thing is fixed, and the Lord will shortly bring it to pass. God's creative power is now unfolding in my friend. Now he knows his own wonderful human imagination is God. That the great I AMness in man is God and that all things are possible to Him. Now the challenge is his. Whatever he wants is! All he has to do is adjust his thinking to the state desired until it becomes alive within him, and at that moment the state will objectify itself in his world.

341. If a lady can return and so merge with the past that she can relive an experience of long ago in detail, and a man can advance into the future and interview those who will be taped the following Friday . . where is the experience of the past and where is next Friday's show? Is everything already finished and we simply tune in on certain states? Yes, for this is a dream which you can modify or radically change. In fact you are called upon to revise every day of your life and sometimes even to eradicate it. This is your human imagination.

342. But until it is revealed to you, use his name as revealed through his prophet Moses. "And when you go to them just tell them 'I AM' has sent me unto you." Lead them out of the wilderness into light by my name. When you can lead yourself today, no matter where you are, whether you are now bewildered, whether you are unwanted (as you think you are), or unemployed, (as you may be) . . lead yourself from these states of barrenness into states of fruition, a fruitful state, in the name. Just simply assume "I AM", and you

name it, hear it, smell it, see it to the best of your ability, and to the degree that you remain loyal to what you are imagining and hearing, you will actually externalize it in your world. Don't judge it before you try it.

343. Don't neglect the law of God which is: An assumption will harden into fact. If an assumption creates its own reality then there is no such thing as fiction. I may forget what I assumed today and when it appears I may not recognize my own harvest, but it could not enter my world had I not brought it in by an imaginal act.

344. By imagination we have the power to be anything we desire to be.

345. If you start to imagine that things are as you desire them to be regardless of reason and your senses denial and lose yourself in that end just as though it were true, by feeling the thrill of accomplishment; and rest in confidence that it is done; and your desire projects itself on a screen of space so you can see it in your world . . then you are the one they are talking about in scripture. Are you not told that by him all things were made, and without him was not anything made that was made?

346. I tell you: your own wonderful human imagination is Jesus Christ. There never was another and there never will be another. One day He will awaken in you and all that is said of him will be experienced by you in the first person present tense; and may I tell you: far from being ashamed, you will be thrilled beyond measure. All you have ever done as a man in this world of mortality of which you are ashamed will be wiped clean. It is necessary for you to go through the muck and mire of this world so that this seed may erupt. And when it does you are one with God, who is perfect, and your entire past is wiped out as though it never were.

347. Everything in your world is produced by imagination. There isn't a thing that was not first imagined, yet when it becomes an objective fact it seems so independent of your perception of it, that you forget its origin and do not realize it was produced by you. Everything that appears without was first an image, nothing more than a dream which was created by the dreamer in you, who is the Lord Jesus Christ.

348. Don't neglect the principle of your wonderful imagination. Use it lovingly on behalf of everything, for when you do, you are using it on yourself, as there is no other. The world is yourself pushed out. Imagine and then drop it.

349. Test your imagination, for there is no other God. If you test him and discover that it is he who creates all things by producing tangible proof of his reality in what you did, then no one will be able to persuade you that what happened was a coincidence.

350. Concerning the Law, I can only acquaint you with the Law and leave you to your choice and its risk; but we have Scripture for it . . to tell it, regardless of what they do with the Law. In the 18th chapter of the Book of Matthew you read these words: "If any two of you agree on earth about any request that you must make, that request will be granted by my Heavenly Father." Find two who agree, and that request will be granted. Well, can you conceive of something greater? If two agree on earth concerning any request . . it doesn't have to be good, it doesn't have to be this, that or the other, but any request . . "that you must make, that request will be granted by my Heavenly Father." Here we are told the greatest secret in the world concerning the human imagination. We are told that: "With God, all things are possible." Then we are told: "All things are possible to him who believes"; so he equates God with the human imagination: that God is the human imagination, and all things are possible to the human imagination.

351. God, as your imagination, can never be so far off as even to be near, for the nearness implies separation. Wherever you are, I AM! To say: "I AM" is near, is to claim God is another . . but there is no other. You and God are one, for He is your wonderful human imagination!

352. God dreams in you and you can test him any time if you are alert, for He steals into your conscious mind least disguised in the form of creative fancy. Sit down and think of a friend and watch this wonderful, moving being create mental images of him. The God of the universe is one with your wonderful human imagination. He works in your depth, underlying all of your faculties, including perception. Then suddenly you find him moving in a serpentine manner in the form of creative fancy. When you think of someone you can catch Him; and then you will discover who God really is, for He is all within you.

353. Now, if you should change on the outside and I become aware of it, the corresponding change would take place within me relative to you. Your change could take place socially, intellectually, financially, or even in your physical appearance; but if I encounter the change, it penetrates me. My acceptance of it will cause me to modify the image of you that I hold. Now, must I wait for the change to appear on the outside before I can change my image of you; or can I produce the change in me first, and then see a corresponding change on the outside? I can if I know that the potter is my own wonderful human imagination and is creating everything that is taking place in my world. "O Lord, thou art our Father, we are the clay. Thou art our potter, we are the works of thy hand." The potter, the Lord, and the Father, are the same being; the same awareness; the same Imagination. Believe my words! Trust your imagination! Having reproduced himself in you, all things now exist in your imagination. If you desire changes, produce them first on the inside. Penetrate that which exists in you, as that penetration will

compel the outside to conform to the changes which you, the potter brought to pass. The only way to prove this is to try it. Imagine a scene which would take place after your desire has been fulfilled.

354. Everyone in this world is bearing fruit . . poverty, wealth, health, being known, being unknown, everything . . and you who know this law can take anyone from the state where you find them and put them in the state you desire to see them. You don't need his consent or knowledge. Don't tell him what you are doing. Trust this power in your own being. Persuade yourself that this imaginal act is true and real, and to the degree that you are self-persuaded it is real it becomes real.

And so I tell you: if you forgive anyone he is forgiven; if you retain his sin it is retained. Don't blame him if he does not find the good job you think he should find. Don't give him an argument. Does he need a good job, and you tell him to go and to make a greater effort? You are not applying this principle. Only after you become self-persuaded that he is employed are you forgiving his sin. Sin means missing the mark. If he misses it and you know it, you can help him. Listen to the words: "If I had not come and spoken unto them, they would not know sin, but now they have no excuse for their sin." He comes and shows man that causation is mental, that it is not physical . . and now man has no excuse for his sin, missing the mark.

If man has a mind, an imagination. he can exercise it. "You have heard of old that you should not commit adultery, but I say unto you to look on a woman lustfully you have already committed the act in your heart." He raises it out from the physical state. He makes every man responsible for missing the goal. If I do not get the job, he does not condemn me. He only asks me to apply the law as it is revealed. "They read from the book the law of God clearly, and they gave the sense so that the people understood the reading." He reads from the

Book (God's revealed Word) that causation is mental, that imaginal acts create facts. So what are you imagining?

I can say morning, noon, and night that I am holding the thought for you, and hope you get it. But I must so persuade myself, that I can't see anything else in the world. That is what he taught us to do. And I tell you the day will come (it begins in one moment when you least expect it) when suddenly the whole thing begins to awaken and the flower begins to unfold in you.

355. There is quite a difference between being awake to your imaginal activities and being asleep to them. Awake, you can trace the event taking place on the outside to an imaginal act; but asleep you will find someone or something on the outside to be its cause. But causation is within the one observing the effect. Causation is symbolized as the foot in the 40th and 69th Psalms, as well as in the 10th chapter of Romans. In the end, man will overcome and put all things under his foot.

356. I say imagination creates reality, and if this premise is true then imagination fulfills itself in what your life becomes. Although I have changed the words, what I am saying is not new. Scripture says it in this manner: "Whatsoever you desire, believe you have received it and you will." This statement goes back two thousand years, yet even before that Jeremiah tells of the same principle in his story of the potter and his clay. But until imagination becomes a part of your normal, natural currency of thought, you will not act consciously. Like breathing, this awareness must become so much a part of you that you will not turn to the left or the right to praise or blame anyone. When you know this presence it will not matter if you started life behind the eight-ball, or in a palace; as a poor, or a rich child; you will realize that life is always externalizing what you are imagining. Lacking the knowledge of this principle, you can reproduce your environment . . be it pleasant or unpleasant . .

forever and ever, as you feed your imagination on what your senses dictate. But knowing this principle, you can ignore the present, and untethered by the so-called facts of life, you can imagine the present as you desire it to be and feed upon your desire, rather than its omission.

357. Man lives by committing himself to invisible states, by fusing his imagination with what he knows to be other than himself, and in this union he experiences the results of that fusion.

358. Now I know that Man is all Imagination, and God is Man and exists in us and we in Him. The Eternal Body of Man is the Imagination and that is Jesus, the divine body of which we are His members. I know this because if He makes all things and I imagine, remain faithful to my imaginal state and it happens. I have found him, not as someone divorced from me, but as my own wonderful human imagination.

359. Today, as in that day, men cannot believe that imagination is the cause of the phenomena of life. They will agree that an artist can imagine a lovely picture and bring it forth on canvas, but they cannot relate the same technique to a toothache. Yet there is only one cause! I, the Lord, am the cause and there is no other. Besides me there is no God. I form light and create darkness. I make weal and create woe. I, the Lord, AM He who does all these things. You cannot blame anyone for your misfortune. You could claim a friend betrayed your trust, therein causing your misfortune; but your friend was not the cause, your dream prompted you to confide in your friend. Causation is not on the outside, it comes from within. As you begin to awake, you discover there is only one God, who is your own wonderful human imagination.

360. Every scriptural miracle is an acted parable. It is imagination who enters the boat called man and falls asleep in order

for the journey of life to begin. Then the financial, marital, physical storms arise according to man's dreams. He could dream of something lovely and know healthy, happy storms. But if he does not know that the cause of the weal is his imaginal activity, he will continue to dwell in the storms of life until the disciples rouse him to remembrance. Awake, you are aware of the thoughts you are creating every moment of time, and carry this awareness into your dream world. You will not falter, for . . knowing the world you want to build and its cause . . you will be constantly aware of what you are imagining. You will no longer seek your desires among things, but will turn within to find they are all waiting to be fulfilled in God's temple.

361. You cannot think without the use of words, for words clothe thought. If you meet someone, you may think he looks remarkably well. It is a thought, being said without using audible words. Believe he does look well and you have sent your word. Think of the good news you just heard about your friend. That he is making so much money he doesn't even know what to do with it. You may hear his laughter in your mind's eye, but feel the reality of your words and let them happen. Don't try to determine how it will come to pass; simply assume it is already a physical fact. Do that and you will know the power of your word, for God became man, clothed in these mortal garments of flesh and blood, that man may become God. When you see a disturbance in your world you may question why, but it appeared because you did not control your imagination. You may enjoy carrying on arguments with your children, your parents, or friends, from premises that are stupid and need not be; but if you know that all things must come to pass, why are you doing it? If you believe that every thought produces what it implies, then stop a negative, undesirable thought, and change the record by putting on a new one. Then one day this fundamental revelation of the unfolding of the word within you will come to pass,

and the sacred word of God will unfold and cast you as the actor in the central role. Then you will know who Jesus really is.

362. Imagination and faith are the only faculties of the mind needed to create objective conditions.

363. Until man has the sense of Christ as his imagination, he will see everything in pure objectivity without any subjective relationship.

364. When people say Jesus Christ is coming again do not believe them, for Jesus Christ has never left you. Did he not say: "Lo, I AM with you always, even to the end of the age?" Then how can you look for him to return? Scripture states that Christ was taken up into the kingdom of heaven (which is within) and that he will come in the same manner as he was taken up. If Christ (God's creative power) is in you, he cannot come from without. Although he seems to be invisible, Christ has never left you, as you cannot detach yourself from imagination.

365. This morning's paper contained an article saying that scientists have discovered that the so-called throne Peter was to have sat upon 2,000 years ago is only 900 years old. They have now taken the chair out of its encasement, but are keeping it as a holy relic, when it was never any more than a piece of wood upon which some self-appointed nut sat while calling himself the emperor, the pope, or holy one. But now after a thousand years of nonsense the truth has been revealed. What are we going to do when man does not want to hear the truth that he is responsible for his own life, that his imagination is the only God? When you look out on the world you may think you had nothing to do with its creation, but you did. You do not know it yet, because its purpose has not been revealed to you. But by the restriction and limitation of your own creative power, you became your created world that you may expand beyond it and

create a still greater world for even further expansion of yourself. God is ever expanding his illumination. He took upon himself the limit of contraction called man, the limit of opacity called man, that he may break the limitation and expand. That's the glory of it all.

366. This "I remember when" principle can be used in a destructive or constructive way. You can say: “I remember when this was a glorious building and look at it now” as you become aware of rubble where once a glorious building stood. Or you can stand on rubble and say: “I remember when this was all rubble,” as you imagine a glorious building. You can say: “I remember when my friend had nothing and now he has much,” or: “I remember when he had much and now he is so poor.” You can say: “I remember when she was healthy,” which could imply she is now ill, or “I remember when they were unknown,” implying they are now famous. So you see what power was in that revelation. It's entirely up to you how you use your imagination, but the operation of your creative power is completely up to you. You make the decision, and are therefore responsible for its effect on the world.

367. Do not let anyone tell you that Jesus is coming again, for he has never left you. In you as your own wonderful human imagination, Christ is crucified in all and will eventually awaken in all as he gathers us together into himself, into his one body, one Spirit, one Lord, one God and Father of all.

368. Look at yourself in the mirror and dare to see radiant health and happiness reflected back to you. Then say within yourself: “I remember when my reflection was so different.” Persist in seeing your new image reflected there and you will resurrect that state. Your image, your concept of yourself or of another, is in your own wonderful human imagination who is Christ and Christ is the only God. God the Father and Christ your creative power are the same being, therefore he has never left you!

369. Start now to remember when your friend wasn't well by imagining he is healthy. Remember when your daughter was single by imagining she is married. Go through life remembering when. Haven't you heard people say: "Who does he think he is? I remember when he had nothing and was a nobody!" Now, you may have heard a little jealousy in their tone and that is good because envy adds fire to the statement, which causes the one spoken of to have more! He may never know who caused his success, but it was done by an act of remembrance with intensity.

370. Start now to mold every being in your world into the form of love. But love, divided from imagination, is eternal death. If you do not know you are dealing with a state, you can love someone dearly yet keep him forever in an unlovely state. But you can take him out by the use of your imagination. We are here in this world of experience for a divine purpose: to know imagination. The world is dead but you can begin now to overcome the last enemy of the world . . the enemy of death . . by imagining your friend is noble, wanted, and loved, and watch him become it. Save your friend from the state of poverty and you are saving yourself! Don't be concerned as to how and when it will happen; it will happen, for the world is yours and all within it. Like the seed, you have to be detached from the Father and fall into the ground to be made alive; for unless a seed falls into the ground it remains alone, but if it falls into the ground and dies it brings forth much. The creative power of your human imagination is the seed which falls into your fleshly body (the red earth called Adam). Hearing the word and applying its truth, your seed is made alive and begins to awake, and you realize who you really are.

371. Tonight, regardless of whether your dreams are beautiful or horrible, you are aware of them because Christ has never left you. And when you awake in the morning Christ (your imagination) awakes with you, or you could not remember your dreams. The

human imagination is the God the world honors (as they should) for imagination is the creative power of the world. Learn to control your wonderful imagination and you will discover that the whole vast world is yourself pushed out.

372. If I have a desire to help you, or to help anyone, all I need do is simply to imagine that I have heard them; then I actually hear them tell me what I wish they would tell me. Then there are two: this one that I am hearing and I, the one who is listening and hearing; and these two agree. If two agree in testimony, then it is conclusive; and because imagining creates reality, it must externalize itself in my world. "The whole vast world is only the imaginal act "pushed out." And so, we are told: "With God, all things are possible," and "All things are possible to him who believes." Well, am I not equating God with the believing one? And the believing one, isn't that one's own human imagination? That's all that it is.

373. Now, imagination cannot be observed as we see objects in space, for imagination is their reality. Fawcett gives the name, "God" to the cause of the universe, saying: "God, the creator, is like pure imagining in ourselves. He works in the depths of our soul underlying all of our faculties, including perception, and streams into our surface mind least disguised in the form of productive fancy." Listen to your thoughts and you will hear God's words! A thought that is not felt produces nothing. But a thought producing motor elements reproduces itself! Catch God in a moment of a motor element such as anger, fear, or frustration, being congratulated or congratulating, and you will know what is going to happen in your world. Unless, of course you arrest your thoughts and revise them. Most of us, however, are not aware of what we are doing, so we do not observe the creator. But we can catch him as he streams into our surface mind least disguised in the form of productive fancy. If, while riding the bus, driving the car, sitting at

home, or standing at a bar, you hear a remark and react by moving on the inside, that remark will fulfill itself in what your life becomes. This principle sets you free, if you are willing to assume its responsibility. But whether you assume it or not, you will fulfill your every motor element thought anyway. So in the end you will not sympathize or condemn, but simply tell those who may be going through an unpleasant experience of this principle, and . . if they accept it . . let the principle work in their lives.

374. So, I tell you, your own wonderful human imagination is the only cause of the phenomena of life. There is no other power! That is the God spoken of in Scripture! That is the only God . . your own wonderful human imagination. Do you know what you want tonight? All right. Don't minimize it. It doesn't matter how big it is, state it; and then listen in your own wonderful manner to your own voice for that matter. Or, tell a friend without his knowledge; you can hear a friend of yours tell you that he heard the good news about you. You know what you want. You actually write it out in your mind's eye, and then have a friend whose voice you know well . . and listen to his voice as he is confirming that you have it. These are the two who agree. You don't need another's voice in the sense that you let him come into your world.

375. We are told that when Job forgot himself in his love for his friends and prayed for them, his own captivity was lifted. Then all that he seemingly had lost was returned, multiplied one hundredfold. As you forgive another by thinking of him as you would like him to be and persuading yourself of the reality of your imaginal act, you are forgiving him for what he appears to be by putting him into an entirely different state. Do that and you are substituting a noble concept for an ignoble one. That's forgiveness! Forgiveness tests the individual's ability to enter into and partake of the nature of the opposite. A priest will say: I forgive you, yet when he passes you on the street he remembers what was confessed. If he can remember, he

has not forgiven! The memory of what was done or said must be replaced by something else, so that the former can no longer be remembered.

376. I ask you to take me seriously. Imagination will fulfill itself, so do not limit yourself by anything that is now happening, no matter what it is. Knowing what you want, conceive a scene which would imply you have it. Persuade yourself of its truth and walk blindly on in that assumption. Believe it is real. Believe it is true and it will come to pass. Imagination will not fail you if you dare to assume and persist in your assumption, for imagination will fulfill itself in what your life becomes.

377. To the imaginative man everything is a manifestation of the mental activity which goes on in man's imagination, without the sensuous reasonable man being aware of it.

378. Imagination is the beginning of the growth of all forms, and faith is the substance out of which they are formed. By imagination, that which exists in latency or is asleep within the deep of consciousness is awakened and is given form.

379. We are all actually one. So, if I stand here now and lose myself in an imaginal act, I AM influencing the entire world . . influencing every one who can be used to aid me in the objectification what am imagining. So, do it lovingly. Whatever you do, do lovingly, . . I don't care what it is. And if you are ever in doubt, do the loving thing, which is called by the simple, simple term the "Golden Rule'. "Do unto others as you would have them do unto you." So, if you are ever in doubt, use that as your rule, and you can't go wrong.

380. May I tell you: you have the power within to create anything! Let people be what they want to be, while you set goals

for yourself. It doesn't matter what has happened in your life or what the evidence of your senses tells you, the power of the universe is in you. That power is the Lord Christ Jesus, whose name is I AM. You will never know it however unless you test him, for only then will you realize that Jesus Christ is in you. I was taught Christ was on the outside somewhere in space. But I took the challenge and tested myself, to discover that I AM creative. That I create from within and that my life is the fulfillment of my own imaginal acts. I haven't always been wise in my choice, for imagination is always fulfilling its imaginal state and I have imagined unlovely things and reaped them by becoming the fulfillment of what I was imagining. Then I became more alert and discovered I could catch Christ as he streamed into my mind least disguised in the form of a creative fancy. If my thoughts were motor driven and they were unpleasant, I knew what to expect unless I revised them. But whether they were pleasant or unpleasant, I knew I would fulfill them.

381. If I read John correctly, not only my salvation is dependent on it; I must actually believe in him. Who is the being? My own imagination. If I don't believe and test it . . even though I fail . . well then, I don't believe in Christ, for Christ is really my imagination, your imagination. So you imagine something lovely of another, and if you don't believe in the reality of that imagination, then you don't believe in Christ. Though you can go to church every day and give ten per cent of your income to the church of your choice . . all these things are lovely, give them if you feel that way about it . . but that is not Christ. That is not believing in Christ. To believe in Christ is to see someone in this world, and have a sweet feeling towards that one that hasn't yet realized how to be lovely, something without his knowledge. Then represent him to yourself as though it were true, and believe in the reality of what you have done mentally.

Believe in Christ, for all things are possible to Christ. Bring him before your mind's eye and see him as he would like to be seen by himself, as he would like the world to see him. But you do it and believe in the reality of what you have done. That is believing in Christ. You will be surprised beyond measure how it works. At that very moment, because: "All things by a law Divine in one another's being mingle."

At that very moment that you interfere with his life, you reshuffle the entire deck, and all things will completely rearrange to mirror the change that is going to take place in him; and everyone in this world who can aid that change will be used to bring it about without their knowledge or consent. You don't need the consent of any being in the world; if they can be used to externalize what you have imagined, they will be used. And when you least expect it, because you believe in Him, then God resurrects you. Then you will live it out, and you stand bewildered when you see what God did for you.

382. Now he asks me, and you who read his letter, to test ourselves: "Test yourself, do you not realize that Jesus Christ is in thee." And he made all these things . . well then, let us put him to the test in us. I say he is our imagination, that is the power, the creative power of the universe. Look around. Do you know anything in the world of man that man has created . . from the clothes that he wears to the homes that he inhabits . . that wasn't first imagined? Do you know of anything in this world that is now proved as fact, as a concrete reality, that wasn't first imagined . . only imagined, and then it externalized? Yes, using hands, using implements of the world, but it first began as an image, and an image is simply the product of this reforming image-making faculty in man, which is man's imagination. Now, if "All things were made by him and without him was not anything made that was made," I can't come to any other conclusion than the fact that Christ of scripture is my imagination.

383. I ask you to take the same responsibility. To not pass the buck to any person, organization, situation, or circumstance, but to discover for yourself that imagining truly does create reality. If the cause of all life is God, then God must be all imagination. And because you can imagine, then . . like God . . you are pure imagination in yourself. Regardless of what reason and your senses deny, you can imagine anything and bring it to pass if this premise is true.

384. If you will let it, reason will take this divine gift from you and leave you poor, indeed. For you have the gift of possessing whatever you imagine, if you are faithful to that which you have assumed!

385. Everything in this world is God's creation and God is all Imagination. Even the clothes we wear, the chairs we are sitting on, were once imagined and then brought into being. Let no one tell you this is wrong. Those who tell you to kill out desire have not gone far enough, for if I wanted to kill desire I would have to start with the desire not to desire, and where would [I] go? How far? So, go out and do what you want to do and fulfill your dreams. Someone without academic background is telling you this. I am going out on a limb to tell you that everything in the Bible is true on a higher level, but it is revealed figuratively, and man confused literal truth with metaphor. I do not crawl on my belly and no little serpent spoke to me, as it says in Genesis; yet what is meant is true in metaphor. The serpent was called the most subtle of all the creatures and it represents the wisdom of man, who takes all his arts and religions for his own glamour and dedicates them to the creator. And then comes one who never went to any school (Blake) and shows them reality. And now those who thought themselves so wise are figuratively crawling on their bellies in the presence of such as he. In the Bible things are told on a higher level and told in metaphor,

but I know from mystical experience things I could not have found in any book.

386. The creator of the world works in the depth of your soul, underlying all of your faculties, including perception, and streams into your surface mind least disguised in the form of creative fancy. Watch your thoughts, and you will catch Him in the act of creating, for He is your very Self! Every moment of time you are imagining what you are conscious of, and if you do not forget what you are imagining and it comes to pass, you have found the creative cause of your world. Because God is pure imagination and the only creator, if you imagine a state and bring it to pass, you have found Him. Remember: God is your consciousness, your I AM; so when you are imagining, God is doing it. If you imagine and forget what you imagine, you may not recognize your harvest when it appears. It may be good, bad, or indifferent, but if you forget how it came into being, you have not found God.

387. But now let me share with you a story I know well, the story of my father. He was born a very poor white man in the Island of Barbados. My mother was born poor. She had nothing; he had nothing. And they proceeded to have children. Twelve children were born; two died at birth, ten survived. He had nothing. How he got hold of this, I do not know, but the first time he heard me speak in New York City was a Sunday morning, and when we went back to the apartment, he said, "You know, everything you said his morning is true. But why do you tell the people to close their eyes? Don't close your eyes. Keep them partly shut. You can control your imagination and you can control your attention better if the eyes are not completely closed. When you see me in the morning after breakfast reclining in my chair, you might think that I am just sleeping it off," because he's heavy drinker, " you might think I'm simply sleeping it off. I am not sleeping off anything. I am doing my day's work then. I bring before my mind's eye the men I want to

deal with that day, and I control the conversation. I tell them exactly what I want to tell them, as though it were true. I let them tell me . . confirm that it is true; and then when I am completely satisfied with my inner conversation, then I go to town. And it works that way."

388. Jesus never violated the law of Caesar. Looking at a coin he said: "Render unto Caesar the things that are Caesar's. If Caesar wants more taxes, ask your heavenly Father to provide more money for you by imagining you have it." Your heavenly Father, who dwells within you, has the power to set you free, while a god believed to be on the outside will enslave you.

389. But while we are here, let us learn the rules of the game of life and play it. Life itself is caused by the assemblage of mental states, which occurring creates that which the assemblage implies. My friend mentally heard the words he would hear if his desire for his friend were fulfilled. Its assemblage, occurring within him, created the event to be played out in the game of life. After you have assembled your mental state and allowed it to occur within you, you do not have to repeat the act. You cast your bread upon the water the moment you felt relief. Although you do not have a physical expression in a sexual manner, relief is possible; and of all the pleasures of the world, relief is the most keenly felt.

When someone you dearly love is late, you anxiously await that key in the door. And when you hear their voice, your relief is keenly felt. That is the same kind of relief you will have when you have imagined correctly. If you find it necessary to recreate the act every day, you are not casting your bread upon the water. You may imagine over and over again, but you are only going to impregnate once; and if you reach the point of relief, your bread has been cast upon the water to return, perhaps in the matter of an hour. I have had the phone ring . . minutes after I have imagined it . . to hear confirmation that it has happened. Sometimes it has taken days, weeks, or months; but I do not repeat the action once I have done it and felt the feeling of relief, for I know there is nothing more I need to do.

Learn to consciously play this game of life, for you are unconsciously playing it every day. I am sure the millions who are on relief feel the government owes them a living; but there is no government, only we who pay taxes. The government has no money and can only give what it takes from our pockets. Those on relief are complaining, claiming they are not getting enough out of our pockets, and that mood persists throughout their day. Their mood never varies, so they see no change and recognize no law between the mood they are sustaining and the outer world they dislike. If they were told that their mood was causing the phenomena of their life, they would deny it. No one wants to feel that he is solely responsible for the conditions of his life, yet there is no other cause. God is the only cause and he is man's own wonderful human imagination.

390. Whether you believe me or not, I know from experience that God and you are one grand Imagination, and there is no other God! One day, Imagination in you will awaken and you . . fully aware of who you really are . . will know that all things are subject to you. That is your destiny.

391. I tell you: imagining creates reality! If you want to change your life you must become aware of the ideas you are planting in the mind of others! When you meet someone who is negative, put a lovely idea in its place. Then, whenever you think of him, imagine he is telling you something lovely. And, because you now walk in a world that is not disturbed by his negative state, when he finds himself no longer thinking negative thoughts, he will never know you were its source. You will know it and that is all that is important. Become aware of the thoughts you are thinking and you

will know a more pleasant life. It makes no difference what others do; plant loving, kind thoughts and you will be blessed in the doing.

392. I urge you to shape your world from within and no longer from without. Describe yourself as you would like to be seen by others and believe your words. Walk in the assumption they are true and . . because no power can thwart God . . what He is imagining, you will experience. You are not someone apart from God, for I AM cannot be divided. The Lord, our God, is one I AM, not two! If God's I AM and your I AM is the same I AM, define what you would like to be. Then believe you are the Lord! Be like the lady who transformed a streetcar into a cruise. Lose yourself in your new state, while your world on the outside remains, momentarily, the same.

393. All forms of the creative imagination imply elements of feeling. Feeling is the ferment without which no creation is possible. There is nothing wrong with our desire to transcend our present state. There would be no progress in this world were it not for man's dissatisfaction with himself. It is natural for us to seek a more beautiful personal life; it is right that we wish for greater understanding, greater health, greater security. It is stated in the sixteenth chapter of the Gospel of St. John, "Heretofore have ye asked for nothing in my name; ask and ye shall receive, that your joy may be full."

A spiritual revival is needed for mankind, but by spiritual revival I mean a true religious attitude, one in which each individual, himself, accepts the challenge of embodying a new and higher value of himself as Dr. Millikan did. A nation can exhibit no greater wisdom in the mass than it generates in its units. For this reason, I have always preached self-help, knowing that if we strive passionately after this kind of self-help, that is, to embody a new and higher concept of ourselves, then all other kinds of help will be at our service. The ideal we serve and hope to achieve is ready for a new incarnation; but unless we offer it human parentage it is incapable of birth. We must affirm that we are already that which we hope to be and live as though we were, knowing like Dr. Millikan, that our assumption, though false to the outer world, if persisted in, will harden into fact.

394. Now to come back to tonight's theme: Imagining creates reality! Have you imagined something and it hasn't come to pass? Then what are you imagining right now? Are you imagining you are John Brown? You were not born knowing you were John Brown. You were born and others began to call you John. As time passed you began to assume you were John Brown and began to respond when you heard the name John. When you imagined being secure did you forget the feeling? Are you imagining you are secure now? You may have no evidence that you are secure, but as you allow others to tell you how much you are loved and wanted, how successful and famous you are, you will begin to assume it, and imagination will have created its reality. Try it, for that reality you already are!

395. So, everyone will get it, for everyone will be resurrected. Then you will not be wearing these bodies, wonderful as they are for us, filled with all the passions of the world, and they are all wonderful . . but it is not the body you will wear. You will be completely above the organization of sex. No need for this kind of creativity. Imagination becomes completely awake and you will create at will, and your imaginal act will become an immediate objective fact. And what we call reality today, all this fabulous world of ours . . may I tell you I have seen it . . it is all imagination.

When man has played his part and God has completed his purpose (which is to bring forth from us himself and make us all gods with him) then these garments . . made up of all the elements that feel so permanent and so wonderful . . they will vanish like smoke. There isn't an element that wasn't brought into being by the creative power of God, by his own wonderful divine imagining, and it is sustained in me because he sustains it by his imaginal act. When he ceases that imaginal act all the elements will melt, all vanish, and the world will be as though it never existed. But you and I will be lifted up above it all into an entirely different world, an eternal world.

396. The imaginative man not realizing that all that he encounters is part of himself, he rebels at the thought that he has chosen the conditions of his life, that they are related by affinity to his own mental activity.

397. When you imagine for a seeming other you are blessed, for there is no other and you are giving your imaginal gift to yourself! Hear your friend tell you his good news, see the joy on his face, feel the thrill of fulfillment, and let it take place in your world. And as it does, recognize your harvest. Realize you are responsible for its consummation. The world is yourself pushed out. Ask yourself what you want and then give it to yourself! Do not question how it will come about; just go your way, knowing that the evidence of what you have done must appear, and it will.

398. God is divine imagination and he limits himself to the very limit of contraction, called human imagination, and actually dies in the sense that all the power and all the memory of his glorious being had to be completely forgotten. So the cry on the cross is true: "My God, my God, why hast thou forsaken me." He himself has cried out, because he so completely gave himself to us he suffered total amnesia, complete forgetfulness of his divinity as he became us, and that was divine imagining becoming human imagining. Then we, building our little world . . lovely as it is to many of us . . it is so different, and the power we exercise is so fragile, compared with

that same power when raised up, when lifted up and the great name which is above all names is conferred upon us. And the day will come, without loss of identity you will bear the name "Jesus." Everyone is destined to be Christ Jesus . . that power, with the name exercising infinite power . . without loss of identity. We will know each other and all glorified, everyone. There is no limitation to the gift. Some will exercise it more than others, but certainly the gift is the same, the gift of Christ Jesus.

399. I tell you: behind the mask you wear is the only God. Divine Imagination reproduced himself in you as your human imagination; and because Divine Imagination contains all, everything is contained in the human imagination. One day you will awaken to this fact and discover that the world is yourself pushed out, just as the world is God pushed out. As this knowledge awakens in you, you begin to expand in the bosom of Divine Imagination, for you . . human imagination and God, Divine Imagination . . are one creator.

400. I know from experience that Jesus Christ is your own wonderful human imagination where all things exist. Buried in you, the human imagination unfolds as scripture fulfills itself in you. Not knowing you are human imagination, you imagine all kinds of things and cause the blows of life. Unwilling to apply your imagination, you . . as the enemy of Christ . . recoil from what I am telling you. You would rather go to church, light your candle at Mass, and think that's enough. I have letters from people who believe that I who make this statement am a devil. But I know that one day they will awaken and everything they have done will be forgotten and never brought to mind again. They are doing and saying these things because they are struggling within themselves.

Unable to believe that their own wonderful human imagination is God, they are the sinner who is missing the mark in life . . the sinner Judas betrays Christ to. Tell the sinners of the world that the cause of the phenomena of life is in them and they are going to resent it, for they cannot believe that God is in them as their own wonderful human imagination. They cannot believe that the only God so loved us He became us that we may be as He is. Unable to accept the truth, they will try to tear the revealer apart. That is why he was told to "Lead him away safely." The violent simply leave your world. They depart because they cannot accept the truth.

401. Believe me! The story of how God became man that man may become God, is the most glorious story ever told. But man must be constantly reminded that this God is his imagination, and the powerhouse of the world! Infinite power resides in your Imagination. You could be in prison and imagine yourself free. Believing in the reality of your imaginal act, it would make no difference to you how you are released. But when it happens and you find yourself where you imagined you were, you will have tested and recognized the infinite power you are. Imagining, you set yourself free; and when God sets you free, you are free indeed.

402. The imaginative man does not deny the reality of the sensuous outer world of Becoming, but he knows that it is the inner world of continuous Imagination that is the force by which the sensuous outer world of Becoming is brought to pass.

403. Now who is Jesus? If Christ is the power and the wisdom of God, and God sunk himself in us, that was his sacrifice. He actually became us that we may live; for were it not for this sacrifice of God, to actually limit himself to the state called "man," man would . . like the earth . . wear out like a garment. As we are told in Isaiah 51:6: "Lift up your eyes to the heavens, and look at the earth beneath; for the heavens will vanish like smoke, the earth will wear out like a garment, and they who dwell in it will do likewise; but my salvation will be forever and my deliverance will never be ended." That word

"salvation" means Jesus. The word "Jesus" is "Jehovah saves." That is salvation. That is forever. Were it not that God became man that man may become God, to save man and lift him up to immortality, because the promise is: "The earth will wear out like a garment."

404. I have disclosed the one and only source of the phenomena of life. Everything that has ever happened, is happening, or will happen to you, comes from God, who is your own wonderful human imagination. I urge you to use it wisely.

405. Everything said in scripture is all about you, for you are the being called God, but unless you claim it you cannot attain it. How can you when you are the only power? You must walk conscious of being imagination, or die in your sins and never attain that awareness. No physical man made the statement: "Unless you believe that I AM He you will die in your sins." The one speaking is He who said these words: "I AM from above. You are from below. You are of this world, I am not of this world." When Jesus Christ was publicly portrayed as crucified (remember, this play did not take place on earth save as a parable), he came before Pilate, who said: "Do you not know that I have the power to set you free or the power to crucify you?" And Jesus answered: "You have no power unless it has been given you from above."

Your I AMness is from above. Having come to do the Father's will, I who am now aware of being you, will drink the cup of experience to the very end. But no one has any power over me save I, by my assumption, give it away. I do it by assuming I am less than another, thereby forcing him to play the part of one superior to me. Everyone reflects my assumptions and plays their part relative to that which I have assumed, for there is nothing but Imagination, and I AM He. Assuming I am afraid, I live in a world of fear, for there is no other. Being protean, I am playing every part in my dream of life, be it for my good or for my ill.

406. So, God became man that man may become God. In becoming man (as God is the only creative power in the world) what in me creates? My imagination. I may not have the talent to put it on paper, I may not have the ability to execute it the way artists can, but I can imagine it. I can imagine a book and the joy of having a book. I can imagine a picture. Without being an artist I can dream. I cannot conceive of a picture that a man can paint on canvas that is more alive than my dream, yet I can't put a thing on canvas. But I go to sleep and I can dream. And what is doing it, if not my imagination? And here when I lose the conscious faculty, this restricted area, I can actually dream. Dream as no artist in the world conveys; put color upon it, put motion upon it, and have the most wonderful drama . . and that is my imagination.

407. There is enormous power in wealth, as well as the atomic bomb; but their power is as a firecracker compared to the power of Imagination. Without any background or degree behind you, you can dwell in any state in your imagination just as though it were true; and in a way no one knows your power will take you (without a topaz, a friend, or a car) into the state of your choice.

408. I have entered scenes just as solid and real as this room, knowing that if I arrested an activity in my imagination everything will stand still. I have entered a restaurant and, observing people being served, I have arrested an activity within me and everything stills. Releasing it, everything continues as intended. The world is a play which has already been written. The players are merely actors on the stage, but getting carried away with the action you weep and laugh, for becoming involved in the emotions of the unfolding acts you do not realize it is only a play. Imagination is buried in his predetermined play, from which he is born and dies over and over again until the Word buried with him awakens. That is God's awakening and your extraction from the play, as told us in the Psalms: "To the Lord God belongs my redemption from death." God

doesn't redeem you from the outside, for every character in scripture is in you! All things exist in the Human Imagination, which is the Divine Body!

409. Someone may be a rascal and take from you what is yours; but when you know that imagining creates reality, you will acknowledge that no one could come into your life unless you called him. And he could not have taken from you unless you . . by your attitude towards life . . had allowed it. The world is yourself pushed out, and you either control it or you don't. That's the story of scripture. There is no other God other than your own wonderful human imagination. If, when you speak of Jesus Christ, you mentally bow your head (if not physically) do the same thing when you think of your imagination, for that is he. Imagination is the Word of God who is God Himself. The world was created, is supported, and sustained, by your own wonderful human imagination. Change your imagining! Believe the change into being and you will live in a wonderful world of life.

410. Believe me. Make imagination your one solid foundation. Do this and you will enjoy a freedom you have not known before. It is a fantastic freedom! Just imagine and it's done! Imagination is the only foundation. No other foundation can anyone lay than that which is laid, which is Jesus Christ. Man has tried to lay other foundations in the many isms of the world. These are not Jesus Christ, for he is man's I AMness, man's human imagination, and there is no other God. Hear, O Israel, the Lord our God, the Lord is one, whose name forever and ever is I AM! Accept awareness as your way of life, and you will find a freedom you have never known before. You will become aware of the fact that everyone and everything is yourself pushed out. You will awaken as God, the father of all life, to realize that although things appear to die they do not, for nothing dies in (imagination) Christ.

411. Prayer is an art and requires practice. The first requirement is a controlled imagination. Parade and vain repetitions are foreign to prayer. Its exercise requires tranquility and peace of mind, "Use not vain repetitions," for prayer is done in secret and "thy Father which seeth in secret shall reward thee openly."

412. But while we are here, we are given a law whereby, through its operation, we may know who God is. The law is simple. It is stated many ways, one of which is: "As a man sows, so shall he reap." As you imagine you are the man (the woman) you would like to be, you are sowing that imaginal thought in your mind. To the degree that you are faithful to that assumption, you will reap its fruit in your world; but first you must know what you want.

413. Take the challenge of scripture and assume the feeling of the wish fulfilled . . not only for yourself, but for your family and friends. When you imagine for another, you are really giving it to yourself, as there is no other. The whole vast world is only yourself pushed out.

414. Now, "The hour has come when the son of Man is betrayed into the hands of sinners." Who are the sinners? Those who recoil from the revelation of the truth that the human imagination is God! Tonight one billion who say they believe in Christ will recoil from the thought that their human imagination is God, and do not know they are sinners, enemies of the truth; for the true Christ is God's power and wisdom housed in Man as his own wonderful human imagination. Those who do not accept the truth but see only its embodiment would destroy him, but he who recognized the personification of truth embraces him with extended arms.

415. There is nothing that appears in perception which cannot be duplicated in fancy, and what the world perceives is all imaginative in character. Here is a graphic example: I am sure everyone knows

what it is to detect the fragrance of a rose. Now smell is a chemical sense and depends upon contact for perception. But does one really need a rose to detect its fragrance? Cannot its fragrance be reproduced imaginatively? Having smelled an Easter lily, can you not discriminate between the smell of a rose and a lily, imaginatively? Then they do not exist independent of you, but live on some level (or levels) of your imagination! Can you call upon your memory of an experience of long ago, bring it back, and duplicate it in fancy? If so, then this world is no different from your imaginal one! In 1820, William Blake wrote “The Presence of the Divine Teacher,” in which he said: "Man is all Imagination and God is Man and exists in us and us in Him. The Divine Body Jesus, we are his members." In this statement Blake does not separate the members from the one body, the one spirit, one hope, one Lord, one faith, one God and Father of us all. There is only one Imaginal Body. We are all His members, for we are all Imagination!

416. I admire the great, inspired poets. Shakespeare is marvelous. Blake is altogether wonderful, and Einstein truly great in his field. These were inspired men; but they did not have any influx of spirit that made them greater than your human imagination, for their imagination and your imagination are one grand, divine imagination, imagining! Their work did not come from something outside of themselves, but from their own imagination, awakening. That same imagination is yours because there is only one spirit. The spirit of man is one with the spirit of the universe and there is no other! Start now to capture the feeling of being this one spirit. Fall asleep in the feeling that you are God, and as you come hurtling back from the depth of unconsciousness toward this level, you will have numberless crazy little dreams based upon this person you are coming through.

You will give importance to these dreams; but oh, what depths you will reach in that which is unconscious relative to this level! Let no one frighten you, for you are an immortal being who cannot die. Although I have awakened to my Godhood before you, I am no better because I got there first, for there is no such thing as being first. Everyone is moving toward that level, and no one can fail. And when all have returned, what joy will be expressed as we form the one body, the one spirit, the one Lord, the one God and Father of all! Everyone will have the vision and prove to himself that he is God the Father.

417. Test your own wonderful human imagination this night and believe in the reality of Christ, your creative power. Believe that all things are possible to him. Imagine the state you desire to express in this world, and as you go about your business you will see how quickly it will come to pass. Then one day scripture will unfold in you, casting you in the central role, but in the interval you are free to choose whatever you want to be or do.

418. But tonight believe me: your own wonderful human imagination is the one and only God, so put him to the test. Know what you want and let him create it for you. Search for and find the feeling that would be yours if things were as you desire them to be. Look at your world . . would you see it differently? Would those in your world see a different you? Create that scene, catch the feeling of reality and don't let go! Don't forget what you saw and how you felt, for he who creates in you must have a model to work with. Don't be the double-minded man Jesus speaks of: "The double-minded man is unstable in all of his ways. He looks into the mirror of life and sees what he looks like, then he turns and forgets what he was like." Do not turn away from what you have just imagined and forget what you really look like, but persist in the new state. Remain faithful to it and let the one within you (who is Christ the Lord) externalize it, for you and He are one. I don't mean you and the Lord, but you are the Lord. There is only God in this world and you will know one day that you are He.

419. God is your own wonderful human imagination and there never was another. He actually took upon himself all of the limitations and weaknesses of the flesh that you . . in turn . . may discover who God is, believe in yourself, apply your belief, and awaken one day to the realization that you are He in every sense of the word.

420. So, be careful what you imagine. I don't care how trivial it is, it will come to pass. The whole vast world is nothing more than the confused imaginations of men and women. So, if it seems confused, it is because man is not in control of his imaginal acts. He thinks he can imagine anything with impunity, but he cannot. It all comes into the world to confront him, and to show him what his harvest is. He planted it somewhere along the way; and now here comes his harvest, and he doesn't recognize his own harvest. It's not the easiest thing in the world to watch one's imagination morning, noon and night, and to actually control it as you would a boat at sea when you steer it in the direction you want it to go. But, it has to be done eventually. Therefore, get started now.

421. Those who are not awake will continue to fight shadows in this world, for everything here is imagination made visible. Shelley once said:

"He has awakened from the dream of life.
'Tis we who, lost in stormy visions,
Fight with phantoms and unprofitable strife."

Those who are fighting against the establishment do not realize that they are fighting against the objectified images of their own mind. But the day will come when he who is dreaming his world into being, will awake within himself to know he is its foundation, the one the Bible calls Jesus. The words "Jesus" and "Joshua" mean

"Jehovah, the Lord's salvation." A man is saved from his dream by returning to the state he occupied before the dream began.

422. How do you occupy a state? By asking yourself how you would feel, what you would see, hear, touch, taste, and smell if your dream were real. Take time to set the stage. Being the star of your production, place yourself center stage, then allow a friend to enter and see you in your new state. Write the script . . the words he would say when he sees you. Feel his touch. Clothe yourself with the reality of the state you have just created in your imagination. You need not ask anyone's permission or help, but moving into the new state in your imagination, simply remain there until you feel its reality. Then let the feeling go its way toward fulfillment.

423. If you imagine a state, remain faithful to it, and it externalizes itself, you have found the creator of the world for by him all things are made and without imagination is not anything made that is made. When you discover how to make something, you have found him of whom Moses and the prophets wrote, your own wonderful human imagination, the Everlasting Sustainer of all life.

424. In Paul's 1st letter to the Corinthians he said: "No other foundation can anyone lay then that which is laid, which is Jesus Christ." And in his 2nd letter he asked: "Do you not realize that Jesus Christ is in you?" Now I ask you: who is this Jesus Christ who is in you? He is your own wonderful human imagination . . the foundation stone of your world! Your dreams create your world, and the dreamer dreaming those dreams, is your human imagination scripture calls Jesus Christ. You may think of Jesus as someone other than yourself, someone separate and apart from you, but I tell you, Jesus Christ is in you as your wonderful human imagination. He is the dreamer, the foundation of your day as well as your night dreams. You may not be able to write a letter, paint a picture, or

carry a tune, but you can dream because (Imagination) Jesus Christ is in you.

425. So tonight please believe me. There is no other God other than he who is your own wonderful human imagination. Turn to any other and you have turned to a false God. Now, make no graven image of God. "I AM" has no face. Unnumbered artists have drawn pictures of what they conceive Jesus to be, but he has no face. He is simply "I AM."

426. I did not know that the story of Jesus Christ was mine. I did not know Jesus interpreted the Old Testament with himself as the very center of it; that the human imagination . . our human I AMness . . was He. But now I know that there never was another Jesus and there never will be another, and those who teach another are false teachers teaching a false Christ.

427. When you dream, do not think that because there seems not a fact to support it, it cannot come. It will come, so dream nobly. If you want fame, have it. But I would suggest that you suggest to yourself that you are awakening and can see this frozen wonderful world and you as the activator. I hope many of you have the desire to do what I am doing and will go out and tell this. First prove it to yourselves. Learn the art of repentance, which means a change of mind. Try it, and try it again, and prove that a change in you will produce an outer change. Go out and prove it and then tell others. Imagine what you want to imagine and continue to imagine until you are confronted with it. It does not matter what your senses tell you; if you learn to live by this you will not fail. Bear in mind that this, the body, is only a garment and one day you will take it off. But you are invisible, and when you [are] completely awakened, you join the Divine Society and become one of the Gods who create. Remember that every moment of time God is begetting himself in us and you cannot fail.

428. Man is looking for a savior to change the establishment and society in the outside world when it is but a reflection of a dream whose reality lies deep within him. A savior will never be found in the midst of shadows. He will only be found when he who laid himself down within the individual man awakens in a wonderful series of events. Everything said of Jesus Christ in scripture is said of you, for you are the dreamer, and the world is your dream pushed out. Fight with it if you will. Do as you like, but you will not awaken until the dream is finished. Then you will awaken to discover that you are its dreamer and creator. There is nothing but your wonderful human imagination! There is no other God. There is no other Jesus Christ. There is no other Lord. Your human imagination is the God of scripture. This I know from experience.

429. I tell you a truth: There is nothing greater than your own wonderful human imagination! It is he who inspired Blake, Shakespeare, and Einstein, for there is only one spirit in the universe! "Hear, O Israel, the Lord our God, the Lord is One." That one spirit is the human imagination! When Blake was asked what he thought of the divinity of Christ he answered: "Christ is the only God, but so am I and so are you." Don't think of Christ as someone greater than yourself. He is the only God, but so am I and so are you! Don't consider yourself less than Christ, for there is only God, who is your own wonderful human imagination. Daring to assume that all things are possible to imagine, put this one reality to the extreme test by assuming you are the person you would like to be. Your reasonable mind and outer senses may deny it; but I promise you: if you will persist, you will receive your assumption. Believe me, you are the same God who created and sustains the universe, but are keyed low; so you must be persistent if you would bring about a change.

430. So you can't see imagination; you see the fruits of imagination. So no one has ever seen God, because you are the

reality called "Imagination." And you don't see imagination, but you see the evidence; you see the fruit of it.

431. My every thought is a vibration, drawing to me that which it is implying." This was set up in the beginning. "As a man sows, so shall he reap." It's the law of identical harvest, called "seedtime and harvest" in scripture. There will be no change. You plant weal, you reap weal. Plant wheat and wheat will grow, all caused by the human imagination. As you imagine you vibrate and call forth that which you have imagined. Your world is forever bearing witness to what you are imagining. You may not recognize your harvest and deny you have ever had such a horrible thought, but no one did it to or for you, you did it yourself. In the beginning you promised that you would take the consequences of your imaginal acts, good, bad or indifferent. And you can try from now until the end of time to change the outside, but only when you change your way of thinking can you change your world. Give a man something on the outside to support him and you have conditioned his world and he will curse you when you stop it. But show him how to use his imagination to attract what he wants and you have given him the gift of life.

432. On this platform we believe that God is all Imagination and God is man (spiritual man, not the garment of skin he wears). Therefore man is all Imagination. We believe also that God, being the only creator, and God being man, then we are creators, that life itself is an activity of Imagination. The whole world in which we live is a world of Imagination. Tonight we hope to show it in such a manner that you will be encouraged to go out and prove it. Everyone can become what he or she desires to be, yet the real being is invisible and you see only its manifestation, for God is spirit, therefore man is spirit, and when we speak of spirit we mean imagining.

433. If you know what you want in this world you can get it. And let no one tell you that you are acquisitive. Those who tell you that would not mind having the same thing for themselves. So be completely disinterested in what people say and go out and live a full, wonderful, rich life, for what you want to do you can do if you know who you are. You are all Imagination and Imagination is God, and only God creates.

434. Experience has convinced me that an assumption, though false, if persisted in, will harden into fact, that continuous imagination is sufficient for all things, and all my reasonable plans and actions will never make up for my lack of continuous imagination.

435. I asked myself many times, "If my imagination is Christ Jesus and all things are possible to Christ Jesus, are all things possible to me?"

436. Through experience, I have come to know that, when I identify myself with my aim in life, then Christ (Imagination) is awake in me. Christ (imagination) is sufficient for all things.

437. Wherever you go, you are always imagining. You cannot leave the Lord behind you. You cannot sit here and wish imagination away as you can the body. I can stand here and assume that I am at the end of the room and imagine that I am looking at this one. But where am I? I am in imagination. I can look at the body as something that I have put away for a while. I return to it. But I can't put away imagination. I cannot get away from the Lord, because, being all imagination, I must be wherever He is in imagination. So, if I now, in imagination feel things as I desire them to be, that's the Lord doing it. And because "All things are possible to the Lord," I must believe in me; I must believe it is the Lord doing it

438. The world is a revelation of the states with which imagination is fused. It is the state *from* which we think that determines the objective world in which we live.

439. We must use imagination masterfully, not as an onlooker thinking of the end, but as a partaker thinking from the end, we must actually be there in imagination.

440. Use your imagination consciously, and after a while you will stop fighting shadows. The conflict within you will cease and your world will be at peace. Let those who are still asleep dream their violence into the world. It's perfectly all right, for in its midst you will walk knowing you are protected, for you are awake. This is your dream, too, and no dreamer can be destroyed by his dream. You can stop dreaming violence and start dreaming peace while you are here, and share your awareness with those who will listen . . but not everyone will. Instead they will call you mad and think you have a devil, just as they did of one called Jesus in scripture.

441. Now remember: nothing appears in perception that cannot be duplicated in fancy. If you can perceive your desire, it exists. You cannot perceive an object that does not exist on some level (or levels) of imagination. Identify your human imagination with God, and because God calls a thing that is not now seen as though it were seen, you can call a state into being by assuming you are in it. And if you believe you have received your desire, you will, for belief will lead the way to its fulfillment. If you look to reason rather than imagination, you are seeing the devil instead of God. The devil is the doubter in you. He questions your belief saying: "If you are the son of God then turn this stone into bread. Cast yourself down and his angels will lift you up." All of these challenges are made by self-doubt. I urge you to practice the art of imagination. If you do, I promise you will prove it in the testing, even though you may have started out to prove it wrong!

442. And the Son of God, in whom there is life, is your own wonderful human imagination. Imagining is life itself. What you imagine becomes animated, it takes on life, it takes on motion, vibration.

443. You can reproduce and duplicate any perception you have ever encountered, in your imagination. A friend or dear one does not need to be physically present for you to think of him. Nor do you have to be in your living room in order to see its contents. You can see the plains of Kansas, the mountains of Colorado, or the great Mississippi River without being there. So when we think from the premise of this as a world of imagination, we start on solid ground, for imagination is He who creates reality. There is no fiction in the true sense of the word, for when a state is imagined, it is created. Prayer is imagination drenched in feeling. A desire, drenched in the feeling of fulfillment, objectifies itself. This I know to be true; so regardless of what the world thinks, when you reproduce anything in your mind it takes on form in your outer world.

444. Begin now to actively, constantly, use your imagination; for as you prove its creative power on this level, you are awakening to a higher level and birth into the spirit world where you know yourself to be God. Prove to yourself that you are God by feeling your desire is now an accomplished fact. Listen to your friends talk about you. Are they rejoicing because of your good fortune, or are they expressing envy? Imagine their words are true. Persist in imagining they are true. Continue to imagine your desire is already an accomplished fact; and when it is objectively realized, proof will be yours. Think of something lovely you would like to give another. Then ask yourself if you gave it to him and he wouldn't accept it, would you want to keep it for yourself? If, for instance, you gave a friend a million dollars and he would not accept it, would you be willing to keep it? I'm sure you would. Then imagine giving the money to him, then give to others in the same way. You may not

even have a bank account; but you can still give, because there is no one to give to but yourself! There is only God whose name is I AM!

445. It is the imaginative self that must be awakened.

446. Man's ability to identify himself with his aim, though reason and his senses deny it, is proof of the birth of Christ (imagination) in him.

447. The ultimate purpose of imagination is to create in us "the spirit of Jesus", which is continual forgiveness of sin (always obtaining our goal), continual identification of man with his ideal.

448. Whatever place or state we convey our imagination, to that place or state we will gravitate physically also.

449. A man can be seen where in imagination he is, for a man must be where his imagination is, for his imagination is himself.

450. If imagining creates reality, and you practice repentance by radically changing your mind, you can take anything that displeases you and change it. Then persuade yourself that the change is real. Expect it to mold itself in harmony with what you are thinking, and the man, woman, or room, will bear witness to your repentance. When you change your attitude towards another, he must change his attitude towards you. Are we not told: "We love him because he first loved us?" It always starts with self! If you want him to be different, you must initiate the change. And as you do, you are practicing repentance, for the time is fulfilled and the kingdom of heaven is at hand. It is now time to repent and believe the gospel!

451. The world thinks of numberless gods, but there is only one. That one is your own wonderful human imagination. Possessing only one son, when imagination awakens, God's only begotten son

will reveal you as God. The same thing will happen to another, then another . . and eventually everyone will see the same son, who will reveal the individual as God the Father. This world is a play, where divine imagination becomes human imagination by inserting himself into an olive skin, a black skin, a white skin, and a red skin. Although we appear to be different, we all will see God's only begotten son . . proving that there is only one God. The purpose behind the play is to expand imagination's creative power. Here we are fragmented into numberless parts, destined to gather ourselves together into the one God, the one Father of all.

452. Although the churches teach that another, greater than yourself, said: "Unless you believe that I AM He, you will die in your sins" . . these words were spoken by the human imagination! And because imagination is one, and you can't get away from that oneness, don't think of another. Accept these words in the first person, present tense; for unless you believe that you already are what you want to be, you will die in your sins by leaving your desire unfulfilled. If you do not believe you are all imagination, you will continue in your former belief, worshipping a God on the outside and not within.

453. There is nothing God cannot do! Do not think that one who is fabulously rich has an influx of spirit which differs from yours. He is imagining wealth, either wittingly or unwittingly; but you can do it knowingly. If he does not know what he is doing, he can lose his wealth and not know how to recover it. I am asking you, regardless of your financial situation, to assume wealth, knowingly. If, tomorrow you would again return to your former state, bring wealth back by claiming "I AM wealthy," for there is only one God. He who creates poverty also creates wealth, as there is no other creator.

454. You don't have to be a brilliant scholar to use your creative power. In fact, the more brilliant you are, the less you are likely to try it. The so-called brilliant mind believes only in that which is physical and visible, and therefore does not believe a desire can be fulfilled by a simple imaginal act. But I know the power of imagining, for I have sat quietly in my chair in my living room, constructed a scene which implied the fulfillment of my desire, gave it all of the qualities of naturalness so that it felt right . . and let it be. Then, just as I would drop a seed into the ground and wait for its maturity, my seed of desire matured and fulfilled itself in my world. Imagine whatever you desire. Believe you will receive it and go about your business in the world with patience and confidence, knowing your desire will erupt and become a reality. Use the law while you remain in the city waiting to be clothed with power from on high, for it will come.

455. How many times have we heard someone say, "Oh, it's only his imagination?" Only his imagination . . man's imagination is the man himself. No man has too little imagination, but few men have disciplined their imagination. Imagination is itself indestructible. Therein lies the horror of its misuse. Daily, we pass some stranger on the street and observe him muttering to himself, carrying on an imaginary argument with one not present. He is arguing with vehemence, with fear or with hatred, not realizing that he is setting in motion, by his imagination, an unpleasant event which he will presently encounter. The world, as imagination sees it, is the real world. Not facts, but figments of the imagination, shape our daily lives.

It is the exact and literal minded who live in a fictitious world. Only imagination can restore the Eden from which experience has driven us out. Imagination is the sense by which we perceived the above, the power by which we resolve vision into being. Every stage of man's progress is made by the exercise of the imagination. It is only because men do not perfectly imagine and believe that their results are sometimes uncertain when they might always be perfectly certain. Determined imagination is the beginning of all successful operation. The imagination, alone, is the means of fulfilling the intention. The man who, at will, can call up whatever image he pleases is, by virtue of the power of his imagination, least of all subject to caprice. The solitary or captive can, by intensity of imagination and feeling, affect myriads so that he can act through many men and speak through many voices.

456. The imaginative man sees the outer world and all its happenings as projections of the inner world of Imagination.

457. The imaginative man realizes that every man must become conscious of this inner activity and see the relationship between the inner causal world of imagination and the sensuous outer world of effects.

458. It is a marvelous thing to find that you can imagine yourself into the state of your fulfilled desire and escape from the jails which ignorance built.

459. To the world it is the height of insanity to believe that imagining creates reality, yet every mystic knows that every natural effect has a spiritual cause. A natural cause only seems to be. It is a delusion of this world, as man's memory is so poor he cannot relate what is taking place now to a former imaginal act. Always looking for physical causation, man cannot believe he imagined anything that could have produced such a physical effect; yet I tell you: as you sit alone and imagine you are setting a cause in motion, and when you see its effects you may deny the imaginal state, but your "now" is alive and real to you because of an imaginal act on your part and for no other reason. Your imagination sets everything in motion, but your memory is faulty; therefore you may look upon

one who claims life is caused by imagination as a fool . . yet Blake would call you an idiot reasoner, not a man of imagination.

460. It is my belief that all men can, like Dr. Millikan, change the course of their lives. I believe that Dr. Millikan's technique of making his desire a present fact to himself is of great importance to any seeker after the "truth." It is also his high purpose to be of "mutual benefit" that is inevitably the goal of us all. It is much easier to imagine the good of all than to be purely selfish in our imagining. By our imagination, by our affirmations, we can change our world, we can change our future. To the man of high purpose, to the disciplined man, this is a natural measure, so let us all become disciplined men.

461. In the Book of Romans, the 4th chapter, the 17th verse, Paul tells us: "God calls things that are not seen as though they were seen and the unseen becomes seen." How does he do it? By the act of movement. I move and that which was invisible becomes visible. I see you now, but you have told me your desire. It is invisible, but by the act of movement I can see your face radiantly happy because your desire has now taken on life and substance. I have moved, and in so doing I see you differently. Now, if I move from that I AM into what I would like to be, you will still be my friend; so in my imagination I let you see me as you would have to see me if things were as I want them to be, and there I remain. I can't be double-minded and let you see me in my former state, but must persist in my new state until it becomes natural and out pictures itself in my world. This is true of everything you do, I don't care what it is. If you want to be known, you will be, regardless of the fact that you start your assumption with nothing to support your claim. Simply dare to assume that you are, for your assumptions . . although denied by your senses . . if persisted in will become externalized facts in your life.

462. Learn to live in your imagination morning, noon, and night. This gentleman whose experiences I shared with you tonight told me that when he first heard me he thought I was crazy; but he tried it, and although it didn't make sense it worked. I know the law and the promise do not make sense from a worldly point of view, yet I tell you: there is a plan of redemption buried in you which will erupt in the fullness of time and you will experience all that is said of a man called Jesus in scripture. Then you will know he was never a physical being, but the name of a plan. Jesus is Jehovah, who is your own wonderful I AM.

463. Truth depends upon the intensity of the imagination, not upon external facts.

464. Facts are the fruit bearing witness of the use or misuse of the imagination.

465. Man becomes what he imagines.

466. Imagination is the way, the truth, the life revealed.

467. I ask you to use this power called the law. Simply determine what you want and imagine a scene which would imply you have realized it. Enter into the spirit of the scene. Participate in it by giving it sensory vividness. Then relax as you feel its reality. Don't consider the means. Know your desire is already an accomplished fact and you are now reveling in it. Then have faith, for faith is loyalty to your unseen reality. Your imaginal act, although unseen, is reality for God did it. If I asked you who is imagining it, you would respond: "I AM" and that is God's name forever and forever.

468. As we awaken to the imaginative life, we discover that to imagine a thing is to make it so, that a true judgment need not conform to the external reality to which it relates.

469. The future dream must become a present fact in the mind of him who seeks to realize it. We must experience in imagination what we would experience in reality in the event we achieved our goal, for the soul imagining itself into a situation takes on the results of that imaginary act. If it does not imagine itself into a situation, it is ever free of the result.

470. "Now is the acceptable time to give beauty for ashes, joy for mourning, praise for the spirit of heaviness; that they might be called trees of righteousness, the planting of the Lord that He might be glorified." Now is the time to control our imagination and attention. By control, I do not mean restraint by will power but rather cultivation through love and compassion. With so much of the world in discord we cannot possibly emphasize too strongly the power of imaginative love. I hope to be able to bring to each of you present the true meaning of the words of Zechariah, "Speak ye every man the truth to his neighbor and let none of you imagine evil in your hearts against his neighbor." What a wonderful challenge to you and to me. "As a man thinketh in his heart so is he." As a man imagines so is he. Hold fast to love in your imagination. By creating an ideal within your mental sphere you can approximate yourself to this "ideal image" till you become one and the same with it, thereby transforming yourself into it, or rather, absorbing its qualities into the very core of your being. Never, never, lose sight of the power that is within you. Imaginative love lifts the invisible into sight and gives us water in the desert. It builds for the soul its only fit abiding place. Beauty, love and all of good report are the garden, but imaginative love is the way into the garden.

471. There is only one foundation, and that is your own wonderful human imagination, and there is no other. Now, let me tell you of another lady who is here tonight. She said: "Ten days ago I heard from my mother that she believed she was afflicted with the same problem she had experienced a year ago. When I received the letter I sat right down and wrote her saying: ‘The God in me is speaking to the God in you, telling me that you do not have this affliction and that you are perfect.' I wrote so convincingly that when she received the letter she believed me, and when the tests were made they came out negative. I have never been able to use the word `imagination' to my family, so I use the word `God' and they understand.”

472. Prayer is a controlled waking dream. If we are to pray successfully, we must steady our attention to observe the world as it would be seen by us were our prayer answered. Steadying attention makes no call upon any special faculty, but it does demand control of imagination. We must extend our senses . . observe our changed relationship to our world and trust this observation. The new world is not there to grasp, but to sense, to touch. The best way to observe it is to be intensely aware of it. In other words, we can, by listening as through we heard and by looking as though we saw, actually hear voices and see scenes from within ourselves that are otherwise not audible or visible. With our attention focused on the state desired, the outer world crumbles and then the world . . like music . . by a new setting, turns all its discords into harmonies.

Life is not a struggle but a surrender. Our prayers are answered by the powers we invoke not by those we exert. So long as the eyes take notice, the soul is blind . . for the world that moves us is the one we imagine, not the world round about us. We must yield our whole being to the feeling of being the noble one we want to be. If anything is kept back, the prayer is vain. We often are deprived of our high goal by our effort to possess it. We are called upon to act on the assumption that we already are the man we would be. If we do this without effort . . experiencing in imagination what we would experience in the flesh had we realized our goal, we shall find that we do, indeed, possess it. The healing touch is in our attitude. We need change nothing but our attitude towards it. Assume a virtue if you have it not, assume the feeling of your wish fulfilled. "Pray for my soul; more things are wrought by prayer than this world dreams of."

473. A controlled imagination and steadied attention, firmly and repeatedly focused on the idea to be realized, is the beginning of all magical operations. If he persists through weeks and months, sooner or later, through meditation, he creates in himself a center of power. He will enter a path all may travel but on which few do journey. It is a path within himself where the feet first falter in shadow and darkness, but which later is made brilliant by an inner light. There is no need for special gifts or genius. It is not bestowed on any individual but won by persistence and practice of meditation. If he persists, the dark caverns of his brain will grow luminous and he will set out day after day for the hour of meditation as if to keep an appointment with a lover. When it comes, he rises within himself as a diver, too long under water, rises to breathe the air and see the light. In this meditative mood he experiences in imagination what he would experience in reality had he realized his goal, that he may in time become transformed into the image of his imagined state.

474. Claim you are as free as the wind! Live nobly in your imagination. Dwell upon all the lovely things in life for yourself and others, as there is no other. Without loss of identity, you are going to know you are the one God who created and sustains the world. You will know you did not begin when you came here, but have been traveling for unnumbered centuries. You have done violent, horrible things; yet God in his infinite mercy has re-moved their memory so that you could live with yourself. And in the end, when God invades

you with the eternal history of salvation, all of your past will be forgiven. It will be wiped out as though it never was. And you will be redeemed with no memory of the horrors you knew in this world of time. All things begin and end in time, but there is no beginning or ending in eternity. It just is! The history of Salvation was not composed by God. It was always so. It was His plan to be inserted into time and redeem humanity!

475. Truth is an ever-increasing illumination. No one who seeks sincerely for truth need fear the outcome for every raising erstwhile truth brings into view some larger truth which it had hidden. The true seeker after truth is not a smug, critical, holier than thou person. Rather, the true seeker after truth knows the words of Zechariah to be true. "Speak ye every man the truth to his neighbor and let none of you imagine evil in your hearts against his neighbor." The seeker after truth does not judge from appearances . . he sees the good, the truth in all he observes. He knows that a true judgment need not conform to the external reality to which it relates. Never are we so blind to the truth as when we see things as they seem to be.

Only pictures that idealize really depict the truth. It is never superior insight but rather, purblindness that reads into the greatness of another some littleness with which it happens to be familiar. We all know at least one petty gossip who not only imagines evil against his neighbor, but also insists upon spreading that evil far and wide. His cruel accusations are always accompanied by the statement, "It's a fact," or "I know it's the truth." How far from the truth he is. Even if it were the truth as he knows the truth, it is better not to voice it for "A truth told with bad intent beats all the lies you can invent." Such a man is not a seeker after the truth as revealed in the Bible. He seeks not truth so much as support for his own point of view. By his prejudices, he opens a door by which his enemies enter and make their own the secret places of his heart. Let us seek sincerely for the truth as Robert Browning expresses it:

"Truth is within ourselves;
it takes no rise from outward things,
whate'er you may believe.

There is an immortal center in us all where truth abides in fullness. The truth that is within us is governed by imaginative love. Knowing this great truth, we can no longer imagine evil against any neighbor. We will imagine the best of our neighbor.

476. It is an intuitive desire of all mankind to be a finer, nobler being, to do the loving thing. But we can do the loving thing only when all we imagine is full of love for our neighbor. Then we know the truth, the truth that sets all mankind free. I believe this is a message that will aid us all in the art of living a better and finer life. Infinite love in unthinkable origin was called God, the Father. Infinite love in creative expression was called God, the Son. Infinite love in universal interpenetration, in Infinite Immanence, and in Eternal procession, was called God, the Holy Ghost. We must learn to know ourselves as Infinite Love, as good rather than evil. This is not something that we have to become; it is, rather, for us to recognize something that we are already. The original birthplace of imagination is in love. Love is its lifeblood. Insofar as imagination retains its own life's blood, its visions are images of truth.

Then it mirrors the living identity of the thing it beholds. But if imagination should deny the very power that has brought it to birth then the direst sort of horror will begin. Instead of rendering back living images of the truth, imagination will fly to love's opposite . . fear and its visions will then be perverted and contorted reflections cast upon a screen of frightful fantasy. Instead of being the supremely creative power, it will become the active agent of destruction. Wherever man's attitude to life is truly imaginative, there man and God are merged in creative unity. Remember that

Love is always creative, causative in every sphere from the highest to the very lowest.

There never has existed thought, word or deed that was not caused by love, or by its opposite . . fear of some kind, even if it were only a desire of a not very worthy aim. Love and fear are the mainspring of our mental machinery. Everything is a thought before it becomes a thing. I suggest the pursuit of a high ideal to make a fact of being become a fact of consciousness and to do this by training the imagination to realize that the only atmosphere in which we truly live and move and have our being is Infinite Love. God is Love. Love never faileth. Infinite Creative Spirit is Love. The urge that caused Infinite unconditioned consciousness to condition Itself into millions of sensitive forms is Love.

477. The abundant life that Christ promised us is ours to experience now, but not until we have the sense of Christ as our imagination can we experience it.

478. Imagination is our redeemer.

479. Creativeness is not an act of will, but a deeper receptiveness . . a keener susceptibility. The acceptance of the end . . the acceptance of the answered prayer . . finds the means for its realization. Feel yourself into the state of the answered prayer until the state fills the mind and crowds all other states out of your consciousness. What we must work for is not the development of the will, but the education of the imagination and the steadying of attention. Prayer succeeds by avoiding conflict. Prayer is, above all things, easy. Its greatest enemy is effort. The mighty surrenders itself fully only to that which is most gentle. The wealth of Heaven may not be seized by a strong will, but surrenders itself, a free gift, to the God-spent moment. Along the lines of least resistance travel spiritual as well as physical forces. We must act on the assumption

that we already possess that which we desire, for all that we desire is already present within us. It only waits to be claimed. That it must be claimed is a necessary condition by which we realize our desires. Our prayers are answered if we assume the feeling of the wish fulfilled and continue in that assumption.

480. Is it not true that the teachings of the Gospels can only be received in terms of faith and that the Son of God is constantly looking for signs of faith in people . . that is, faith in their own imagination?

481. Is not the promise Believe that ye receive and ye shall receive, the same as "Imagine that you are and you shall be"?

482. Let us watch our feelings, our reactions to the day's events. And let us guard our feelings even more zealously in the act of prayer, for prayer is the true creative state. Dignity indicates that man hears the greater music of life, and moves to the tempo of its deeper meaning. If we did nothing but imagine and feel the lovely, the world's reform would, at once, be accomplished. Many of the stories of the Bible deal exclusively with the power of imagination and feeling. "Feeling after Him" is the cry of the truth seeker. Only imagination and feeling can restore the Eden from which experience has driven us. Feeling and imagination are the senses by which we perceive the beyond.

Where knowledge ends, they begin. Every noble feeling of man is the opening for him of some door to the divine world. Let us measure men, not by the height of their cities, but by the magnificence of their imaginations and feelings. Let us turn our thought up to Heaven and mix our imagination with the angels. The world that moves us is the one we imagine, not the world that surrounds us. In the imagination lie the unexplored continents, and man's great future adventure. This consciousness of non-finality in "feeling after God" has been the experience of all earnest God-ward feelers.

They realize that their conception of the Infinite has constantly deepened and expanded with experience. Those who endeavor to think out the meaning of the experience and to coordinate it with the rest of our knowledge, are the philosophic mystics; those who try to develop the faculty in themselves, and to deepen the experience are the practical or experimental mystics. Some, and among them the greatest, have tried to do both. Religion begins in subjective experience. Religion is what a man does with his solitude, for in solitude we are compelled to subjective experience.

483. Even though you once considered Christ as human, when he is quickened in you, you will regard him thus no longer and speak out. You will be bold and tell everyone that their human imagination is the only creative power in the world. That God is imagination. He is the Father of all life. Imagining is his son, his creative power, and that is Jesus Christ.

484. Any kind of meditation in which we withdraw into ourselves without making too much effort to think is an outcropping of the subconscious. Think of the subconscious as a tide which ebbs and flows. In sleep, it is a flood tide, while at moments of full wakefulness, the tide is at its lowest ebb. Between these two extremes are any number of intermediary levels. When we are drowsy, dreamy, lulled in gentle reverie, the tide is high. The more wakeful and alert we become, the lower the tide sinks. The highest tide compatible with the conscious direction of our thoughts occurs just before we fall asleep and just after we wake. An easy way to create this passive state is to relax in a comfortable chair or on a bed. Close your eyes and imagine that you are sleepy, so sleepy, so very sleepy. Act precisely as though you were going to take a siesta. In so

doing, you allow the subconscious tide to rise to sufficient height to make your particular assumption effective.

When you first attempt this, you may find that all sorts of counter-thoughts try to distract you, but if you persist, you will achieve a passive state. When this passive state is reached, think only on "things of good report" . . imagine that you are now expressing your highest ideal, not how you will express it, but simply feel HERE AND NOW that you are the noble one you desire to be. You are it now. Call your high ideal into being by imagining and feeling you are it now.

485. There is only one body. Everyone who awakes is incorporated into that universal body to know you are it. And while your physical body sleeps, you will be all over the world. Your voice will be heard and you will be seen. That is the being you become after you have awakened from the dream of life. Tonight I urge you all to use the word imagination, for I have come to set this new idea against the old. Although people may rebel, when you get the results you want, it doesn't matter how they object. The term to be used now is your own wonderful human imagination

486. This creative power is buried in everyone, and that power is God himself. There is no intermediary between you and God. Jesus Christ is the creative power of your own wonderful human imagination! That is Jesus Christ and there is no other! God the Father is buried in you as your I AM, and your human I AMness is Jesus Christ. This is the being Paul speaks of when he says: "Test yourself; Do you not realize that Jesus Christ is in you? Unless, of course, you fail to meet the test." Now let me share a letter from a friend. She said: "I am a freelance designer. I never seek work, but as I sit at home and imagine I am working, they call. In the past six months I have received very few orders from a company that kept me very busy in the past, so I called them to discover that they had

employed a full-time art director and would no longer require my services.

After hanging up the phone I revised this conversation. I heard them tell me they had lots of work for me, and I felt the thrill in their words. One week later they called, asking me to design a 26-page book of institutional advertising, plus four ads for Harper's Bazaar. This was more than they had given me in the past at any one time. Now I am busier, happier, and making more money than ever before, and my technique is simple. Sitting in my chair I quietly listen for the phone to ring, answer it in my imagination and hear the orders I desire to create . . and they come."

487. The best defense against the deceptive assault upon our mental and moral eyesight is the spiritual eye or the Eye of God. In other words, a spiritual ideal that cannot be changed by circumstance, a code of personal honor and integrity in ourselves and good will and love to others. "Not what thou art, nor what thou hast been, beholdeth God with his merciful eyes, but that thou wouldst be." Through the veins of the humblest man on earth runs the royal blood of being. Therefore, let us look at man through the eyes of imaginative love which is really seeing with the Eye of God. Under the influence of the Eye of God, the ideal rises up out of the actual as water is etherealized by the sun into the imagery cloudland.

Things altogether distant are present to the spiritual eye. The Eye of God makes the future dream a present fact. Not four months to harvest . . look again, If we persist in this seeing, one day we will arise with the distance in our eyes, and all the staying, stagnant nearby will suddenly be of no importance. We will brush it aside as we pass on to our far-seen objective. The man who really finds himself cannot do otherwise than let himself be guided by love. He is of too pure eyes to behold iniquity. Our ability to help others will be in proportion to our ability to control and help ourselves. The day a man achieves victory over himself, history will discover that to have been a victory over his enemy. The healing touch is in an attitude, and one day man will discover that one governs souls only with serenity. The mighty surrenders itself fully only to the most gentle.

488. Having imagined what you want in the world, if doubt appears in thought or personified by another, say to yourself: "Get thee behind me Satan (get out of my sight) . . I will have nothing to do with you."

489. Discouraged people are sorely in need of the inspiration of great principles. We must get back to first principles if we are to speak with a voice that will kindle the imagination and rouse the spirit. Again, I must repeat, in the creation of a new way of life, we must begin at the very beginning with our own individual regeneration. Man's chief delusion is his conviction that he can do anything. Everyone thinks he can do . . everyone wants to do and all ask, "What to do?" What to do? It is impossible to do anything. One must be. It is hard for us to accept the fact that "We, of ourselves, do nothing." It is especially difficult because it is the truth and the truth is always difficult for man to accept. But, actually, nobody can do anything.

Everything happens . . all that befalls man . . all that is done by him . . all that comes from him . . all this happens, and it happens in exactly the same way that rain falls . . as a result of a change in the temperature in the higher regions of the atmosphere. This is a challenge to us all. What concept are we holding of ourselves in the higher regions of our soul? Everything depends upon man's attitude towards himself. That which he will not affirm as true within himself can never develop in his world. A change of concept of self is the right adjustment . . the new relationship between the surface and the depth of man. Deepening is, in principle, always possible, for the ultimate depth lives in everyone, and it is only a question of becoming conscious of it.

Life demands of us the willingness to die and to be born again. This is not meant that we die in the flesh. We die in the spirit of the old man to become the new man, then we see the new man in the flesh. "Subjection to the will of God" is an old phrase for it and there is, I believe, no new one that is better. In that self-committal to the ideal we desire to express, all conflict is dispersed and we are transformed into the image of the ideal in whom we rest. We are told that the man without a wedding garment reaches the Kingdom by cleverly pretending. He does not believe internally what he practices externally. He appears good, kind, charitable. He uses the right words, but inwardly he believes nothing. Coming into the strong light of those far more conscious than himself, he ceases to deceive.

A wedding garment signifies a desire for union. He has no desire to unite with what he teaches, even if what he teaches is the truth. Therefore, he has no wedding garment. When we are united with the truth, then we will put off the old nature and be renewed in the spirit of our mind. Truth will strip the clever pretenders of their false aristocracy. Truth, in its turn, will be conquered and governed by the aristocracy of goodness, the only unconquerable thing in the world.

490. Do not look for any physical causation, for causation is invisible. The world is all imagination, as you imagine you are Jesus Christ. Do you believe in your imaginal act? On this level the made reveals the mistakes of the maker. Learn from your mistakes. In a moment of anxiety perhaps you made that which you do not want. Learn from that which you made, where you made your mistake. Don't deny your harvest. Reap it, then plow and plant again, this time in the moment of joy and thanksgiving. Learn to believe in your own wonderful human imagination. There is nothing in the

world but God and his creative power. God needs no intermediary between you and himself because he is buried in you. Learn to trust this creative power in you and then God will reveal himself to you.

491. If anyone ever asks you what you think of Christ, tell them that he is your own wonderful human imagination; that he became you, with all of your weaknesses and limitations, that you may be God the Father. May I tell you: when you really believe this your outer world will change to conform to the inner changes that radiate from you. Your world is forever mirroring and reflecting all of your beliefs, so any modification of a belief will cause a change in your outer world. So instead of working on little things like wealth, health, and fame, work on the major concepts of Christ by learning to know him through exercising your own wonderful human imagination.

492. Not everyone sought Christ. Some found him and brought others. In the Book of John we are told that Andrew found his imagination to be Jesus and told his brother Peter. Philip found him and brought his friend Nathaniel. Peter and Nathaniel were not seekers, but were introduced to the truth. And who did they find? The one of whom Moses and the law and the prophets spoke, Jesus of Nazareth. Where is he? Come and you will see that the drama is supernatural. Having heard the truth from one who has experienced it, do you reject my words or do you accept them? If you accept my words and toy with this idea to the degree that you become enamored, you will modify your former belief concerning Christ Jesus. Tonight one billion believe in a little personal being who walked the earth 2,000 years ago, because they do not understand the concept that is the vision of Jesus Christ.

493. I ask you to believe me, for "Unless you believe that I AM He you will die in your sins." You will miss the mark and never reach your goal unless you believe that you are right now the man

you want to be. Is happiness your goal? Then assume it, for unless you assume "I AM happy," you will remain unhappy. You want to be secure? Then assume "I AM secure." That is the only way you will attain it. I AM Imagination, the only power in the world, for Imagination is God. Unless I imagine I AM the man I want to be, I will continue to imagine I am the man I do not want to be. No power on the outside can make me other than what I think I AM. I must assume my own divinity, and as I do it will unfold within me.

494. I do not care what the world will tell you, imagination creates its reality. All of these precepts must be accepted literally, for they are literally true. What person truly believes that he was born to be what he is today? He may have been born into a family of great wealth, and . . being surrounded by it . . he takes wealth for granted; but that is an assumption. He may even believe he is entitled to it; but if you checked into his family tree, you would discover that his father or grandfather had a vision which became his reality. And if he who was born into wealth does not know the principle that supports it, he can lose the money and never regain it again. But you who know that everything is based upon an assumption realize that no one can take anything from you that you really want!

495. Believe me. Dwell upon my words, for as you do the visions will unfold; and as far as your outer world is concerned you will never have to question what you shall eat or drink or wear, for you will have no need to be concerned about the marginal things of life. Start now to center your focus on Imagination and don't be concerned about the fringe. Seek the kingdom of heaven by turning your thoughts inward, and wonderful things will appear to come out of the nowhere. In my own case I never thought of or contributed to any money my parents made, yet when my father made up his will, all ten children shared equally. So while I was about my Father's business, completely absorbed in the kingdom of heaven and not

concerned with dollars and cents, money grew in a foreign field. I had no knowledge or concern for its growth. Trusting my brothers implicitly, I have never once entertained the thought that anyone would ever take advantage of me, and no one has.

496. From this platform I teach that I and my Father are one. Being one, my Father can never be so far off as even to be near, for nearness implies separation. What is there in you that can't even be near? Imagination! You cannot separate yourself from imagination. You can't claim: "I AM" and point to it as something on the outside. It is impossible to separate yourself from the sense of being, so in the sense of I AMness, you are imagining. If this sense of oneness is your Father, do you really believe in him? If so, to what extent does your confession in words conform to your deep, deep conviction?

497. Feeling is the secret of successful prayer, for in prayer, we feel ourselves into the situation of the answered prayer and, then, we live and act upon that conviction. Feeling after Him, as the Bible suggests, is a gradual unfolding of the soul's hidden capacities. Feeling yields in importance to no other. It is the ferment without which no creation is possible. All forms of creative imagination imply elements of feeling. All emotional dispositions whatever may influence the creative imagination. Feeling after Him has no finality. It is an acquisition, increasing in proportion to receptivity, which has not and never will have finality.

An idea which is only an idea produces nothing and does nothing. It acts only if it is felt, if it is accompanied by effective feeling. Somewhere within the soul there is a mood which, if found, means wealth, health, happiness to us. The creative desire is innate in man. His whole happiness is involved in this impulse to create. Because men do not perfectly "feel," the results of their prayers are unsure, when they might be perfectly sure.

498. Blake, claiming that his great poem "Jerusalem" was dictated from on high, stated: "All that you behold, though it appears without, it is within, in your Imagination of which this world of mortality is but a shadow." Blake meant us to take that statement literally. All that you are conscious of is within you. Where else could it be? Looking out, and seeing this world as mechanical and not spiritual, causes you to remain lost in your search, for the world is your mirror. You are its source. Everything you perceive is within, for it is in the head that God created the heavens and the earth. I am not speaking of your mortal head. It is only a symbol, a reflection of your immortal one.

The day will come when your mortal head will return to dust, but there is a head that survives this one. A head capable of instantly restoring and clothing you in a mortal frame just like your present one . . only young . . to find yourself in a terrestrial world just like this. That is the head in which God sleeps. It is there that the pattern is buried. And it is in that head that the pattern man unfolds to reveal you as the source. Man finds it difficult to believe he is the cause of all life, yet I say there is no other. Look into the eye of your friend . . or enemy . . and you will see only yourself.

499. We are told that whatever we desire, when we believe we already have received it, we will. This promise is based upon the premise that imagining creates reality. There is nothing you cannot become or have as an objective fact, if you believe you already have it. No restriction or condition has been placed upon the power of belief. If you will deny the evidence of your senses, suspend your reason, and persuade yourself that you are now the person you want to be, you will become it! Ask yourself how your friends would see you if you now embodied the idea you desire. Your true friends would rejoice, would they not? Then, if this statement is true, all you have to do is persist in believing your assumption is true, and it will harden into fact.

500. Now, in the earliest gospel, the Gospel of Mark, we find these words: "The time is fulfilled and the kingdom of heaven is at hand; repent and believe in the gospel." The word "repent" means "a radical change of attitude (of thinking) towards anything that you either dislike or want to change." A radical change on your part will produce a corresponding change in your outer world. So now you are urged to examine yourself to see whether you are holding to the faith. Are you accepting as facts the headlines you see in the paper? The telephone call you just received! The morning's mail or the news on TV which suggest unlovely, horrible things to you? A friend calls, and pouring out all the bilge in the world tells you how bad things are and how they are destined to get worse. As you listen, their woes enter and are assumed by you. Now, if you understand this law that imaging creates reality, you should, like a computer, choose what you are going to allow to enter. And when the conversation is finished and your friend's voice is still fresh and clear in your ear, hear her changed words, the changed tone of her voice, and feel the joy emitted there.

501. "Every natural effect has a spiritual cause, and not a natural. A natural cause only seems. It is a delusion of the perishing vegetable memory." (Blake, from "Milton") If man could only bear in mind that every simple little imaginal act sends a quiver through Omniscience, right through Omnipotence, and right through Immanence so the whole thing is like a huge, big computer, . . your imaginal act instantly is added to the sum total of it all; and instantly the whole. thing is changed, and the world is reflecting every imaginal act in this world of man, and keeping it all perfectly recorded, so that there is no such thing as a natural cause. It is all a spiritual cause. "All things were made by Him, and without Him was not anything made that was made." And where does He dwell? He dwells in us, for He is Spirit, and "the Spirit of God dwells in us." He dwells in us, and I have, by experiment, discovered what that Spirit is; and I tell you from my own experience, the Spirit of

God and the human imagination are one. They are not two. So when you depart this world, your reality . . which is the Spirit of God . . is your own wonderful human imagination; and that gives cubic reality to everything in this world if you enter it. Now, the secret is to enter it. Can I enter the state of my wish fulfilled? Those other states were simply experiments. Can I enter the state of the wish fulfilled? I have done it. On several occasions I have. When it seemed essential, I did it. If someone asked of me, I tried my best to do it. And how do I do it? By feeling.

502. The story recorded in the Old Testament lays the foundation of which the New Testament is its fulfillment, but "Even to this day when Moses is read a veil is over their minds and they cannot understand it." When the mind is veiled, one cannot understand that the God spoken of by the prophets is imagination; but I tell you: at night when you go to bed God is dreaming, and when you awake in the morning he is still dreaming your world into being.

503. We have been talking about God's law and God's promise. God's law is conditional. You cannot be in one state and not suffer the consequences of not being in another state, and you and I are free to imagine any state in the world, and imagining that state we can occupy it. Occupying the state, we fertilize it; having fertilized it, it has its own appointed hour for fulfillment. Every vision has its own appointed hour it will flower; if it seems long, wait for it . . it is sure and it will not be late. Some things will grow overnight, and some things will grow in a week, then in three weeks, and then in a month, and some things will take years. It could be a problem over which we seem to have no control. We have told you the story here, where on one occasion it took five years, but oh! the joy of reaping the fruit then. It was the relationship of a mother and son-in-law. I have told you unnumbered stories where it took intervals of time, but it doesn't matter, if we apply the principle.

504. Grant to everyone the good he asks of you, without putting your hand in your pocket. Grant it by an imaginal act on your part. Try to be as faithful as you can to that imaginal act; believe in the creativity of that imaginal act, and as you do it, they will all become the embodiment of what they asked of you.

505. "I, even I, am He, and there is no God beside me. I kill, and I make alive; I wound, and I heal; and none can deliver out of my hands." And the God spoken of in that chapter is seated here in everyone who is seated, for that one in you is the Spirit of God, and the Spirit of God is your own wonderful human imagination. So blame no one in this world for anything that befalls you.

506. Right now you can use your powerful imagination to assume you are what at the moment your senses and reason deny. Walk in this assumption, knowing you are all imagination, and all things are possible to you. Dare to believe in the reality of your assumption and watch the world play its part relative to its fulfillment. Your assumption may appear to be false when first imagined; but if you will persist, it will harden into fact, because God is he who is doing the assuming. All of the objective facts you see here on earth are only shadows, which fade because imagination is their reality.

507. This platform is concerned only with the great secret of life. Here we are convinced that the Supreme Power that created and sustains the universe is Divine Imagining, and it does not differ from human imagination save in degree of intensity. So God-in-man is your wonderful Imagination; that is God. We tell you that Imagination creates Reality, but bear in mind that at this human level on earth it takes time and persistence. If we will persist in the image, live in it, sleep in it, breathe in it, it will crystallize into tangible form. Night after night we take different facets of this truly great secret, and as we turn to the greatest book on Imagination in

the world, we treat it differently. So, as we turn to it, bear in mind that the Bible is addressed to the Imagination, not to the man of sense or the man of reason . . the one that is "lost" or "dead" or "sound asleep."

508. Whatever your inspiration may be, you will draw to yourself that which you have assumed you want to be. If in your mind's eye a certain person is great and you want to be as great as he is, you will draw him out of yourself to instruct you. You are only instructing yourself, however, for every vision takes place within the human imagination. "All that you behold, though it appears without, it is within your imagination of which this world of mortality is but a shadow." Choose an image you would like to express. Feel you are that image. So appropriate it that it must come forth in your world of shadows. Do that and you are praying, for prayer is your own wonderful human imagination, drenched with feeling.

509. God is real. You may not question it . . I don't . . but in 1963, the scientific world would question it. I don't know all the uses of the word, "God," but I like it. But if it will help you any, I use the word I use most: "imagination," because to me when I think of God I mean the same as when I say "divine imagination." When I speak of Christ I mean divine imagining, God in action. We are told: "God is Christ reconciling the world to himself." Imagining is Christ, which is God in action. So imagination in Christ with his imagination, imagining, is reconciling the whole vast world to himself. But if it offends you, go back to the word, "God," but don't put God on the outside of something separated from you, because he is not.

510. The most creative thing in us is to believe a thing into objective existence. Can you believe that something is already objective to you, even though your mortal eyes cannot see it? Can you walk, drenched in the feeling that it is an objective fact, until it

becomes so? That's how everything is brought into being, for all things exist in the human imagination, who is God himself. Imagination is the divine body called Jesus, the Lord. If you are willing to step out, asking no one if it is right or wrong, and dare to walk in the assumption your image is true, it will come to pass.

511. Let me define Imagination for you. It is spiritual sensation, but the word "spiritual" is to most of us something that is not practical . . the incorporeal as opposed to the corporeal. But Imagination is the power to perceive what is absent from the senses. Take a rose . . there is not one here . . but right now could I sense it in any way? Smell it? Touch it? I can, though it is absent from the senses. That is Imagination. If Imagination creates reality, such perception of what is absent from the senses makes it so. We have unnumbered case histories to prove it. Imagination is the power to perceive what is absent from the senses, and if you persist, you go beyond the sense man and go beyond the rational man. "The natural man receives not the things of the spirit of God for they are foolishness unto him."

512. God's revealed name to this world is "I AM." That is his great name. Can you say, "I AM?" That is God. What am I doing? I am thinking you are no good . . well, that is what you're doing, that is God in action. And do you know: you will live to see the day you are right. So "I AM" doing what? Anything in this world, all things are possible to God. When you say: "I don't believe so and so." Perfectly all right, that's your privilege, but who is not believing it? "I AM," you say . . well, that is God. Don't believe it. "I am no good, I can't make a living." Well that is your privilege; believe it and may I tell you how true God is: he'll prove it. Finally you are relieved and you will say to me: "I told you it's no good." Can't you realize that you are setting it in motion and you were fertilizing it in your world, for God's only revealed name is "I AM." So, what are you imagining?

513. Ask yourself: "If I now believe that I AM He that the world worships as the Lord, and all things are possible to me, then I must test myself and according to my faith in myself will it be done unto me." It is up to the individual to perform the action, for the evidence always follows the action. Act as though things are as you would like them to be. Persuade yourself that it is true and let the results follow. This is how you are called upon to operate in this world. This is imagination. It is not written in detail, but only sketches that you fill in with your life.

514. Start examining yourself. Do you believe that imagining creates reality? If you do, then test yourself. Do you not realize that Jesus Christ (imagination) is in you? Do you have the courage to claim; "I AM He and besides me there is no other?" In the 8th chapter of John, the statement is made: "You will die in your sins unless you believe that I AM He." This is not a statement of another telling you that you must believe he is God. No! You are forever talking to yourself! Limited by the five senses, "I" . . Christ (Imagination) in you . . will miss my goals in life unless "I" believe that "I AM" that which "I" formerly desired to be.

515. Everyone will fulfill scripture, for life is not finished until this happens. No man is going to come from outer space, or from some holy womb, and save you! Christ (imagination) comes to you from within you, because that is where he is buried. Your body is his sepulcher, from which he rises and unfolds. And only when this happens will you know the truth and be set free. Now, you either believe me, and use your imagination . . consciously, or you do not. If you do not act now, you will eventually, as no one will be lost. If you die tonight your belief will not be transformed, but you will be restored to life in a world just as real as this one. You will know the same limitations as you know here. You will suffer, be deceived, betray and be betrayed, until you believe to the point of action. Then scripture will unfold within you, and you will depart this age of

death to enter the age of life by controlling your own wonderful human imagination.

516. The average person, believing only that which can be seen and touched physically is real, will think I am crazy. A very intelligent, wonderful man who attended my meetings in New York City, once told me he enjoyed listening to my words; but when he did, he planted his feet into the carpet and held the sides of the chair to remind himself of the reality and profundity of things. Otherwise he would take off into some dream world. Call it a dream world if you will, but if there is evidence for a thing, does it matter what others think? I had evidence for my belief and I tried to share my experiences with him, but he would not even test his imagination. Not everyone who hears the truth will believe it, even though he seems to be so wise in the eyes of the world. So I say: I have yet many things to say to you, but you cannot hear them now. I am not speaking of the law. Mark puts that quite simply: "Whatever you desire, believe you have received it and you will." I am speaking of the promise and urge you to search the scriptures, for if you do you will find me there. And when you find me, you will know, from experience that you and I are one.

517. If you will but control what you are imagining, not a thing is impossible to you. And you will discover that when you find God, your values change. You will no longer worship things, rather you will worship God, the creator of the things. It is so thrilling to imagine something for a friend and watch it come into being, then to give thanks to the one who did it within you. When you thank God, you worship God and serve God. When your friend gives you the good news that he has what you had imagined for him, thank him for telling you; but your real thanks will go to God, for . . having found him, you now honor him, knowing he will never let you down. You don't have to burst a blood vessel when you imagine. Just let it be so. Knowing your request is genuine, imagine it as

already accomplished and then trust him implicitly. This has nothing to do with any moral or ethical code, but your trust in God. Knowing that when you imagine, God is acting and God is faith, trust him to bring it to pass for he will, and in a way you could never devise.

518. As we are told, "Do you not realize that Jesus Christ (imagination) is in you?" Then test yourselves to see if you really realize it. Put yourself to the test If I say, "Jesus Christ," and your mind jumps on the outside to something other than yourself, you have failed the test, for you are told: "Do you not realize that Jesus Christ is in you? . . unless, of course," said he, "you fail to meet the test!" Well, you have just had the test. So, when I use the words, "Jesus Christ," and something on the outside comes to you, you have failed the test!, for Jesus Christ is in you. If I go to Him in my prayer, where would I go but to myself? He became as I AM, that I may be as He is. He actually became me. He is in me as my own wonderful human imagination, for "by Him all things were made, and without Him was not anything made that was made," so I go within and appropriate the state.

So, the subjective appropriation of my objective hope is my prayer. And having appropriated it, I drop it, as I would the seed into the earth. The seed must fall into the earth and rot before it can be made alive. Well, just drop it, and then in its own good time it will come into harvest. It takes an interval of time between my appropriation and its fulfillment; so having done it, I drop it, and go about my "Father's business" appropriating other states . . not only for myself, but for myself pushed out," which I call "others." For, in the end, there is Only One.

519. Your imagination is the true vine from which everything in your world is drawn. Any misuse of your imagination causes the deformities in your life. It is a shock, I know, to realize that you are the sole cause of your life; and what a responsibility you have, to

prune this true vine of awareness! Since the Father and the Son are one, I . . as Father AM the true vine and must prune myself. Not realizing a seeming other was a branch growing from me, the true vine, I allowed myself to entertain unlovely thoughts of him. But I didn't cut the branch, for the pruning is not in that way. Called repentance in scripture, pruning is revision . . which is a radical change of attitude towards an individual or a situation. I revised my thoughts relative to that seeming other and accepted this unseen imaginal act as reality. Then I watched, and in time I became aware of a change in my world relative to this person or that condition. Having found the true vine and the Father who pruned it, I know I must prune it every day; for if I do it will knot and form itself into these full, clean clusters to repay the hand of the vinedresser (the Father) who pruned it.

520. Anything is possible if you can feel it; but if you are going to use reason it will never happen, because failure becomes your image. You don't realize it but there are two of you, and it is your deeper self that tells you it can't happen. But no real belief can ever be suppressed for long, for your inward conviction (Imagination) must find some external objective habitation, and it will.

521. I tell you: the only God in the universe is your own wonderful human imagination. When you say: "I AM," that is God. There is no other God other than he who is encased in the limitation of your little garment of flesh. How can you call upon him, when you do not believe you are he? And how can you believe in him of whom you have never heard? What preacher ever told you that your own wonderful human imagination is God? They paint a word picture of a god outside of you, but that is not the true God. And when someone comes and tells you who He really is, the idea is blasphemous. No one wants to believe that he is creating the conditions of his life; but God is the only causative power, as there is nothing but God. Everything is caused by Imagination. He is the

only reality. So, how can you believe in him of whom you have never heard? And how can you hear of him unless there is a preacher? And how can there be a preacher unless he is sent?

522. Take my message to heart. The God spoken of in scripture is seated right here. He is in everyone as their wonderful human imagination. When you say, "I AM," that's God. If, right now you are assuming that you are other than what reason says you are and I ask you, "Who is imagining?" you would say, "I AM." At that very moment you have spoken God's name and all things are possible to God. So without the consent of anyone you can move from where you are to where you would like to be by a simple change of attitude. But your move must be fixed so that when you wake or sleep you remain in that attitude, for the state to which your thoughts constantly return constitutes your dwelling place, and your world is forever externalizing your dwelling place.

523. Don't try to be holy. God isn't making good people, holy people. God is making creators, just like himself. If you think you are holy, that is not the key in to paradise. No matter how good you are, no matter how holy you think you are, holiness is not the key that allows you to enter that special grace, your creativity. God is doing it for you, working on you, bringing you to complete fruition and fulfillment. Try this principal of imagining, and if there is one thing I think man could do to aid . . as something within a shell could aid the bird . . the key is given to us in the Book of Job. He complained and complained of all the things that were happening to him, but his captivity was lifted when he prayed for his friends. If you would use your imagination lovingly on behalf of another and rejoice in his good fortune without any reward to you, you will see how this thing will begin to unfold within you.

524. Your true environment is in your imagination! All that you behold, though it appears without, it is within, in your imagination . .

of which this world of mortality is but a shadow. No matter what is taking place on the outside, it is but a symbol telling you what is taking place within; for the world is nothing more than yourself pushed out. Its image, alive in your imagination, overwhelms you.

525. I wanted a trip I could not afford, yet I traveled over 5,000 miles by being still and saying to myself: "My awareness is God and all things are possible to him. therefore what I am imagining will come to pass." Then I began to imagine I was on a ship sailing towards Barbados. I remained faithful to that act, when suddenly . . after twelve years . . I received a letter from the family saying they would take care of all of my expenses if I would come home for Christmas. So I proved it. Then I tried it again and again, and the more I tried it the more I realized that the statement in the 46th Psalm was true: that God really is my own wonderful consciousness, for I learned to be still and know that I am God.

526. In Genesis, the story is told of Isaac . . who was unable to see, but capable of feeling . . calling to his son, Jacob, saying: "Come close my son that I may feel you. Your voice sounds like my son Jacob, but you feel like Esau." At that moment Jacob . . the imaginary, purely subjective state . . possessed the qualities of Esau, the objective world. So Isaac gave the imaginary state the right to be born. As Isaac, you can sit quietly and with your imaginary hands you can feel the difference between a tennis ball, a baseball, a football, and a golf ball. If they are nothing (because they are subjective and not objectively real to you at the moment) then you could not discriminate between them. But, if you can feel the difference between these so-called unrealities, then they must be real, although not yet made objective to your senses. The moment you give them reality in your mind's eye, they will become real in your world. Try it just for fun. Take an object and thank the being within you for the gift. Then thank the one on the outside, for within

and without are vicarious, as is life; for by observing an odor, a look, or a feeling within, you will discover you are life itself.

527. The law operates by faith. If you believe, no effort is necessary to see the fulfillment of your every desire. If you go to the bank and have money deposited there equal to your check, you will give them your check in the belief that . . because of your faith . . they will give you the money you desire. Treat your desire in the same manner. Knowing your desire exists in your imagination, simply expect its fulfillment in your outer world. Try it. I have lived by this law all of my life and know, that by applying this principle, all of your desires will be fulfilled.

528. So, in this world that profound story of the twins, Esau and Jacob, is not understood because it does not make sense, but it is so very practical. The outer world may tell you that you can't have what you want, that you do not have the necessary education, experience, or means to achieve your goal. But your husband hates that outer you, and loving his bride (your human imagination), he gives you whatever you want.

529. Now, the power of any imaginal act is in its implication. If he is congratulating you on your good fortune, then you must have already received it, so accept his congratulation as a fact. Do that and you have subjectively appropriated your objective hope. Hoping that one day he will know of your good fortune and congratulate you, you have gone ahead in time, entered the state and allowed him to congratulate you. Now, go about your business and when you think of him, let him know (in your imagination) that he knows of your good fortune and that the day will come when it will be externalized. And when it does (and he will know of it) he will congratulate you on your good fortune on the outside, just as he did first on the inside.

530. Imagination can see, touch, hear, taste and feel things other than what your senses are experiencing right now. If you persist in acknowledging what your inner senses are telling you until you are persuaded of their reality, you will see their evidence. Then you will know from experience who Christ really is. Imagination is the only Christ Blake ever heard of. The apostles knew of no other, and any other belief was a false religion Blake called the devil. When you believe in someone on the outside, you have put him in conflict with the Second Commandment. You have made a graven image, yet [you were] told to "Make no graven image unto me." And when you think that someone other than yourself is Christ, your religion is false and you have a devil.

531. If you attempt to change the world before you change your attitude towards it, your struggle will be in vain. That which you dislike will change only to the degree that you change your attitude towards it. Until you do it cannot change, for the dislike is coming from within you. “Man is all Imagination, and God is Man and Exists in us and we in Him. The Eternal Body of Man is the Imagination and that is God himself.” The secret of imagining is the greatest of all secrets, and everyone should try to unravel this mystery. Do you not realize that Jesus Christ is in you as your human imagination? Test yourself and see. You do not test another. Test yourself! See if what I tell you is true. I say your own wonderful human imagination is Jesus Christ, the life-giving spirit of all things. If this is true, you can test him who is your very self, and when you prove it you will know where, what, and who you really are. If I told a pillar of the Episcopal church (as the lady whose story I shared, was) that her imagination was Jesus Christ she would think me blasphemous.

When the lady came to me for help I did not call him Christ in her presence, but spoke of her imagination. She could use that and still have her little icons. She could assume her apartment in New

York City was rented, but she could not believe that the being who made the mental transfer was Christ. Yet we are told that all things were made by him and without him was not anything made that is made. She mentally moved, and in less than twenty-four hours the move was physically accomplished. Now if all things are made by Christ and she knows exactly what she did, didn't she discover him? No, she didn't. She calls Christ her imagination, but separates her imagination from the Maker of worldly things.

Although she knows she brought about the rental of her apartment by her imaginal act, she still cannot bring herself to believe that her imaginal act was God in action. Raised to believe Jesus Christ was someone on the outside, she still worships a man based upon an artist's concept of him. But when you discover who Jesus Christ really is, you will know him as your very self. It does not yet appear what we should be, but we know that when he appears, we shall know him, for we shall be like him. "When scripture unfolds from within you, you will know that you and Christ are one."

532. You are infinite love, but without the power of imagination, love itself is eternal death. Start now to change your world to conform to your acts of love, but you cannot do it without imagination. Begin with self! Change your world and prove God's power is within you. Then you will know what it is to drink the cup which the Father has given you. It was God's infinite love that detached and allowed you to fall, for this separation is a fall and yet a beginning of a new creation. Just as the seed falls from man and a new creation begins, you fell and began a new creation, for God came with you as your human imagination.

533. Now, the Bible teaches that permissible lies are allowed. An assumption not based upon fact is a lie, is it not? We are told to emulate the story of the unjust steward who . . when told he might

lose his job . . asked the one who owed one hundred measures of oil to give him fifty, another eighty, and still another sixty. And when he returned to his master the steward was commended for his wisdom. This steward falsified the record, the facts of life which memory claimed to be correct. Perhaps memory says you only have ten dollars in the bank, the rent is due, and there are no prospects of more money on its way. Or that your friend is ill or out of a job.

These are facts memory has recorded. You can falsify that record by a permissible lie, by seeing a thousand dollars in the bank and the rent as paid. By seeing one who is ill . . as well, or one who is unemployed . . as gainfully employed. That which appears so real is based on fiction anyway, and fiction is fact in the sense that it is all imagination! You can lift anyone out of the state into which he has fallen and place him in another, be it a state of want, illness, or failure. There are infinite states into which man may fall. If you will but believe that imagining creates reality, and there is no fiction, you can rewrite your life and give yourself and those within it beauty for ashes, gladness for mourning, and praise for faint-hearted. Believe in the reality of your unseen act, then watch it fulfill itself.

If you have proof that imagining creates reality, it will not matter what others think. All that matters is that you try it and allow imagination to prove himself in performance. I encourage you to live as fully and as graciously as you desire to, while you wait for God's Son to reveal himself in you. But don't think that because you do not live fully and well, you are better off in the eyes of your Father . . for you are not. He is only interested in the work He is doing in you; and when it is completed, you will be born from within, for until that happens you cannot enter the kingdom of God.

534. Stop for a moment and see if you cannot relate the world round about you to an imaginal act. Then honor your imagination as God. Do not continue to simply acknowledge that your thoughts

create your reality, but accept those thoughts for what they are, and that is God in action. And do not give your creative power over to a mortal man, believing he was the cause of your good fortune (or misfortune). Man is God's image . . the created, and not your imagination . . the Creator.

535. Your Imagination knows all, is all, and is all powerful! If you should forget something, knowing that your own imagination is Jesus Christ, say: “Thank you Father that you always hear me.” Do that and in the matter of moments the thought will return. Recognize your own wonderful human imagination as the only God, the only Lord Christ Jesus, for besides him there is no other. So the outstanding need this day is for a new Christology, a new knowledge of Christ, a completely new thinking of the human imagination. Until this is done unnumbered billions will be appropriated to fight poverty to no avail. You can never give a poor man enough to satisfy him, and the day you stop giving he will cut your throat.

536. The whole vast world is no more than man’s imagining pushed out. I must qualify that by saying that the world outside of man is dead, but Man is a living soul, and it responds to man, yet man is sound asleep and does not know it. The Lord God placed man in a profound sleep, and as he sleeps the world responds as in a dream, for Man does not know he is asleep, and then he moves from a state of sleep where he is only a living soul to an awakened state where he is a life-giving Spirit. And now he can himself create, for everything is responding to an activity in man which is Imagination. "The eternal body of man is all imagination; that is God himself." (Blake)

537. Then wait in confidence for ways to open that you could not devise. No one knows how or when it will happen, but it will. You will find yourself walking across some bridge of incident that

you did not consciously devise, which takes you to your freedom . . whatever that end may be. I tell you, "Man is all Imagination and God is Man and exists in us and we in Him. The Eternal Body of Man is the Imagination and that is God Himself." When this God awakes within you, His birth clothes you with everything said of Him in scripture. It is said that He is the light of the world; that He is love; that He is the power and the wisdom of the universe. May I tell you, when He awakes in you, you will be clothed with power, with wisdom, with light, and with love. And those whose eyes are opened into the inner, eternal world of thought will see you clothed as God.

538. Leave the good and evil and eat of the Tree of Life. Nothing in the world is untrue if you want it to be true. You are the truth of everything that you perceive. “I AM the truth, and the way, the life revealed.” If I have physically nothing in my pocket, then in Imagination I have MUCH. But that is a lie based on fact, but truth is based on the intensity of my imagination and then I will create it in my world. Should I accept facts and use them as to what I should imagine? No. It is told us in the story of the fig tree. It did not bear for three years. One said, “Cut it down, and throw it away.” But the keeper of the vineyard pleaded NO”! Who is the tree? I am the tree; you are the tree. We bear or we do not. But the Keeper said he would dig around the tree and feed it . . or manure it, as we would say today . . and see if it will not bear. Well I do that here every week and try to get the tree . . you . . me to bear. You should bear whatever you desire. If you want to be happily married, you should be. The world is only response. If you want money, get it. Everything is a dream anyway. When you awake and know what you are creating and that you are creating it that is a different thing.

539. Do not look to another as the cause of your misfortune. If you are perceiving a thing, it is penetrating your brain; therefore it exists in you. That which you are perceiving appears to exist in the surrounding world independent of your perception of it, but don't

wait for it to change. If you desire a change in that which you are perceiving, you must produce the change in yourself. Ask no one to help you; simply persist in your new thoughts and let your changed thinking reproduce itself in your outside world, for it is only an out picturing of the world of thought within you. Try it. You can change your world as this prisoner did. In his imagination he moved in time to the day after his escape. You can do the same. Would your friends know of your success the day after it was achieved? Would they get together to discuss it? Make their gathering the scene from which you start. What would they say? Would some of them be jealous? Some happy for you? Put them all together and eavesdrop on their conversation. Then believe in what you have heard. Persist and your success is assured.

540. In the Book of John, he tells an incredible story, saying: "I AM God the Father. When you see me, you see the Father. Do you not know that I AM in the Father and the Father in me?" Making one fantastic statement after the other, he adds: "I have told you before it takes place, so that when it does take place you will believe that I AM He." For we are told: "Unless you believe that I AM He, you die in your sins." John emphasizes over and over again that you must believe you are the one you would like to be, or you will never become it. Rather, you will remain what you believe yourself to be right now. Your belief is always externalizing itself on the screen of space. It has to, for it is in you and not out there. When your belief becomes a fact and appears solidly real on the outside, it is because it is supported by you on the inside. The day you cease to believe in it, it will fade, for everything must be built on the foundation of belief. I believe I AM a success. I will remain a success only to the extent that I continue to believe I AM.

The day I stop believing, failure enters and success fades. You must believe you are in a certain state. You cannot forget it if you want to externalize that state. You may drop it after reaching a certain point, but if you want to keep it alive, you must do it within yourself; for nothing comes into being unsupported by an imaginal act, and nothing remains unless supported by that act. The day imaginal support is withdrawn the thing begins to vanish, and ceases to be in your world. This is true for a marriage, a friendship, or a business. If you know what you want, give it to yourself, for there is only one source of causation. That source is God (imagination). He is the dreamer in you who will awaken from this wonderful dream of life; and when he does, you will realize you have been dreaming all along. Many great poets have tried to tell this, but man cannot comprehend that the poet . . in touch with a deeper layer of his own being . . was awakened and recorded his experiences, until it happens in the individual.

541. Isaiah tells you: "Your Maker is your husband; the Lord of hosts is his name. He has called you like a wife forsaken and grieved in spirit, and will love you with everlasting love." In spite of everything you do, have done, or will do, God will forgive you . . for you are his emanation, his wife till the sleep of death is past. Regardless of the garment you wear, be it male or female, you are God's wife in this world. In symbolism however, God's wife appears in the form of a female. Blake tells us that He is God only, and She is God in you. As you journey you are God's emanation. But when the journey comes to its end you will know only God as your Maker, your husband, for you will inherit God. You will no longer be two, but you will become one being as you inherit yourself! Remember: you have only one lover, only one husband. He is your own wonderful Human Imagination, called God. It is he who gives you everything you fall in love with. But if you pray to a little statue made by human hands you are serving a false God. One day you will know that this world, which seems so real, is a dream.

542. Although it doesn't seem possible, you and I were detached from that infinite field of beauty by an act of love. We were made

subject unto futility, not by our own will but by the will of him who intended to give himself to us. But in order to do it we had to be individualized by complete incarnation, complete insulation where we think we are human. Being a member of a family, having friends, and living in a world of people, you are insulated and completely separated. This incarnation is essential to your individuality, and when you begin to awake you awaken to the realization that you are he who subjected yourself, for you become the very being the world calls God the Father.

543. Believe my words! Trust your imagination! Having reproduced himself in you, all things now exist in your imagination. If you desire changes, produce them first on the inside. Penetrate that which exists in you, as that penetration will compel the outside to conform to the changes which you, the potter brought to pass. The only way to prove this is to try it. Imagine a scene which would take place after your desire has been fulfilled. Do not concern yourself as to how it is going to happen; simply go to the end. The most creative thing in you is your power to imagine a thing into existence. We are told in the Book of Hebrews that, "The things which are seen are made out of things which do not appear." No one can see your thoughts when you sit down to imagine. They are unseen by the outer world, but you know what you have done. Now, because imagination and faith are what creates and sustains your world, if you do not have faith in what you have imagined, it will not come to pass. It cannot, because imagination and faith are two sides of the same coin.

544. Take me seriously. When you know what you want in life, construct a scene which would imply your desire is fulfilled. See it as clearly as possible. Feel its naturalness. Experiment until you know the scene and all it implies is real. Now, to the degree that you believe in its reality, your experiment will become your experience. Do not stop there. Keep on imagining and share your results with

others. Tell them how to free themselves from this bondage to Caesar. When you know who you really are, you will not envy anyone. How could you, when you know you are God . . imagination, and they are only yourself pushed out? If tomorrow, something comes into your life that is not to your liking, do not accept it, for this fact blinds the I of imagination. Remove the blindness by asking yourself what you would like, in place of what seems to be. Enter into that thought. Revel in it as though it were not a fact. Persuade yourself that it is. Believe in its reality and it will become your experience.

545. Everything is created by the human imagination. There is no other God. You can use your imagination wisely and create a heaven here on earth, or use it foolishly and create the world's havoc; but there is only one power, called the Lord God Jehovah in the Old Testament, and Jesus Christ in the New.

546. Tonight ask yourself: “Who am I? Where am I?” If you do not like your answers, assume you are the person you would like to be, living where you would like to live. Persist in this assumption and . . although denied by your senses and reason . . if you persist your desires will harden into fact. Start now to take God’s gift of his creative power and create! God detached and dropped you in love, for God is love. And when he did, he buried the gift of his creative power . . imagining . . called Jesus Christ . . in you. So now, like him, you can create, and as you do, your creation comes to life. Then you know that you no longer have to argue with the world, but can instantly change it to conform to the ideal that is in your being.

547. Everyone should be completely consumed with the desire to know how a thing is made. I’ll tell you how I make it. Knowing what I want, reason may tell me I can’t get it and my senses may deny that I have it; but believing that my own wonderful human imagination is Christ and trusting myself, I assume I have it and

drop it right there. I do not concern myself with what means will be employed for me to get it, I simply believe I already have it! I believe that my own wonderful human imagination is Jesus Christ and all things are possible to him, even the recording of something that I have struggled all day to remember and cannot. Like Blake I turn to my human imagination, my divine body, for I know thee O Lord, when thou ariseth upon my eyes, even in this dungeon. So when I awake in the morning and imagination returns to make me alive, I trust it implicitly. Perhaps I can't remember something, but would like to, so I say: "Thank you Father, you always hear me." Then as I walk the earth memory appears out of the nowhere. Perhaps it is a poem, a saying, or an article I have misplaced; but when I turn to Him and in thankfulness request its memory, my Heavenly Father always gives it to me. This I know from experience.

548. No matter what you are doing, can you see clearly what you want to do and carry on a conversation inwardly with a friend which will imply that which you desire is now a fact? Then do it. For on higher levels of Imagining inner activity is revealed by inner conversation. If man would listen to what he is inwardly saying, he would know what he is setting in motion. As man walks the street if he would pause and say "what am I saying now?" he would find that 99% are justifying failure. But we are told, "You are without excuse for you have seen him and his work, yet you deny it." When you hear the word God or Jesus Christ you think of some being external to your own imagining, but there is none for Imagining is God. That is what lights every being in the world, and as you imagine, so you will become. So no matter what your present limitations are, you can start now to dream the most noble dream, and you can walk through this door tonight as though it is true knowing that your Imagining is God. There is no fiction. You can write your own novel and realize it. Even someone in a dungeon may be imagining and who knows what he may call forth. If I were in a dungeon I would move the

world if necessary to get out. A body may be physically confined, but you cannot confine God. Man only sees the proximate cause; the real cause of something you cannot see; for the invisible power is what is creating.

549. Your assumption, though false in the sense that it is denied by your reasonable mind, if persisted in will harden into fact. You do not need to know the means that will be employed to bring your assumption to pass; all you are required to do is persist in your assumption and allow your own wonderful human imagination to give it to you. All things are possible to your imagination. It's up to you to provide the necessary link between your assumption and its fulfillment. That link is faith. Having assumed your desire is fulfilled, your faith in that assumption will cause it to harden into fact. That is the law.

550. Everyone here . . your invisible presence is God, but if you imagine money into being and you make a million, suddenly you worship the million, not the power that made it possible. You enter a certain social circle and then you forget that you brought it into being by imagining and now you think this group is what is all-important. So man forgets and exchanges the glory of the immortal God for the image of a mortal man or something that vanishes. For everything visible will vanish; but you will not vanish. Even this great land will one day be washed by the sea but you will not be. That which brought things into being cannot cease to be.

551. I say: everything is possible to anyone who knows who he is. The average person does not know God, for if he did he would honor his imagination as God. Those who know God have discovered that when they imagine a state something happens and it takes form in their world.

552. You can attain any goal if you believe that your own wonderful human imagination is the Lord Jesus Christ. Imagine something, accept it in gratitude and watch it come to pass. May I tell you: you have always been doing it, but your memory is so short you do not recognize your own harvest. If your memory awoke you would see that everything happens because you at one time imagined it, (mostly in fear) and then dropped it. You planted the seeds of the tares and the wheat, the events and circumstances of your world, but have forgotten the planting. So I tell you: you are as free as you want to be if you will believe in Christ. He is not on the outside but in you, as your own wonderful human imagination!

553. Forever justifying our world . . claiming he slapped me first, or she pushed me . . we speak with the voice of hell, the voice of self-justification. But in heaven it is all forgiveness of sin, because all things exist in heaven, the human imagination! Nothing happens on the outside that did not first take place in you, so you must forgive by changing the cause. If you try to justify or condemn, you live in the state of hell, for everything is taking place in you! Now seemingly separated from the Father, don't despair; for he was built in you from eternity.

554. If you believe what the churches teach you may think that you are not entitled to the good that you desire (read Romans 1:20) Ever since the creation of the world his invisible nature, namely, his eternal power and deity, has been clearly perceived in the things that have been made. So they are without excuse; for although they knew God, they did not honor him as God or give thanks to him, but they became futile in their thinking and their senseless minds were darkened, claiming to be wise, they became fools, and exchanged the glory of the Immortal God for images resembling mortal man or birds or animals or reptiles . . . "and then they worshiped and served the creature rather than the Creator."

555. So I say to all: the one who makes everything is the human imagination. This may seem cruel to one who is now experiencing pain, but it is true. I have suffered. I have known physical pain. Even though I may say I caught the flu, I know I caught it within me. I read the paper where I learned that 50 per cent of the people had the flu, and . . becoming a statistic . . I made it fifty-one. I have experienced its aches and pains, and learned a lesson. Now I know that even though I have experienced the drama of Jesus Christ, I am still subject to everything man is subject to. I know that I cannot point to any other cause other than my own imagination, as cause cannot come from the outside. If I am in pain, the cause is mine. We are told in Galatians that God . . your imagination . . is not mocked. That as you sow, so shall you reap.

556. You can prove you are all imagination if you believe it, for you live by your beliefs. Lip service is not enough. Belief must become alive. Do you really believe your imagination makes all things? Then test yourself and see. When confronted with any problem, immediately construct an imaginal solution. Enter into that image and abide in its truth. Always remember who the maker is, for he makes things out of that which does not appear. He is like quicksilver, but you can test him best in a daydream. Fawcett said: "Divine imagining is like pure imagining in ourselves. It lives in the very depth of our soul underlining all of our faculties, including perception, but streams into our surface mind least disguised in the form of creative fantasy." All dreams proceed from God whether they be in the day, or night. Everything is preceded by a dream, called an imaginal act!

557. In the 64th chapter of the Book of Isaiah we read: "O Lord, thou art our Father; we are the clay. Thou art our potter; we are the work of thy hand." When you hear the words Lord, Father, and potter, do you think of another? I certainly hope not. The word "Lord" is Jod He Vau He [pron. “Yod Hey Vav Hey”] which is

defined as “I AM”. Your own wonderful I AMness is the Lord, your Father. And the word "potter" means "imagination; that which is shaping your world." Imagination is the Lord, the potter, the shaper of your world, molding it into its present form.

558. At the end of the drama it is said that one who knew Jesus betrayed him. Now, in order to betray someone, you must know his secret! So the one who knows the secret betrays him. That one is self! God is self-revealed. Unless God reveals himself to you, how will you ever know him? Turning to those who did not know him, Jesus said: "Now that you have found me, do not let me go, but let all these go." Let every belief of a power on the outside go, but do not let the belief in your powerful imagination go . . for truth is within you. When you find the Maker in yourself, then no matter what arguments the priesthoods may give, do not believe them, for the Christ you seek is the human imagination. Tomorrow you may forget and be penetrated by rumors which disturb your body and cause you to suffer.

When this happens you must reestablish your harmony by imagining things are as you desire them to be. Living in this wonderful world, we cannot stop the penetration. To perceive another, that other must first penetrate your brain; therefore, he is within you as well as on the outside and independent of your perception. Cities, mountains, rivers and streams, must first penetrate your brain for you to be aware of them. At that moment of awareness they are within you, even though they still maintain a certain independence of your perception and are without. Treat this inner penetration seriously and you will discover all you need to do is adjust your thinking. That you are all imagination and must be wherever you think you are. If you want to contact a friend, simply adjust yourself to his community by making there . . here, and then . . now. Visit him in his home by penetrating it within yourself. Give him your message and see his eyes light up with the pleasure of your words.

559. We are told that Daniel oriented himself at an open window, where he looked toward Jerusalem. And those in the Mohammedan world pray looking towards what they call Mecca. But because Christianity takes place within, scripture is speaking of the Jerusalem within, and not on the outside at all. When you pray you do not prostrate yourself on the ground and look towards some eastern point in space, but adjust yourself mentally into your fulfilled desire. Although this technique is simple, it takes practice to become its master. Your true direction is to the knowledge of what you want. Knowing your desire, point yourself directly in front of it by thinking from its fulfillment. Silence all thought and allow the doors of your mind to open. Then enter your desire. Stay with your imagination as your companion. Start by thinking of your imagination as something other than yourself, and eventually you will know you are what you formerly called your imagination. It is possible to amputate a hand, leg, or various parts of the body . . but imagination cannot be amputated, for it is your eternal Self!

560. Your own wonderful human imagination is the being that I speak of when I speak of God. When I say, "God became as we are, that we may be as He is," I am speaking of your imagination. And you cannot get away from your imagination. "And by Him all things were made, and without Him was not anything made that was made." That's your imagination. There isn't a thing in this world that you see now and call it a fact that wasn't first only imagined: the building; the clothes you wear; the chairs on which you are seated; this little mike; . . everything was first only imagined, and then executed.

Well, if all things were made by Him, and without Him was not anything made that was made, . . good, bad or indifferent, try to find some other maker than your own wonderful human imagination. Try to find it. You may say: "Edison did it" . . in his imagination; "Einstein did it" . . in his imagination. Show me one other instrument other than the human imagination that conceived anything in this world, and that is God. "If all things were made by Him, and without Him was not anything made that was made," then you conclude that He must be the human imagination. So, I tell you, your own wonderful human imagination is the God of Whom I speak! That is the Being that actually will awaken within you. But, now, to get things in this world, assume that you are. "All things are possible to Him."

Assume that you are the man that you want to be . . or the woman that you want to be. And, although at the moment of your assumption your reason and your senses deny it, if you dare to persist in that assumption as though it were true, that assumption . . in a way unknown to your rational, conscious mind . . will harden into fact. It knows how to actually build that series of events necessary to make it so in your world. If you really want to be what you call "secure", . . say, in finances, dare to assume that you are secure, and live as though you were; sleep as though you were; and then it will happen in your world that will cause you to leave your present environment and move on into the state that you have assumed. If you wait for things to change before you dare to assume, you will wait forever. Circumstances cannot change of themselves. You change them by changing your concept of Self. To attempt to change the world before you change your own imaginal activity is to struggle against the very nature of things.

Now, you say: "Well, I am reaping these things in my world, and I didn't make them." No, . . you have forgotten the blossom time. What you are now reaping is simply the fruit of some forgotten blossom time. You have a very faulty memory. We all have. We can't remember when we set in motion what we are now reaping as a harvest; but everything in our world was once planted as an imaginal act, and it has not a physical cause, . . it has an imaginal cause. Every natural effect in this world has an imaginal cause, and not a natural cause. A natural cause only seems; it is the delusion of a faulty memory, because man cannot remember the blossom time when he actually set it in motion.

561. Everything, that can be seen, touched, explained, argued over, is to the imaginative man nothing more than a means, for he functions, by reason of his controlled imagination, in the deep of himself where every idea exists in itself and not in relation to something else. In him there is no need for the restraints of reason. For the only restraint he can obey is the mysterious instinct that teaches him to eliminate all moods other than the mood of the fulfilled desire.

562. That is what I mean by imagining creating reality, for an assumption is faith; and without faith it is impossible to please your own wonderful human imagination. Divine Imagination, containing all, reproduces itself in human imagination; therefore, the human imagination contains all. The world is the human imagination pushed out. Not knowing this, man cheats himself, murders himself, declares war against himself, and does all sorts of evil against himself; but do not let yourself be intimidated by the horror of the world. Leave it alone, for it is only the misuse of the power exercised by sleeping mankind.

563. Now, you have friends. They know your present position and the conditions that surround you. If they are not as you would like them to be, let your friends know . . not verbally or outwardly . . but in your imagination. See them seeing you as they would have to see you, the day after they know things are just as you want them to be.

564. "The secret of imagining is the greatest of all problems, to the solution of which every man should aspire; for supreme power, supreme wisdom, and supreme delight, lie in the solution of this great mystery." Imagination is the Jesus Christ of scripture, and when you solve the great mystery of imagining, you will have found the cause of the phenomena of life. Imagination is called "Jehovah" in the Old Testament and "Jesus" in the New, but they are one and the same being. Divine Imagination, containing all, reproduces itself in the human imagination; therefore, all things exist in the human imagination. When you solve the problem of imagining, you will have found Jesus Christ, the secret of causation.

565. Eventually we are all going to know we are the Father; but in the meanwhile, persistence is the key to a change in life . . more income, greater recognition, or whatever the desire may be. If your desire is not fulfilled today, tomorrow, next week or next month . . persist, for persistency will pay off. All of your prayers will be answered if you will not give up. My old friend, Abdullah, gave me this exercise. Every day I would sit in my living room where I could not see the telephone in the hall. With my eyes closed, I would assume I was in the chair by the phone. Then I would feel myself back in the living room. This I did over and over again, as I discovered the feeling of changing motion. This exercise was very helpful to me. If you try it, you will discover you become very loose with this exercise. Practice the art of motion, and one day you will discover that by the very act of imagining, you are detached from your physical body and placed exactly where you are imagining yourself to be . . so much so that you are seen by those who are there.

Being all imagination, you must be wherever you are in imagination. Moving in your imagination, you are preparing a place for your desires to be fulfilled. Then you return, to walk through a series of events which will lead you up to where you have placed yourself. In imagination, I can put myself where I desire to be. I move and view the world from there. Then I return here, confident that . . in a way unknown to me . . this being who can do all things and knows all things, will lead me physically across a bridge of incident up to where I have placed myself. You can move in imagination to any place and any time. Dwell there as though it were true, and you will have learned the secret of prayer.

566. Everyone here, you can be what you want to be, no matter what your dream is, if you are willing to let God do it, God being your own Imagining. You walk completely suspended above appearances and you will become what you desire. This is the only Christianity I know . . the freedom to exercise this divine art of Imagining. Now you try it. If you are here for the first time I challenge you to disprove it. Everyone has the same power. Because one has a million does not make him any more a creator than you are. Be careful what you are imagining for what you are Imagining you will create, though it may convulse the world. I hope you have the Revised Version of the Bible for it is from what I have quoted tonight. It is more accurate in meaning if not as orally beautiful as the King James Version.

567. In my Father's house are unnumbered mansions. Unnumbered states of consciousness. If it were not so, would I have told you that I go to prepare a place for you? And when I go I will come again and receive you to myself, that where I am you may be also. In this statement Imagination is telling you he is the Father for "No one comes to the Father but by me." Only when you come to the awareness that your human imagination is the phenomenon, the source of all life, will you find the Father.

568. So tonight, you take me seriously; and when you go home . . or start it here, . . you put into practice this greatest of all secrets; the secret of imaging. There is no greater secret in the world. Every

child born of woman is alive because it was imagined. And imaging is God in action. That's the soul of man . . imaging; and that is the power of God. And the power of God is Christ. And that is the wisdom of God, and the wisdom of God is Christ. A child can imagine. Well, that's Christ. That is Christ crucified on that little tiny garment, and it suffers with everything that that little child imagines, or it enjoys with everything the little child imagines. It wears all the stripes and all the blows that man in his misuse of that power will do. He doesn't criticize him. He waits upon me as indifferently . . and as quickly . . when the will in me is evil as when it is good. That way, He bears all my stripes. He bears all of my misuse of His power, knowing that in the end, I will awaken and use it only lovingly.

569. Having been taught God was another, I had formed a mental concept of him that comforted me and allowed me to pray to someone other than myself. But when I found him, I found him in myself, as myself! Then I knew I could not pray to another; I must turn within and appropriate, for everything is contained within my own wonderful human imagination!

570. No matter what it is you desire, remember: nothing is impossible. What is now proved was once only imagined, so begin by imagining a state and persuading yourself that you are in it. Blake said: "The ancients believed that if you are self-persuaded, it was so. There was a time in Imagination when a firm persuasion removed mountains." You can remove the seemingly mountainous obstacles which confront you by simply ignoring them and assuming the end. And if you have to go over the mountain, you will, or the mountain will be removed. Whatever is necessary to be removed for you to fulfill what you have assumed, will be done for you as long as you remain faithful to yourself, the source of all life.

571. Browning began his wonderful poem, "Easter Day" with the words: "How hard it is to be a Christian." And Chapman said: "Christianity has not been tried and proved wanting. It has been tried and found difficult and therefore given up." Why? Because a Christian cannot pass the buck and blame another. Christianity is built upon the foundation that all are one. That man is forever drawing conformation of what he is doing within himself. That your world bears witness to what you are doing to yourself. This is difficult to accept, yet it is Christianity. No man comes unto me, save my Father . . imagination . . who sent me calls him. I and my Father are one, therefore I call all those who enter my life to reveal to me what I am doing in my imagination.

572. Now, in order to prove that the law works, you must try it. Have a goal. Your goal may be peace of mind, health or marriage. You name it. Knowing your own wonderful human imagination is the one and only cause of your life, conceive a scene which, if true, would imply the fulfillment of your goal. Do not allow yourself to observe the action, but put yourself in the center of the scene and allow your friends to congratulate you on your good fortune. Accept their congratulations without embarrassment. Enter into the spirit of the scene and remain there until it feels real, then drop it in confidence that the imaginal act was performed by God. How do I know this? Because God's name forever and ever is I AM. If at the time of your imagining I had asked you what you were doing, you would have said: "I am imagining." At that moment you called forth your desire with His name. Every time you imagine, God is acting and all things are possible to him. All you need to do now is wait patiently, confident that your desire will externalize itself, and when it does you have found the cause of creation. Then tell your sleeping brothers, who wait patiently for their world to change while they activate its continuance. Nothing happens on the outside! Everything has to be initiated on the inside first. Read the morning paper, turn on the television or radio, and react to what you hear and see, and

that reaction is an imaginal act which will cause unlovely experiences to people your world. As you reap your harvest, you may not relate your present experience to what you did, but you had to have done it or you couldn't be aware of it now, for everything is yourself pushed out, for you and God are one.

573. You must forget the concept of Jesus Christ as a little man external to yourself, for it is Christ in you who is your hope of glory. All things are made by him, whether they be good or ill, lovely or unlovely. An artist doesn't have to create only the beautiful, but can create anything, and so it is with God. You can find him by testing your wonderful human imagination. I have searched for and found Jesus Christ to be my own wonderful human imagination. I now know that everything in my world was first imagined by me. I may not always remember the imaginal act relative to the unlovely things I have experienced, but I have imagined and watched its fulfillment in my world. I know that although I may not remember the imaginal act, I must have committed it, for I cannot reap that which I have not sown.

574. I urge you to set your hope fully on the grace that is coming to you at the unfolding of Jesus Christ in you. Use the law towards beautifying your world and getting all of the lovely things you feel you need. Don't ask anyone's permission; simply appropriate it in your own wonderful human imagination. Imagine and live by imagining, . . morning, noon, and night. It will not fail you, but remember: you are the operant power. Knowing what to do is one thing. Doing it is another; and we are called upon to be doers of the word and not just hearers only, deceiving ourselves. You can read one of my books over and over again. You can tell others what the book says, but if you never apply its message, the mere reading of its words will not benefit you. But if you will test your imagination, it will prove itself in performance.

575. All cause is spiritual! Although a natural cause seems to be, it is a delusion of the vanishing vegetable memory. Unable to remember the moment a state was imagined, when it takes form and is seen by the outer eye its harvest is not recognized, and therefore denied. "There is a moment in each day that Satan cannot find, nor can his watch fiends find it, but the industrious find this moment and it multiplies. And when it once is found, it renovates every moment of the day if rightly placed." (William Blake) The word Satan means doubt. Desiring a certain state, reason may tell you it will be difficult to attain, and your friends may say it is impossible. If you listen to them and doubt your desire's fulfillment, Satan has made himself known to you. Your protractors . . God and Satan . . are always with you, for one is faith and the other doubt. Can you imagine you are the one you would like to be, and remain faithful to that assumption? If you can and do, it will appear, and you will realize that its spiritual cause was the moment of assumption.

576. No one would ever agree with another as to what is right and what is wrong, for we all have different values. What is right to one is wrong to another. We came down into the world of death because we ate of the tree of knowledge of good and evil, and we are told that the only thing that displeases God is the eating of that tree, and unbelief. If you think another is the cause of your misfortune, you are sinning and missing your mark in life. There is only one cause for all of the phenomena of your life, and that is God, whose eternal name is I AM. When you really believe this, you will not deny the harvest you are reaping. It may be unpleasant, but you will know that it couldn't happen unless you sowed it, so accept your harvest and then plant something lovely in its place. Never deny that one and only cause, which is your own wonderful human imagination!

577. If you confine yourself to the human belief of truth, you will be stuck in that groove; for every moment of time you are

confronted with the facts of life. Knowing your social, intellectual, and financial background, you could not get out of the environment in which you were placed. My family did not accept these so-called facts of life. They climbed out of poverty by using their imagination. Knowing what they wanted, they imagined their desire was an external fact. They remained faithful to this imagined state, and in time they became what they imagined themselves to be. That is the law.

578. In the parable of Isaac and his two sons, Esau and Jacob, Isaac is blind. Desiring to be felt as his brother Esau was, Jacob clothed himself with the skins of a goat. Clothed so that his blind father could feel him through the sense of touch, Jacob deceived his father into giving him his blessing. Let us extract the psychological meaning from this story. Reason says you are not the man you want to be. Closing your eyes to the obvious facts of life, you deny everything reason dictates by mentally clothing yourself in your desired state. Let people see you there. Imagine until you are actually standing where you want to stand. Actually doing the things you would do if your desire was now an obvious fact. Do this, and you are clothing yourself in the outer garment of naturalness.

When you open your eyes to the facts of life, they will deny everything you have done . . but you know what you did. You caught a precious moment which doubt cannot find, or his help-mates find. You have become one of the industrious, for you found the moment and clothed yourself with the feeling of fulfilled desire and . . like Isaac . . you have given your blessing to the moment and cannot take it back. Isaac would not retract his blessing; so when Esau (the reasonable, rational mind) returned, its right to live had been taken away by Jacob (the smooth-skinned desire). Jacob was rightly named, for the word means "the supplanter." Isaac explained to Esau that, even though Jacob deceived him, the moment could not be called back. It was on its way toward fulfillment. And when it appears, its suddenness is only the emergence of a hidden continuity.

579. I urge you not to despair. If you have tried and tried to imagine, yet failed, don't give up, try to be more intense. Try to be more believing concerning the reality of your imaginal act. Man, believing in the mechanism of the universe, finds it difficult to see it as imaginal, but it is. Tell the story of the Kennedys to the average man and he will say: so what? He cannot see that story as confirmation of the fact that imagining creates reality. You could tell him a hundred such stories, but . . steeped in believing that this world is mechanical and must be moved on the outside . . man finds it difficult to understand that the world will reshuffle itself to reflect any change that takes place in the individual. But the change takes place in the imagination, not in the world!

580. In the 2nd chapter of the Book of Jeremiah, the Lord said: "I planted you a pure seed, O Israel. How did you become degenerate?" I will tell you how! By going after foreign gods; by worshipping the gods of astrology, numerology, wealth, or so-called important people. By believing in things on the outside and seeing other causes for the phenomena of your life and not the only cause, who is God, your own wonderful human imagination, whose name is I AM! One day you will awaken to discover that you are the one and only God. But you aren't going to rob anyone, for it takes all your brothers, together, to form the one pyramid, and when this is accomplished the top stone will be put in place.

581. God is the only source and there is no other. In the 87th Psalm it is said that when this one is born, the Lord registers his people, and the singers and dancers alike say: "You are my springs." There is no other spring! No other cause! No other source! Whether you are dancing or singing here, you are asleep and your own wonderful human imagination is causing your life to be what it is.

Do not blame another for the events in your life. There is no one you can turn to as its cause, and don't let anyone blame you, as they are creating their own world by what they are imagining. If one imagines unlovely things for another, they are going to produce them . . not in the other, but in themselves.

582. This world is made up of infinite states which you may clothe yourself with. If you do not like the state you are in, you can get out of it by taking a heavenly moment and assuming you have moved. You can put yourself into any state, be it wealth or poverty. If you don't enjoy poverty, don't get into the state. I have no desire for fabulous wealth. I do not want the responsibility connected with it. I can't see how anyone who is fabulously wealthy has any time for spiritual awareness. Morning, noon, and night he must watch his portfolio. The first thing he does in the morning is read the financial section of the newspaper. He reads it as some ladies read the social section . . as though it really matters. There are those who read the obituaries first and make their living from it. My father-in-law was a very prominent man in New York City when he died.

Shortly after his death, his wife received hundreds of letters from people claiming he had ordered something from them and had promised to pay, and many of the writers had misspelled his name! Her lawyer told her to forget the letters, as many people made their living that way. You can't conceive of anything that someone is not already doing. Everything is possible because imagining creates reality. And don't think you can imagine quietly, because your world is a record of your imaginal acts. Nothing appears by accident. You may not remember the moment you imagined it, so you cannot relate your spiritual cause to its natural effect; but every natural effect has a spiritual cause. All causes are spiritual, all imaginal, for "Man is all imagination and God is man and exists in us and we in him. The eternal Body of man is the imagination and that is God Himself." (William Blake)

583. I have told you the story of how Moses did not cross into the promised land, but Joshua did. You may not be familiar with scripture, but Joshua's original name was Hoshea (Numbers 13:16) The word "Hoshea" means "savior or salvation." Put the prefix "Je" before Hoshea and the meaning changes to "he by whom Jehovah is saved." Moses represents the pattern man, and Hoshea . . creative power. When that power is fertilized, Joshua . . the pattern . . unfolds, and the individual occupying the state enters the promised land. What you saw in the beginning was the perfect egg, but it was not fertilized. A sperm must penetrate the surface of an egg in order to fertilize it; yet no hole appears in this perfect egg either before or after penetration, because it is all imagination. Being all imagination, you do not need to go through any door to put yourself into a closed room, or break down any wall when you depart. Having entered without the use of a hole, you can depart without leaving any breakage relative to your entrance or departure. So it is with a little sperm. It penetrates the surface of an egg and it leaves no hole either before or after penetration; but unless it penetrates, that egg remains just a perfect pattern of what could be. It takes the sperm to penetrate and make it alive. I urge you to test your creative power on this level.

Take every moment you can and clothe yourself in the feeling that your wish is fulfilled. Feel its reality and do not forget that moment, for it is productive. In its own good time, that moment will appear in this world, properly clothed as an objective fact. No matter who it takes to aid the birth of your imaginal act, he will appear. If it takes an army to bring it to pass, an army of men will do it. You do not have to determine the way, all you need do is imagine. Just as you would plant a seed in the ground, confident that it will grow, so you can drop your fulfilled desire into your mind, confident that it will appear as an objective fact. If you want to be a man of wealth, assume that you are.

You see: the man of wealth and the poor man are the same being. The individual who occupies the poor state is God's emanation who has fallen into the state of poverty. He does not differ, however, from the individual who occupies the state of wealth. The man in the state of wealth may have lots of money, but he is the same being, in a spiritual sense, as the man who is poor. The only difference is that the poor man does not know he can leave the state of poverty.

584. When you know what you want, use your sense of feeling. Let the feeling of satisfaction so fill your being that the idea ceases to be a desire, but has evoked motor elements. These awaken sensory sensations within you causing the desire's fulfillment. Imagination is nothing more than sensory states. Learn to go beyond an idea by feeling its reality. Then turn to another and still another, as the being who is feeling it begins to awaken within you. Fulfill all of your desires while you are here, and then when you least expect it, the Divine Breath will breathe upon that immortal tomb where you are buried. And you will awaken to find yourself completely sealed in your Holy Sepulcher where you have been dreaming your life into being. This world is made up of horrible dreams which the one within every individual is dreaming. That one must and will awaken, as you hear the story and put it into practice through repentance. The word "repentance" comes from the Greek word "metanoia," which means "a radical change of attitude." This change must be so radical that it gets right down to the root, the I AM! Think of your world as your mirror. Do you like what you see there? You know you can live with it or ignore it, but perhaps you would like to see it differently. If you would, repent by persuading yourself that you are seeing a world to your liking. Persist in your repentance, for to the degree that you are self-persuaded it is so, it will be so.

585. Let the world turn their back upon this law. That is perfectly all right, but you go your way using your talent. And when you least expect it, all that is said in scripture concerning Jesus Christ will be yours to experience in the first person, singular, present tense. Then you will know beyond all doubt who Jesus Christ really is. When you know who you are, it will not matter what the world says. Let the billion Christians and the two billion non-Christians go their way. If they want to question or ridicule you, turn your back and walk away. Having found the real Christ, imagination, you have found the great secret to the mystery of all life.

586. Scripture speaks of the stone, the water, and the wine. The stone is the literal story, the allegory. When man discovers the fictitious nature and character of the story by turning within, he has struck the rock and . . like Moses . . water flows from it. The first miracle, or sign, is recorded in the Book of John, as turning water into wine. The story comes first. That's the stone. If you accept the story as literally true, you have accepted the stone. When you discover the fictitious character and extract the true meaning of the story, you have found the psychological water. A dog is the symbol of faith.

Her faith is now in the psychological meaning of these great truths, and as she applies them she will convert them into wine. Believing that imagining creates reality, dare to imagine you are now what you would like to be. Do that and you are turning the water into wine. We are told that when Jacob brought his flock into the field, the well was covered with a stone. He rolled it away, watered his flock and replaced the stone. Jacob did not turn the water into wine, but removed the stone which covered the tomb of water. This is an allegory. You must use your imagination to extract the water (meaning) and feed your flock. Every scriptural story has a psychological meaning. Find the meaning and you are extracting water from stone.

587. Can you imagine what it would be like if you were the man (the woman) you would like to be? Sustain that imaginal act as though it were true, and no power in the world can stop it from becoming true, because there is no other power. Try it beginning tonight. Take a glorious concept of life. Nothing less than the very best, and simply imagine it to be true about you and those you love. Start with your immediate circle and . . although at the moment your circle may deny it by reason of what they are doing . . persist in your assumption as though it were true, and it will harden into fact. Grant all of your sleeping brothers their right to pursue God in some other direction. They will never find him in any other way, save by experiencing the story of Jesus Christ. Then and only then will they know the true knowledge of God.

588. "Father, forgive them for they know not what they are doing." If you know that you are the cause of your sorrow, can you not forgive the one who submitted it? Must you condemn a shadow, when you are its cause? Everyone who comes into your world is drawn there by your Father, with whom you are one. If he who enters insults or offends you and you know you are the cause of his seeming offense, can you not forgive him? Can you not say: "Father, forgive him for he knows not what he is doing?" Your world is filled with those who are under compulsion to play their part because of what you have imagined. You may have forgotten your imaginal acts, and may even deny you ever entertained such thoughts; but they could not come if you had not called them out of yourself; therefore, you must forgive them, for they only did what you asked them to do.

589. But I tell you, every child born of woman has the greatest talent of them all . . the human imagination. A man sentenced for

life could be in a dungeon imagining himself elsewhere, and if it takes an earthquake to set him free, an earthquake will appear. But if he sits in the dungeon believing the world is against him, he will remain there. But, while there in his body, he can walk the streets as a free man by using his talent. He can view the world from a free state and in a way that no one knows, he will be set free. Whatever your desire may be, is possible and can be yours if you will imagine its possession and dwell in its fulfillment.

But I warn you: Do not imagine with hate in your heart, because you are only hurting yourself. Although you may not realize it, the world is yourself pushed out. It is forever bearing witness to you who are all Imagination. Make no attempt to change the world until you first change your attitude towards it. Change your thinking and the world will reshuffle itself to reflect your new thoughts. This is the talent of which the gospels speak. To one five talents were given. To another, two and another, one. Then came the day of accounting and all those who had expanded their talents were invited to enter into the joy of their master. And those who were afraid to test their Imagination, who wouldn't even try it, were condemned, and the knowledge of the power that they are was taken from them.

The talent is God's gift to you. It is entrusted to you for your use. Use your talent tonight by sleeping in the assumption that you are now . . not tomorrow . . but now, the person you would like to be. In the morning, persist in your assumption by allowing the world to see you as they would have to see you, were you now the one you would like to be. Although your reason and senses deny your assumption, if you persist your desire will harden into fact.

590. Imagination truly creates out of nothing! Thoughts call forth a thing that is not seen, as though it were happening. This is accomplished by an imaginal concept touched by feeling. Hearing of

the success of another and feeling their joy builds a structure which will project itself on the screen of space. Calling the projection reality, one may think it was created from the outside. But what happened had to happen as it did, for there are no accidents.

591. When you have found the cause of the phenomena of your life, let every other belief go. Should people urge you to eat certain food or observe certain days do not believe them, for there is nothing you can do on the outside that will ever commend you to God. You are defiled or purified by what comes out of your heart, not by what you eat or observe on the outside. Are you imagining good or evil for yourself, for the true vine is your own wonderful human imagination, and the world without is nothing more than your branches.

592. Jesus Christ is God himself, who became you, individually. Your awareness is He. When you imagine, God is acting. He is the true vine and the vinedresser, for he is your imagination, imagining you. If you really understand this, you will start pruning your thoughts. If you don't and continue to believe Jesus Christ is other than your Self, you will persist in allowing your wanton energy to run wild, to swell into irregular twigs, and bear unlovely things in your world. When you become aware of those in need, even though you do not know them personally, do you use your imagination to lift them from that state? That is what you are called upon to do. If you represent them to yourself as you would like them to be, and persuade yourself it is true, that branch will change in your world. You do not eliminate the state of need. It remains for anyone to be aware of, but you . . having lifted yourself out of the state . . see it no more. Prune your vine morning, noon, and night; and then . . when you least expect it . . a series of wonderful, supernatural experiences will be yours, as God reveals himself in you . . not as another, but as your very Self. Then you will say, from personal experience, "I AM He."

593. Do not be concerned with the horrors of the world; simply remember that all is ordered and correct. Instead, fall in love with the I AM within you and change your world. God made it as it is now and he can change it, for your husband is a creator. Everything in your world can be traced back to your own wonderful human imagination, who is God. Fall in love with the state you now desire to occupy and to the degree that you are self-persuaded, you will enter it. Don't believe in anyone outside of your own wonderful human imagination! Every coin is inscribed with the statement: "In God we trust" yet I wonder how many trust in God . . and not the coin! If you really believe in God, you can be penniless, yet walk in the assumption of wealth and be wealthy. Learn to trust your own wonderful human imagination, for he is the only God. Do that and you will never go wrong!

594. The entire 15th chapter of the Book of John is devoted to this pruning of the vine. He starts off: "I AM the true vine. My Father is the vinedresser. Every branch of mine that bears no fruit he prunes, that it may bear more fruit." The tree in your garden may be lovely to look at and it may pain you to cut a certain branch, but you know you must do it if you want good fruit next year. That is life. Consciousness (the I AM) is the eternal vine. Your eternal body is the Imagination, which is God himself. We are all members of the divine body . . Jesus; therefore humanity is truly the body of the Lord Jesus Christ. Every child is part of that universal body; and when he knows that Jesus Christ is his own wonderful human imagination, he is confused for the moment, until the realization rearranges itself within him. Then he takes himself in hand, determined to do something about it. I tell you from experience, if you will take yourself in hand and really believe in Christ in you to the point that you will turn to no other causation, but will prune your thoughts morning, noon, and night, your world will change. It will mold itself in harmony with the change which has taken place in

you, for your outer world is forever reflecting your inner, imaginal acts.

595. One must see the whole vast world as a psychological drama. You may think you have never committed adultery, but the moment you lust after anything, the stage is set by your imaginal act. Restraining the impulse is not good enough. The moment you have the impulse to steal, the act is committed. The impulse to hurt is the act of hurting. You may be afraid to carry out any act, but when the impulse appears, the act is committed. Once you understand this, you will forgive all, for there is only one son (who you are), doing your Father's will.

596. You can write your own essay on success if that is your desire, and to the degree that you are self-persuaded it is true, you will give it life in your world. The secret is to imagine to the point of self-persuasion. Can you believe what you are imagining? There are not two of you . . you and Imagination! You are not reshaping a piece of pottery when you imagine, but yourself! You are moving into your desire. If you persist until you see exactly what you want to see, fix your position with the glue of feeling and remain there . . it will be reflected on the screen of space, just as your world is now reflecting the fixed state from which you are viewing it.

There are two worlds: the outer world of effect and the inner world of causation. That inner world, in the depth of your soul, is where the true drama of life goes on. It is there that God is endowing you with life-giving power. Now a living soul, you are being transformed into a life-giving spirit! On that day you will see this world from above, to discover it is dead and you are its animating power. Blake said: "Where man is not, nature is barren." This is true, for nature cannot produce anything by itself. Man, a living soul, causes things to appear alive by his animating power. Although you are now animating all that you behold, you are destined to become a life-giving spirit . . to fashion things in your own image, bring them forth, and endow them with the power to create life. Believe me, there is no fiction! Every thought you think will come to pass. You may think it is just a thought and will never become real, but it will.

597. Born in the little island of Barbados, we kept ducks and chickens for our own consumption. If mother wanted a pair of ducks for a Sunday dinner, ten days prior she would tell one of her nine sons to put a brace of ducks aside. Now, our ducks were raised in the yard and fed on fish, which was cheap and plentiful . . and not on corn, which had to be imported and was very expensive. We could buy a bucket of fish scraps for a penny, so we fed the chickens and ducks fish; consequently they smelled of and tasted like fish. But if they were separated ten days or two weeks before you wanted them for dinner, and stuffed with corn and food of that nature, the entire texture of their flesh changed.

During that interval of time however, they could not be given even a little bit of fish. They had to have a complete, radical change of diet. If mother's command was not remembered until perhaps four days before the meal everyone knew it, because when the birds were plucked and the heat began to express the birds, the entire neighborhood knew the Goddard's were having fish for dinner, and no one could eat them. But if their diet was changed from fish to corn . . and only corn for that interval of time . . we had delicious ducks for dinner which tasted like ducks! Now, although we are not ducks we do feed on ideas. Feed your mind a certain idea for one week and you will change its structure. Continue for two weeks and you will be well fed on lovely thoughts.

You see, this is a fictitious world and you are its author. Nothing is impossible! It's all fiction anyway, so live nobly and dream beautiful dreams; for you are all imagination, and your human imagination is the Lord God, Jesus . . the Christ.

598. There is no sin against the Holy Ghost other than man's belief that something is impossible to his own wonderful human imagination! I want you to go all out! To put no limit on God's creative power. To imagine that which is unimaginable and to walk on the water, through faith. Water symbolizes your acceptance of life as psychological, and its drama as taking place in the Imagination. When you cease excusing yourself or anyone for life's experiences, and begin to rearrange the structure of your mind to feel your desire is fulfilled, you are walking on the water. Scripture speaks of the stone, the water, and the wind. Accept the facts of life and you are stepping down on stone. Change the facts in your imagination, and you have turned them into psychological truth, which then becomes a spiritual experience. When you live by this principle, you are walking on water, towards your birth from beyond.

599. A friend recently shared a wonderful experience with me. It seems a neighbor was forever dropping in on her, constantly telling horrible stories about her friends. She tried to tell the woman how to change things by using her imagination, but she would not listen. And although she imagined her as a fine, positive, happy person, she remained in her negative state. Realizing the lady was a character my friend had to overcome, she began to change her thoughts. In her imagination she told the neighbor that she loved her. This she persisted in doing, until one day she realized she really did. That night she had this dream. She found herself sitting in the shade of a beautiful tree. A figure approached, looking like a goddess, in a long white gown with loose sleeves and a silver belt.

Suddenly she realized it was her friend, who came to say goodbye. They embraced and she felt a surge of love for that woman like she had never known for anyone before. The next day this lady came to her door and said: "I gave my notice this morning and have come to say goodbye." Then my friend added this thought: "If I could fall as much in love with the being within me as I did with this lady, I would be completely transformed . . which in turn, would produce great changes in my outer world of effects, for now I know my friend's transformation took place within me."

600. The true vine is your own wonderful human imagination. When you believe this you will no longer imagine as you formerly did, but will prune your thoughts every minute of every day. You will break the habit of feeling remorseful, depressed, or regretful. You will no longer think unkindly about another, because you will know that he is actually yourself pushed out, and appeared in your world because the Father in you called him. No one can come unto me unless I, who am one with the Father, call him. Even though he brings poison he does it because I gave it to him to bring. This is the story that is reenacted today, but not understood.

601. Blake asked the question: "Why is it that the Bible is more entertaining and instructive than any other book? Is it not because it is addressed to the Imagination, which is spiritual sensation, and only immediately to the understanding, or reason?" The one book, called the Bible, is composed of sixty-six books. Take this challenge. Read each book as though the depth of your soul is speaking to your surface mind. As though the ineffable Imagination is speaking to the human Imagination, and not to your immediate understanding or reasoning mind. Let us examine this thought. In his 2nd letter to the Corinthians Paul says: "We walk by faith and not by sight." When we walk by sight, we know our way by objects that the eye sees.

But Paul tells us to order our life by objects seen only in the imagination. In other words, when you know where you want to go and what you want to be, you are told not to rearrange your physical structure, but to walk by faith, viewing only the rearranged structure of your mind. And if you will remain faithful to that state of consciousness, what is seen only in your imagination will objectify itself in your world.

602. Every event in life contains within itself something beyond its physical experience. Flowers symbolize the growth of plantings. During winter, when nothing grows, he planted seeds, which he will harvest not only in the world of Caesar, but also in the world of the Spirit, as we all do. I urge you now to use your imagination and walk on the water. Plant the seeds of desire in the depth of your soul and allow them to flower on earth. If you do not see their harvest immediately, believe what you did, for it will come whether you recognize it or not. And do not sin against the Holy Ghost by saying something is impossible, for God is your own wonderful human imagination and nothing is impossible to imagine.

603. As the operant power of your imagination, you can tell where you are going and what you are doing by watching your thoughts. If certain events in your past are unlovely and you remember them, you are ordering their experience. But if you turn your back on the past by forgetting what lies behind and stretch forward to what lies ahead, you will order your conversations aright and become what you behold. This truth will never be disproved, but you are its operant power and must live by it. You need nothing on the outside, but can start just where you are; but you must walk in the direction you set up in your imagination. Ask yourself this simple question: What would it be like if it were true that I am now the person I want to be? Then reach for its feeling, its spiritual sensation. What is that? I'll show you in a very simple way. Feel a piece of glass, now feel a baseball. Does the baseball feel like glass? Can you feel a tennis ball? Does it feel like a baseball or a piece of glass? Can you feel a piece of cloth, a violet, a piano? Do they all feel alike? Of course not. That's spiritual sensation . . a vivid way of seeing, hearing, smelling, tasting, and feeling reality.

604. My brother Victor wanted to be a successful business man, and he knew how to remain faithful to what he imagined. In 1924, when our family didn't have a cent, Victor rearranged the name on a building (in his mind's eye) to imply we owned it. This he did for two years, when . . without any more money than when he started imagining . . a casual acquaintance purchased the building for us without collateral for $50,000. Eight years ago we sold the building to a bank for $850,000, and there is no capital gains tax in Barbados! Walking by faith, every day as Victor passed that building, he saw "J. C. Goddard and Sons" on the marquee in place of the existing name of "I. N. Roach & Company". Sight told him the building belonged to another, but faith said the building was his. By simply rearranging the structure of his mind every day for two years, our family's fortune changed. Now, we are told: "Faith is the assurance of things hoped for; the conviction of things not seen, so that what is seen was made out of things that do not appear." (Hebrews 11) Only my brother Victor saw his mental act. Others saw the sign, "J. N. Roach & Company" . . by sight, but Victor saw the words, "J.C. Goddard & Sons" . . by faith.

605. Many times I have heard someone say: "I believe that imagining creates reality, but I once imagined something and it never came to pass." Then I ask: "What are you doing, saying: 'I once imagined it' and not imagining it now?' For God's name is I AM, not I did!" Always thinking of God as someone outside of himself, man finds it difficult to keep the tense, but God is the human imagination and there is no other God. When you imagine you may include others, but do not think in terms of influence. Rather, think only in terms of clarity of form. Perhaps a friend would like a better job, more money, and greater responsibility. Before you imagine, take a moment and clarify the form your imaginal act will take. Are you giving the celebration party or is he? Who will be there? Fill the room with those who would want to share in the celebration. Raise your glass and say: "Here's to your

fabulous new job, your salary increase, and the challenge of your greater responsibility!" Don't think in terms of trying to influence the friend's boss, for he could die or be discharged. Just go to the end. Toast the event, and do not think of influencing others. The law, to be effective, needs feeling with form. Build a structure that would imply your desire is already fulfilled, and enter its form with feeling. You do not have to be concerned about influencing others, as they are not the cause . . your imaginal act is! Those who have a billion dollars are not causing your world. You and you alone are doing it, as your imaginal acts influence people. Everyone is yourself pushed out, so when you imagine, you are influencing yourself!

606. Reality is controlled by feeling, as told us in the 27th chapter of Genesis. The central character in this chapter is the state called Isaac, who has two sons . . Esau and Jacob. Esau is clothed in objective reality, while Jacob wears subjective reality as longings, wishes, and desires. When Jacob disguised himself as an objective fact, Isaac said: "Come near that I may feel you to determine whether you are Esau or not." And when he asked: "Are you really Esau?" Jacob answered, "I AM." Put yourself into a subjective state. Then feel the objectivity of the state by giving it sensory vividness and tones of reality. Then deceive yourself into believing that the image into which you have entered is now objectively real. Do that, and you have entered the state called Isaac. And we are told that when Isaac once more saw his objective world, Esau returned and Jacob disappeared. Then he realized that he had been self-deceived, but could not take back the blessing given to the subjective state. Although your objective world denies the reality of what you have done in your imagination, that which you have subjectively assumed is on its way to supplant your objective world and become your Esau.

You see, in life you are playing the part of Isaac with your two sons: Esau . . your objective world, and Jacob . . your subjective one. Your subjective world may seem to be clothed in unreality; but when you enter into its image in your imagination and clothe that image with feeling, your subjective desire takes on the tones of reality. This is how I do it: When I close my eyes this world is shut out and I, like Isaac, am blind to the outer world. Then I feel myself into the state of my desire. With my inner eye I see it all around me. I sense its solidity, and when my five senses are awakened I have the feeling of relief, knowing it is accomplished. When I open my physical eyes, Esau . . my physical world . . returns and tries to persuade me that what I did was unreal. But having done it time and time again, I know that my desire is moving towards its objective fulfillment.

607. A seamstress and dress designer I know wanted more money. Using her imagination, she held an envelope in her hand and listened to the paper tear as she opened it. Shaking the contents out, she counted the money to the very penny. This she did for seven nights. On the eighth day, a lady called, offering her a job which paid her, to the penny, what she had imagined. Do you know . . that lady could have counted out much more and she would have received it, but she was quite satisfied with the amount she had imagined. Now, if there is evidence for a thing, does it matter what the world thinks? Could you ever take this lady's experience from her? No! The truth, experienced by her parallels scripture, for all things are possible to one who believes. How did this lady believe what she was imagining? She did it by bringing forth all of her senses to bear upon this event. Using her sense of hearing, she heard the paper tear. Shaking the contents of the envelope, she heard the money fall on the table. She felt the envelope and saw the bills inside. Do you know, money has an odor unlike anything else? So you can smell money. She determined what she would do if she had the money and she did it.

608. I ask you to test your imagination! Go all out and believe in what you have imagined. Do not try to influence anyone. Instead, put all of your energies into clarity of form. If a certain desk designates that you are occupying a desired position, occupy that desk. Enter into the image, and you will realize your vision. Sit in the chair behind that desk and view the room. Persist in thinking from that point of view. If you do not physically occupy that chair tomorrow, and begin to doubt, ask yourself: "What am I doing, remembering and not imagining?" Then return to your chair behind that desk!

609. Now we are told by the great Blake: "The spirit of Jesus is continual forgiveness of sin" . . forgiveness of sin every moment of time. Tonight when we go into the silence we can sit here for a minute and forgive each other. Suppose I could hear everyone here rise and tell the most fantastic story in the world about themselves or a friend, or a relative . . or someone. Suppose I, really wanting it to be told from this platform, sit in the silence and listen to that and that only . . the most fantastic story in the world that you could tell me individually. If I walk out of here tonight convinced that I heard it and remain loyal to what I have imagined I heard, I must hear it . . no power can stop it, if I remain loyal. If anyone says it has not worked, I am not asking any questions, but as far as I am concerned, it has worked. I am sure when I know the vision I am holding for you "has its own appointed hour, it will ripen and it will flower. If it seems long in coming, wait. It is sure, it will not be late." If I actually assume things are as I would like them to be of every being here, and I remain loyal, I either know the story is true or it is false. I know it is true. It can't fail. There is no power in the world to make it fail.

610. If you do not believe you are this fabulous being, that your own wonderful human imagination is the cause of the phenomena of your life, you are still searching for its cause. But when you are

convinced, you will begin to awaken and discover that there never was another God. Then you will see how practical this vision of God really is. Your own wonderful human imagination is the Lord Jesus. Prove it! Believe in the only Jesus, for all things are made by him and without him is not anything made that is made. It is he who made the statement in the Book of Deuteronomy: "I kill and I make alive; I wound and I heal." The same being who wounds, heals, because imagination does it all! So you see how practical and wonderful this whole principle is? Tonight, if you really want something . . I don't care what it is . . you can have it. For your own sake I hope it will not injure another. You don't have to hurt anyone to get what you want; all you have to do is accept it! To live as though you had it now! And when you get it (and you will) I urge you to share your good news with others to encourage all.

611. No one is without sin. At some time everyone has mentally coveted or stolen. Describe a man in unflattering terms and you have stolen his good name. Everyone is guilty; therefore, do not analyze yourself, for if you do, you will miss your mark. To worry about what you may have done, is to waste your creative power. You will reap the tares as well as the wheat, as every imaginal act fulfills itself. But start now to plant something lovely . . not only for yourself, but for your neighbor, friend, or child. Fall in love with the idea that he is happy and secure. Feel the satisfaction that comes when one recognizes his harvest, for if a harvest is not recognized, there is no satisfaction. But when you do something consciously and see your harvest, you will receive enormous satisfaction. Prove your thoughts have creative power by consciously imaging constantly, and walk on the water. No matter what happens in the course of a day, revise it. Make the day conform to what you want it to be, and you are walking on the water.

612. I tell you: everything is possible to the individual when he knows who he is. You are the Joshua of the Old Testament and the

Jesus of the New. And Jesus, your own wonderful human imagination, is Jehovah. He is your awareness, but as long as you see Jehovah as someone other than yourself you will not apply this principle. You must be willing to give up all foreign gods, all idols, and return to the one and only God, whose name is in you as your very being! If you were trained in the Christian faith, you were taught to believe that Jesus was on the outside. But how can you put him to the test if he is another? There never was another Joshua or Jehovah. There is only God, the director of the great dance of life whose dancers are himself. God plays the part of the bum and dances the dance of poverty. He also plays the part of a millionaire and dances to the tune of millions, as every part is being played by God. Now, everyone must act from where he is! Ask yourself: where am I? If I AM God, where can I go and God is not? If I make my bed in hell, God is there. If I make it in heaven, God is there, for everything penetrates me! I do not have to physically move. Simply by adjusting my thinking I can move from one state to another.

613. If I desire to visit my island home in Barbados, but do not have the means or the time to go there, I can enter its image in my imagination by approaching it on the fiery chariot of my contemplative thought. I have done it. I do not use this wonder working power lightly anymore, because I know that after imagining, my desire fulfilled (although I may forget it) I will be compelled to experience it in this world of shadows. This wonder working power is to be used for anything you desire. It now penetrates your brain, and it is wherever you are. I know that Barbados is in the outer world, but I also know that I am all imagination. I know that God is Man and exists in us and we in Him; that the eternal body of Man is the Imagination, and that is God Himself. So if I . . imagination . . enter into an image I desire to occupy, no earthly power can stop that image from becoming an objective fact. What is the secret that makes this wonder working power operate? Feeling!

614. Practice the art of imagining, and you will discover you can go anywhere and enter any time without the aid of anyone. Move in your imagination, and people will respond because of your action. Dare to assume you are wealthy, and watch everyone play their parts to provide you with the wealth you claim to have. They will, for they are only yourself pushed out. The world goes on and on, as the actors . . playing their numberless parts . . desire more and more things that vanish. Man is forever fighting for something that passes away; yet he is told: "Do not lay up treasures on earth where thieves can take and the moth corrupt, but lay up treasures in heaven where no man can take from you." The treasures of earth can be withdrawn at any moment, but the treasures in the instructions I am giving you now are forever.

615. Are you willing to become enamored over a desire that much? Are you willing to fall in love with its fulfillment that you imagine it is yours now? If so, I promise you it will out picture itself in your world. And when it does, you will have found Christ, for the words of scripture: "By him all things are made and without him is not anything made that is made," are false. When you test your imagination you will find He who produced your desire and the Maker of all things! I have tested him numberless times. I have taught this principle to others who have tested him and shared their experiences with me. Now I know who Jesus Christ really is. The words, "Unless you believe that I AM He, you will die in your sins," are not spoken on the outside, but on the inside. Now wearing a garment of flesh, my words appear to be coming from without, and one day I will seem to die and become a historical fact. But I am not speaking as an outer man. I am speaking as the true Jesus Christ, who comes in every individual by unfolding his story as recorded in scripture. There is only one story, and only one being to play the part. That being is God. It is he alone who acts and is in all things.

616. Paul found Christ to be his human imagination and urged everyone to test himself. Like Paul, I urge you to test your human imagination. You do not need the money or the time to go anywhere in your imagination, yet you can put yourself there, just as though you had made the trip. If you do, and your circumstances change so that the money and the time appears, allowing you to go, have you not found Jesus Christ to be your imagination? This is what scripture teaches, but man has personified the story and made Jesus Christ into a little idol to bow before, when the true God is the human imagination. All things are made by the human imagination. Imagine something that is not now a fact. Persist in your imaginal act, and when it becomes a fact, you have found God. And once you have found him, never let him go!

617. When you truly believe that imagining creates reality, you will know there is no fiction. How can there be fiction when imagining is forever creating its reality? You may hear something you do not like, but because imagining creates reality what you heard was first imagined, or it could not have happened. When you revise the hearing by stopping the action and rewriting the script you are walking on the water, imagining the reality you desire to hear and appear in your world.

618. At the end of the drama it is said that one who knew Jesus betrayed him. Now, in order to betray someone, you must know his secret! So the one who knows the secret betrays him. That one is self! God is self-revealed. Unless God reveals himself to you, how will you ever know him? Turning to those who did not know him, Jesus said: "Now that you have found me, do not let me go, but let all these go." Let every belief of a power on the outside go, but do not let the belief in your powerful imagination go . . for truth is within you. When you find the Maker in yourself, then no matter what arguments the priesthoods may give, do not believe them, for the Christ you seek is the human imagination.

619. When you imagine a state, do you believe that the scene has the power to externalize itself? Or do you feel you must pray to a being on the outside for help? I tell you: there is no being on the outside. The creative power of the world is housed within you now. Sit down and imagine a state of confidence that it must externalize itself. Believe that because all things are possible to imagine, the state you have imagined must become an external fact. I have tried this time and time again, and it has always proved itself in performance. Now I share this knowledge with everyone who will listen. How many believe my words and put them into practice I do not know. I only know that man finds it hard to keep the tense. Religious leaders speak of God in the third person as if he were on the outside, yet I tell you he comes from within. When Moses heard the words: "I AM has sent me unto you," it seemed to come from without, yet it was whispered from within.

620. “God actually became as we are, that we maybe as He is.” [Blake, from “There Is No Natural Religion”] So when you imagine something, remember: It is God Acting! And God’s actions are His words. “And His word cannot return unto Him void but it must accomplish that which He purposed, and prosper in the thing for which He sent it.” Well, what are you imagining? Whatever you are imagining, you are actually sending into being to be confronted with it. So if you really want a lovely life, be careful what you are imagining, because imagination is God. Imagining is God-in-action! So what are you imagining? That everything is going down? That the whole world is collapsing? Well then, if that is what you imagine, may I tell you? You will have the experience of a collapsed world, but others won’t.

621. If God is in you, is there any place where God is not? And if there is no place where imagination is not, where would you go to be where you want to be? If everything penetrates you, then you must choose what you want and adjust yourself into the feeling that

you are already there. You will know you have arrived when you view the world from there. Motion can be detected only by a change of position relative to another object. While physically sitting in a chair you appear not to move, but because everything penetrates you, by a mental adjustment you can think from the awareness of being the person you want to be. How will you know you have changed? By the expression on the faces of your friends. If they now see the new you, then you have moved. So let them look at you until their faces tell you they are seeing that which you are assuming is true.

622. All things are made by your imagination, for without imagining, nothing is made. Imagination is not limited to this level of consciousness. There are levels and levels of imagination, as your dreams and visions prove. This world is sustained by Divine Imagining, which is human imagining on a higher level. Our imagination is keyed low, but we are called upon to exercise this power, to examine ourselves to see if we are keeping our faith. On this level, faith is not complete until, through experiment, it becomes experience.

Experiment with this statement: "Whatever you desire, believe you have received it and you will." If faith is not complete until, through experiment it becomes experience, you must take an unseen objective and place it in an assemblage of mental states which would imply its fulfillment. Then this desire must be activated by entering into its center, feeling its reality, and walking in the faith that it will happen. I tell you: in a way you could not devise, what you have assumed will come into your world. You do not have to construct a bridge of incident to walk across; you simply move toward the fulfillment of what you have already prepared for yourself. Then fulfill another desire the same way, and when it appears you will know exactly what to do when confronted with any problem. You will simply turn your back upon it by constructing an imaginal scene which would imply the fulfillment of its solution. Activate it and let it come into being.

623. I tell you: God became you, with all of your weakness and limitations, that you may become Imagination. Becoming our imagination, God exists in us and we in him. Our eternal body is the imagination, and that is God Himself. And God alone acts! He can act the part of the fool, or the king, the poor, or the rich man. Every desire is a state. Move into your desire, and God will play that part . . as you! If you desire riches, yet do not know this power, you will remain poor because you are looking for a God on the outside, trying to coerce him into giving you wealth for acquiring merit. You can spend your life acquiring merit and be so good the world will think you are wonderful, yet remain poor. Man must seek and find his true identity within himself, for he and he alone is the revealer and maker of everything in this world.

624. Knowing what you want, assume your desire is already fulfilled by imagining a circle of friends are congratulating you. Fall asleep knowing that those who would empathize with you have already witnessed your good fortune. Knowing you have put the fulfillment of your desire in motion, walk confident that what you are assuming is true. And when it happens, share your experience with others, in the hope that they will try it and it will work for them. It does not matter to me what others think, for I have found my Father . . the one the world worships and calls God . . to be my own wonderful human imagination!

625. So, I only ask you to be as faithful to any imaginal state in this world, no matter what it is. In everyone God resides. Everyone has to say, "I AM." That is God. I AM Einstein, I AM Neville. I AM is God. Neville is a tiny thing resting on the foundation that is God. I AM rich . . that is a tiny thing on the foundation of God, and God is

Infinity, God is Everything. Therefore, whatever you say, before you say it, you say, "I AM".

626. I urge you to use your imagination for everything that is lovely and loving. I don't care what your desire may be . . your imagination will give it to you, for the human imagination is the divine body the world calls Jesus. Because you can imagine and I can imagine, we are members of that one divine body, and all things are possible to him. There is not a thing impossible to God. All you need do is imagine its fulfillment! Faith is an experiment which ends as an experience. Experiment by believing you already have all that you desire, and you will have the experience.

627. Christ is your own wonderful human imagination. That's an awful shock, and when you first hear it your world collapses, for there is no one to turn to but self! Formerly you could point to another as the cause of your misfortune, but you can no longer do that when you discover who Jesus Christ really is. From that moment on you must turn to yourself to blame or praise. And when you have played all of the parts, you will find him of whom you seek, Jesus of Nazareth!

628. A thought acted upon is an imaginal act. Think (imagine) a horrible earthquake and God will give it to you. Imagine (think of) a war and God will provide that, too. Imagine peace and you will have it. God will give you health if you will but imagine being healthy. Imagine success and you will have it. The moment you think, you are feeding your imagination, which is a person. I use the word person deliberately, for you are a person. You are the mask God is now wearing, for God became you that you may become God.

629. *"He was in the world, and the world was made by Him and the world knew Him not. The mystery hid from the ages; Christ in you, the hope of glory."*

The "He" in the first of these quotations is your imagination. As previously explained, there is only one substance. This substance is consciousness. It is your imagination which forms this substance into concepts, which concepts are then manifested as conditions, circumstances, and physical objects. Thus imagination made your world. This supreme truth, with but few exceptions, man is not conscious of. The mystery, *"Christ in you",* referred to in the second quotation, is your imagination, by which your world is molded. The hope of glory is your awareness of the ability to rise perpetually to higher levels. Christ is not to be found in history, nor in external forms. You find Christ only when you become aware of the fact that your imagination is the only redemptive power. When this is discovered, the "towers of dogma will have heard the trumpets of Truth, and, like the walls of Jericho, crumble to dust".

630. *"Now unto Him that is able to do exceeding abundantly above all that we ask or think, according to the power that worketh in us, unto Him be glory."*

Him, that is able to do more than you can ask or think, is your imagination, and the power that worketh in us is your attention. Understanding imagination to be him that is able to do all that you ask, and attention to be the power by which you create your world, you can now build your ideal world. Imagine yourself to be the ideal you dream of and desire. Remain attentive to this imagined state, and as fast as you completely feel that you are already this ideal it will manifest itself as reality in your world.

631. "The mystery hid from the ages... Christ in you, the hope of glory," is your imagination. This is the mystery which I am ever striving to realize more keenly myself and to urge upon others. Imagination is our redeemer, "the Lord from Heaven"

632. Imagination's birth and growth is the gradual transition from a God of tradition to a God of experience. If the birth of Christ (imagination) in man seems slow, it is only because man is unwilling to let go the comfortable but false anchorage of tradition. When imagination is discovered as the first principle of religion, the stone of literal understanding will have felt the rod of Moses and, like the rock of Zin, issue forth the water of psychological meaning to quench the thirst of humanity; and all who take the proffered cup and live a life according to this truth will transform the water of psychological meaning into the wine of forgiveness. Then, like the good Samaritan, they will pour it on the wounds of all. The Son of God is not to be found in history, nor in any external form. He can only be found as the imagination of him in whom His presence becomes manifest.

633. Truth depends upon the intensity of the imagination, not upon external facts. Facts are the fruit bearing witness of the use or misuse of the imagination. Truth cannot be encompassed by facts. As we awaken to the imaginative life, we discover that to imagine a thing is to make it so, that a true judgment need not conform to the external reality to which it relates. The imaginative man does not deny the reality of the sensuous outer world of Becoming, but he knows that it is the inner world of continuous Imagination that is the force by which the sensuous outer world of Becoming is brought to pass. He sees the outer world and all its happenings as projections of the inner world of Imagination. To him, everything is a manifestation of the mental activity which goes on in man's imagination, without the sensuous reasonable man being aware of it. But he realizes that every man must become conscious of this inner activity and see the relationship between the inner causal world of imagination and the sensuous outer world of effects. It is a marvelous thing to find that you can imagine yourself into the state of your fulfilled desire and escape from the jails which ignorance

built. The Real Man is a Magnificent Imagination. It is this self that must be awakened.

634. The moment man discovers that his imagination is Christ, he accomplishes acts which on this level can only be called miraculous. But until man has the sense of Christ as his imagination, "You did not choose me, I have chosen you." He will see everything in pure objectivity without any subjective relationship. Not realizing that all that he encounters is part of himself, he rebels at the thought that he has chosen the conditions of his life, that they are related by affinity to his own mental activity. Man must firmly come to believe that reality lies within him and not without. Although others have bodies, a life of their own, their reality is rooted in you, ends in you, as yours ends in God.

635. I was first made conscious of the power, nature, and redemptive function of imagination through the teachings of my friend Abdullah; and through subsequent experiences, I learned that Jesus was a symbol of the coming of imagination to man, that the test of His birth in man was the individual's ability to forgive sin; that is, his ability to identify himself or another with his aim in life. Without the identification of man with his aim, the forgiveness of sin is an impossibility, and only the Son of God can forgive sin. Therefore, man's ability to identify himself with his aim, though reason and his senses deny it, is proof of the birth of Christ in him. To passively surrender to appearances and bow before the evidence of facts is to confess that Christ is not yet born in you.

636. "You must imagine yourself right into the state of your fulfilled desire", Abdullah told me. The world which we describe from observation must be as we describe it relative to ourselves. Our imagination connects us with the state desired. But we must use imagination masterfully, not as an onlooker thinking of the end, but as a partaker thinking from the end. We must actually be there in

imagination. If we do this, our subjective experience will be realized objectively. "This is not mere fancy", said he, "but a truth you can prove by experience." His appeal to enter into the wish fulfilled was the secret of thinking from the end. Every state is already there as "mere possibility" as long as you think of it, but is overpoweringly real when you think from it. Thinking from the end is the way of Christ.

637. "Does a firm persuasion that a thing is so, make it so?" And the prophet replied, "All poets believe that it does. And in ages of imagination, this firm persuasion removed mountains: but many are not capable of a firm persuasion of anything." . . . Blake *"Let every man be fully persuaded in his own mind."* Persuasion is an inner effort of intense attention. To listen attentively as though you heard is to evoke, to activate. By listening, you can hear what you want to hear and persuade those beyond the range of the outer ear. Speak it inwardly in your imagination only. Make your inner conversation match your fulfilled desire. What you desire to hear without, you must hear within. Embrace the without within and become one who hears only that which implies the fulfillment of his desire, and all the external happenings in the world will become a bridge leading to the objective realization of your desire.

638. To change your life, you must change your inner talking, for "life", said Hermes, "is the union of Word and Mind". When imagination matches your inner speech to fulfilled desire, there will then be a straight path in yourself from within out, and the without will instantly reflect the within for you, and you will know reality is only actualized inner talking.

639. Man's ignorance of the future is the result of his ignorance of his inner talking. His inner talking mirrors his imagination, and his imagination is a government in which the opposition never comes into power. If the reader asks, "What if the inner speech

remains subjective and is unable to find an object for its love?", the answer is: it will not remain subjective, for the very simple reason that inner speech is always objectifying itself.

640. The Real Man, the Imaginative Man, has invested the outer world with all of its properties. The apparent reality of the outer world which is so hard to dissolve is only proof of the absolute reality of the inner world of his own imagination. "No man can come to me, except the Father which hath sent me draw him... I and My Father are One." The world which is described from observation is a manifestation of the mental activity of the observer.

When man discovers that his world is his own mental activity made visible, that no man can come unto him except he draws him, and that there is no one to change but himself, his own imaginative self, his first impulse is to reshape the world in the image of his ideal. But his ideal is not so easily incarnated. In that moment when he ceases to conform to external discipline, he must impose upon himself a far more rigorous discipline, the self-discipline upon which the realization of his ideal depends. Imagination is not entirely untrammeled and free to move at will without any rules to constrain it. In fact, the contrary is true.

Imagination travels according to habit. Imagination has choice, but it chooses according to habit. Awake or asleep, man's imagination is constrained to follow certain definite patterns. It is this benumbing influence of habit that man must change; if he does not, his dreams will fade under the paralysis of custom. Imagination, which is Christ in man, is not subject to the necessity to produce only that which is perfect and good. It exercises its absolute freedom from necessity by endowing the outer physical self with free will to choose to follow good or evil, order or disorder. "Choose this day whom ye will serve." But after the choice is made and accepted, so that it forms the individual's habitual consciousness, then imagination manifests its infinite power and wisdom by molding the outer sensuous world of becoming in the image of the habitual inner speech and actions of the individual.

641. Blessed are they whose imagination has been so purged of the beliefs in second causes they know that imagination is all, and all is imagination.

THE END

Metaphysical / Law of Attraction Books

David Allen - The Power of I AM (2014), The Power of I AM - Volume 2 (2015) , The Power of I AM - Volume 3 (2017)

David Allen - The Creative Power of Thought, Man's Greatest Discovery (2017)

David Allen - The Secrets, Mysteries & Powers of The Subconscious Mind (2017)

David Allen - The Money Bible - The Secrets of Attracting Prosperity (2017)

David Allen - Your Faith Is Your Fortune, Your Unlimited Power

The Neville Goddard Collection (All 10 of his books plus 2 Lecture series) (2016)

Neville Goddard - Assumptions Harden Into Facts: The Book (2016)

Neville Goddard - Imagination: The Redemptive Power in Man (2016)

Neville Goddard - The World is At Your Command - The Very Best of Neville Goddard (2017)

Neville Goddard - Imagining Creates Reality - 365 Mystical Daily Quotes (2017)

Neville Goddard's Interpretation of Scripture (2018)

The Definitive Christian D. Larson Collection (6 Volumes, 30 books) (2014)

1-416-622-1413

CPSIA information can be obtained
at www.ICGtesting.com
Printed in the USA
BVHW08s0016130818
524247BV00002B/70/P

9 780997 280142